The Good Chinese Daughter: Growing up in China and in America

Elizabeth Chiu King

"The Good Chinese Daughter: Growing up in China and in America," is an inspiring memoir of a successful woman, mother and author, looking for unconditional love from her mother who almost "aborted" her. After her mother divorced her first husband, she kept reminding her daughter that she might not have been born.

Elizabeth, born in Shanghai, was traumatized as a child as she watched the cruelty and brutality of the Imperial Japanese Army in Manila, The Philippines. It was there she learned to deal with the fact that the man she called "Dad" was her stepfather.

Her mother, a socialite, spent little time with her daughter who was reared by her beloved amah, Ah Woo. Elizabeth, the "good" Chinese daughter - obedient, loyal and gracious, true to her Chinese tradition and Catholic upbringing - dreamed of closer relationship with her mother and stepfather.

Caught between two worlds - her Chinese upbringing and adjusting to life in the U.S. when the family moved to California, she searched for her true self and personal identity in the shadow of her strong-willed, dominant mother. In spite of the inevitable tensions that marked the relationship, she served as her mother's right hand, helping to raise her five younger siblings and to manage the household.

All of us search, at one time or another in our lives, for the assurance of love and acceptance from loved ones, whether parents, spouse, children or friends. As Elizabeth raised her own family in the U.S. which includes two sons and their spouses, seven grandchildren and a husband of great renown in the field of Bioengineering, she kept looking for the something that was "missing" in her life.

Finally, she found it in Christian Meditation - the peace that serves to bridge the gap between her mother and herself and other relationships in her life. During her Mom's waning years, they came to something of a reconciliation. Elizabeth found peace and a deeper integration of her life experiences through contemplative prayer - a form of communion with the transcendent taking place in total silence and stillness.

Chinese Cultural Publications
P. O. Box 3505
22200 W. Eleven Mile Road
Southfield, MI 48037-9999
USA

Library of Congress Control Number: 2016908835
ISBN 978-0-692-68163-3

Cover Design by Icicle Group
Author Photo by Michelle Andonian

The Good Chinese Daughter:
Growing up in China and in America

Elizabeth Chiu King

Chinese Cultural Publications
Michigan

For Albert, Albert, Jr. and Tom
with love

Chapter Three

Chapter Four

Chapter Five

Chapter Six

Chapter Seven

Introduction

I had wanted to write such a book for a long time to find out who I am. I was hounded by fear, afraid to begin and had no idea where to begin, although I kept detailed journals through the years. Organizing these was the first step.

As I reread my writings, I realized that although I had recorded a lot of facts, they weren't stitched together. Then it dawned on me that in order to truly know myself, I needed to know my mother. Like many daughters, my relationship with her was, and still is, a very intense love-hate one. I had to find out who she is. Unfortunately she never kept a diary. She wasn't in the habit of writing regularly to anyone and she never shared any feelings about her past or present. But, I did keep some of her short notes and postcards.

I dug into my journals to find out where and what I had written about her. I also searched my memory bank to recall what had happened, as well as when and where. I have added what I remember she told me through the years and included my understanding of her words and actions.

In January 2002, a breakthrough between us took place. I finally had the courage to confront and quarrel with her. My feelings were so raw that I couldn't write with honesty. Doing that would be counter to Chinese culture, as well as a betrayal of my Catholic upbringing. The good sisters at St. Mary's taught me to honor my parents. On top of this, my mother "without me you wouldn't be here today," was my caretaker. These are the very words she used, time and again, to control me, to make me submissive to her will and whims.

1

Now I am ready to write about her, our relationship and my life. Mom is very much alive on the West Coast. Now, in her late 90s, she still has a good memory, stubborn pride and a strong will – qualities that have kept her alive and going. My niece, Sherri, calls her "feisty" and smiles at her pride and arrogance.

January 22, 2002 was the day - the day I mustered the courage and stopped being the good and obedient Chinese daughter. At 66, I was ready to cut the apron strings.

And so begins my memoir…

1

The Dreams

Ioften have dreams that I can easily recall in my waking moments. For some strange reason, many of my dreams are about finding a toilet to use. Each time I am rushing, running, in search of a clean toilet. Oftentimes I wait in a long line and end up in a very dirty and poor facility.

Several times I find myself stuck in muck - knee deep in shit. The feeling is horrible. I can't extricate myself. The stench and the slime that cover my feet make me squirm. The surroundings are awful. I am writhing in agony. When I finally wake up, I am thankful that it is after all just a dream.

When I shared this recurrent dream in my memoir writing classes, one comment was, "You must be involved in some shitty circumstances in your life, circumstances you wanted to get out of, but can't." Upon deeper reflection I realized that this was symbolic of my relationship with my mother. Our relationship was not only shitty, but downright ugly and unpleasant, like being stuck in muck.

I had another vivid dream. This occurred during my seven-day intensive Christian Meditation retreat at the Monastery of St. Clair in Fara Sabina, near Florence, Italy.

A little fish with shiny golden scales and a body much like an angel fish is swimming happily in the ocean. Along comes a big stingray, dancing as it unfurls its wings. This stingray is different from other stingrays. While beautiful and graceful as all stingrays are, it has a transparent body, much like that of the jelly fish family.

Soon the stingray spots the little fish and gives chase. The little fish panics and doesn't know where to go. It darts here and there, trying to avoid being captured by its pursuer. Finally, the stingray swallows it whole. It happens so fast, the captive still swims in a desperate attempt to get out of its prison in the body of the stingray.

The stingray, now that it has captured the little fish, is swimming triumphantly. But the captive is busy thinking about how to get out. Finally, she realizes that the only escape is to swim straight ahead through the mouth of the stingray. She has to keep a straight course and pierce through the membrane of the stingray's throat with her sharp snout. Yes, that's the only way she can be free. To do that isn't easy since the stingray swirls around and around. The little fish uses all her energy to keep a straight course while encouraging herself. *I gotta make it, I gotta make it. I know I can, I know I can.*

Now it is the stingray's turn to panic. She becomes aware of what the little fish is trying to do. She wriggles and twists and turns every which way to prevent the little fish from piercing through her throat. She knows that would cause her death.

At last, the determined little fish comes near the stingray's throat, and with one big effort, she points her snout at the throat and gives it a mighty thrust. She pierces the membrane and is free. Before she swims away she turns to eye her captor. The stingray, lethargic and losing her energy, sinks to the bottom of the ocean. When I see what is happening my sympathies are divided. On one hand I want the little fish to be free, on the other hand, I feel sorry for the stingray.

When I related this story to Fr. Laurence Freeman, OSB, my

spiritual teacher, during our interview at the Fara Sabina Retreat, he asked for my interpretation of this dream. I immediately identified myself as the little fish, trying to free myself from my mother, the big stingray who had imprisoned me. Fr. Laurence pointed out the significance of the little fish piercing the throat and causing the demise of her captor. The throat represented the verbal abuses Mom had heaped on me through the years and which I have endured, especially her comments about how I should be thankful to her for not aborting me, otherwise I wouldn't be here today.

Mother

Chiu Sheung at 15

My story began before I was born. It started the afternoon my birth father, Zhou, saw my mother, Chiu Sheung, then a beauty of 15. She went with her No. 3 brother* to dance at the Far Eastern Hotel in Canton (now Guangzhou), China, at tea time. Unbeknown to my mother, General Zhou, a star in the Chinese Military Academy, was seated at a table with his aide and several comrades. He had gone to Canton for a meeting, but took the afternoon off to relax. The six of them were drinking, smoking and chatting, when suddenly he spotted a young couple dancing. The five-piece Filipino band was playing the *Vienna Waltz*. Of the dozen couples dancing, Chiu Sheung and her brother stood out, they were excellent dancers.

It didn't matter to Zhou that he was already married and the father of two in the province of Zhejiang.* It didn't matter that he was 20 years older than this young beauty. She was a budding rose, to be plucked and cherished. And he was determined to have her, for he had the power and the means.

He made inquiries. He enlisted the help of his friends and associates, including the mayor of Canton. They checked and found her home address. She was the younger daughter, the sixth child, of T.S. Luk, the scholar and once affluent land owner and businessman, whose fortunes fell while his name was still linked to many concubines and other women.

Zhou must have thought it fortunate her family had seen better days. He knew her father needed money to support his womanizing and extravagance. He hired people to find the tastes of the family. He sent gifts – oranges, grapes, apples, all imported from abroad. Next came fresh seafood, live crabs and shrimp, followed by several Jinhua hams, one of the best hams in China. Then he called on the Luk family in person, accompanied by the mayor of Canton, who after being wined, dined and richly gifted, sang Zhou's praises and achievements.

The eager suitor discovered that Mr. and Mrs. Luk were avid mahjong* players, the Southern style. He hired a mahjong expert to tutor him in that style of game, so he could ingratiate himself to them by indulging in their hobby. Day after day, he joined in their mahjong games. Many times, he purposely kept himself from winning to allow his hosts to triumph. Within a month, he was accepted as an old friend and treated like a member of the family.

After weeks of mahjong and cups and cups of tea and wine, accompanied by lavish banquets in the best restaurants in the city, he finally had the courage to ask for Chiu Sheung's hand in marriage. That was accompanied by gifts his go-between (match maker) promised the Luks. Aside from depositing $200,000 (Chinese currency) in their bank account, together with 10 ounces of gold, he promised 100 tables at the wedding banquet at the Far Eastern Hotel, 500 boxes of *lo po beng** (wife cake) and 50 cases of the finest wine. The foreigner from the North was heartily welcomed, the marriage contract sealed and signed.

Chiu Sheung's parents never discussed the matter with her. Such familial matters were unheard of. It was the prerogative and duty of the parents to find a suitable husband for their daughter. Zhou was the ideal mate for Chiu Sheung. Not only was he wealthy and generous, but he was well educated and his future was bright. How many girls had the prospect of going abroad someday – to the United States, for that matter, at that time? Marrying an older man was also advantageous – he would protect and take good care of her. Plus this son-in-law was insurance for their old age.

After all, when one considered all the energy, time, patience and money invested in raising a child, especially a daughter, her only worth was how well she could capture a husband of means and education. Chiu Sheung was fortunate and certainly blessed. It never occurred to them that Zhou was a total stranger to Chiu Sheung, that he was a military man from the Zhejiang, obstinate, hard-headed, willful, insensitive, and puffed up by his success and prowess. It probably never occurred to them that they were using her as a pawn to support their affluent lifestyle.

At 15, Chiu Sheung, a gentle beauty of even temperament, barely 4'11", weighing no more than 75 pounds and wearing size 2 shoes, was the promised bride of General Zhou.

Chiu Sheung was shocked. She hardly knew her husband-to-be. She only saw him when he came to play mahjong with her parents. They would bump into each other in the hallway and exchange a polite greeting. She didn't speak Mandarin, the dialect of the North and had never met a man from Zhejiang.

Her fate was sealed. She had no choice, no alternative. She couldn't run to her mother, as some of her friends could, to plead and beg for more time. Her mother, brought up in the household of Sir Robert Hotung in Hong Kong, was herself the pawn of a loveless marriage.

Her mother had left all the nurturing of Chiu Sheung to the maids. Her chief preoccupation was grooming herself each morning before she started her mahjong game. But Chiu Sheung's father was a different matter. He cherished her and was the one who insisted that she, a daughter, should have a good grounding in the classics. When a tutor was hired to teach her older brothers Confucian classics, history and poetry, she was included.

However, she realized it was futile to talk to her father. She knew that Zhou's fortune would salvage their financial woes. It was no use to beg her father to cancel this nuptial. She had no one and nowhere to turn. How could she love this older person? To think that after the wedding, she had to leave her home and travel to Nanking (now Nanjing) and perhaps to the United States, was frightening. Besides, the young man she loved, L.S. Ng, was studying medicine in Japan. They were secretly betrothed. She was trapped. She was to be married at 16 to a stranger.

My mother married my birth father Zhou in the next spring of 1928 when she turned 16. They had an extravagant Chinese traditional wedding in Canton, her hometown. Then she left for

Nanking to be with Zhou where he was stationed. After staying in Nanking for two years where she had her first born, Ford, the three of them left for a year's stay at Fort Leavenworth, KA.

It was there that Chiu Sheung first visited the U.S. and learned English. Two years after their return to Nanking, she gave birth to a daughter, Mimi. Then in 1934, Zhou was sent to the Chinese Embassy in Washington, D.C. This time, Chiu Sheung and Ford accompanied him, but left little Mimi with Zhou's aunt which turned out to be a bad situation. Mimi was alone and unhappy.

This move to the Chinese Embassy in Washington, D.C. was very different from their stay in Fort Leavenworth. As the capital of the U.S., Washington, D.C. had a different ambiance and climate. Here the brightest and most beautiful people worked and lived. Chiu Sheung, now 22, had matured. She was challenged and excited. As the wife of the Chinese Military Attache, she was privy to the social circles.

The time she spent studying English at Fort Leavenworth paid off. She could socialize and hold her own at the many diplomatic teas, dinners and socials. Soon she became the jewel of the Chinese Embassy and the toast of Washington's diplomatic circle with "her charm, beauty and zest for living and dancing" so described an article in the Washington newspaper. They, as a couple, were included in all the diplomatic parties and it was at this time that she decided to use a new name, Rowena.

Me

Rowena and Frank, my parents

I am the third and last child of the arranged marriage of my mother and General Zhou. My nickname is *Lun Lun** in Cantonese, and *Ling Ling* in Mandarin, a mythical creature of wonder and magnificence. By the time I was born, Mom was already divorced from Zhou for six months. My older brother, Ford, was still with Zhou in Washington, D.C., while my older sister, Mimi, was with Mom and me. I don't know why Mom didn't abort me. She told me years later that although her Brother No.2 who was with her in D.C. and several friends advised her to do so, she decided otherwise.

After her divorce, she was just 22, beautiful and rich. Zhou had paid dearly for his womanizing, certainly one reason for the divorce. She told us that she threw the 5-karat diamond ring he had given her in a final act of anger and disgust. It landed on the bathroom floor at Zhou's feet. Zhou knew she was pregnant, so in addition to a U.S. $50,000 settlement, she was given an extra $2,000* in U.S. currency to cover the cost of my delivery. With the money and divorce final, she headed north to Shanghai away from her hometown in Canton to begin a new life. Zhou and I never met and I have never seen my brother Ford. I don't know if he's still alive.

Even though she had no family in Shanghai, it was a natural choice. She knew if she returned to her parents' home in Canton, they would take her nest egg and she would once again be dependent on them for hand-outs. That was the reason for the arranged marriage, to provide a pension for her parents. While living in the Chinese Embassy in Washington, D.C., she met a dashing young man, Frank Chiu, an economics major at George Washington University. He was due to graduate and return to Shanghai about the time Mom arrived with her growing family and he urged her to join him there.

Shanghai, in the mid-30s was the biggest and most cosmopolitan city in China. It was then, as now, the New York of China, the hub of finance, culture and fashion. After her life in Washington, D.C., and her success on the social circuit, a big city attracted her, even though she had no friends or relatives there. She now used her American name, Rowena.

Frank and Rowena were married a year after I was born. This time it was a love match. Frank became the only father I ever knew. We children called him Daddy. He was lean, handsome and bespectacled, with a winning smile, lots of charm and smart. He adopted Mimi and me and we took his surname, Chiu.

Mom and Frank parented five more children: James, Francis, Maria, Shirley and George. James (1938) and Francis (1939) were born in Shanghai, Maria (1941) in Manila, Shirley (1947) in Canton and George in Hong Kong in 1950. We were reasonably happy, and my younger siblings didn't learn of Mimi's and my paternity until many years later. Dad treated Mimi and me no differently than he did his own children.

I didn't learn that Dad was not my natural father until I was 10 years old. But that made little difference, except that Ah Woo, my beloved amah,* would continuously remind me, "The man you call Daddy isn't your birth father. Your own father was a big man in the Chinese government. You're intelligent and beautiful and must study hard to prove yourself. One day you can show your birth father and the whole world how smart you are."

My early years in Shanghai were happy. We lived in a two-story house in the French Concession, a privileged neighborhood in Shanghai. At this time, Dad had a good job in a financial firm, while Mom was the leisurely *tai tai*,* with no household responsibilities, except to plan the daily menu with Ah Woo, who doubled as our cook. Mom was as free as a swallow to enjoy life and not worry about her children.

In 1940, Dad was offered a job he couldn't refuse, as chief financial officer of the Bank of Communications. So our entire family of eight: Mom, Dad, Mimi, James, Francis and myself and our two amahs, Ah Woo and Ah Lo, moved to Manila.

Manila

Our first year in Manila was wonderful. Dad leased a house in Pasay City, a suburb of Manila, recently vacated by the French Consul. It was tastefully furnished so Mom and Dad kept the furnishings and ordered extra beds for each of us. We retained the French chef and the two Filipino maids.

The house on Villawell Street was a well-constructed bungalow with a wide wrap-around porch. It had five bedrooms, three full baths, large living and dining rooms, a fully equipped kitchen, servants' quarters and a separate two-car garage at the back. The house was set in the center of an acre of land, with big front and back yards, and a low wooden fence in the front. Extra large glass windows gave a definite accent to the house while the unusually tall front door had three locks and bolts. It stood securely on a four-foot stilt which came in very handy, during the heavy rainy season and during the war.

It didn't take us long to adjust to our new home. The weather was hot and humid all year long so we kids ran in and out of the showers several times a day. After a month, all of us were tired of eating French fare, so Dad dismissed the chef, but kept the maids, who were efficient, pleasant and kept our home immaculate, especially the shiny wooden floors.

Ah Woo took over the cooking for she was a born chef - a natural who could easily turn out home cooking as well as banquet fare. She had honed her cooking skills as a young girl, helping her father who was the village chef. Soon Ah Woo's fame as a chef spread throughout Manila and our home became the hub of many mahjong dinners and social gatherings. And it must have been at that time that my love for Chinese cooking became a part of my spirit.

Since she was my amah, Ah Woo always saved the choicest piece of fish, duck or chicken for me. That was when I developed my taste for fish fins and tail, duck tongue and chicken wing tips. The sound of her chopping and stir-frying, the aroma of home brewed soup and stews are still vivid.

We got to know the neighbors and their kids and enjoyed our home and the bounty of the fruit trees in our backyard. We played all kinds of outdoor games and very soon, all of my siblings and I could speak and understand English and a bit of Tagalog.

However, our idyllic life was short-lived. On Dec. 7, 1941, the Japanese bombed Pearl Harbor and the United States declared war against Japan. World War II had begun.

In the spring of 1942. the Japanese Imperial Army entered Manila with militaristic flare. I recall the day they came marching in formation into Pasay. Most of the soldiers were young - no more than 18 or 19. They marched in unison, each carrying a big rifle with a bayonet attached and they sang a hauntingly plaintive chant. They took over some big building in our neighborhood as barracks.

For a while, things stayed the same. Ah Woo continued to shop at the market for fresh vegetables, meat and seafood for our meals. Dad went to work as usual. Mom entertained her friends and played mahjong, Mimi and I continued to attend St. Scholastica School, while James, Francis and baby Maria, born in July 1941, stayed home.

Then things began to change. All schools were closed. We had a long vacation. We kids had nothing much to do but climb trees, pick fruit, set up roadside stalls to sell lemonade, play in the neighborhood with other kids, our dogs and my pet pig. At first it was great fun to sleep in late and idle around, reading comics and story books. After a month, it became boring, so we invented more games and continued to play in our backyard with our neighbors.

In 1943-44 things got worse. There was much tension in the air and many of our neighbors reported that the Japanese were preparing for the defense of Manila. We watched them build blockades and bury land mines in the streets.

"Don't go out into the streets," Mom and Ah Woo warned us. Fortunately the homes along our street had big backyards. Each yard had a side door to the neighbors on the right and left. We could easily walk through the backyards to go from one end of the street to the other end. We still played games such as hide and seek, cops and robbers with our friends.

One day, Uncle Ko,* a good friend of Dad's, called to invite us to evacuate to his shoe factory in the center of town.

"It's dangerous for you and your family to stay by yourselves. Come to my factory. I have many able-bodied young men working for me. By staying together, we can protect your family."

Dad and Mom discussed his suggestion and agreed that it was a good solution. We immediately packed a few belongings - clothes, books and toys. Ah Woo bought several of her cooking pots, tools and spices, while Ah Lo packed our bedding.

The Kos had a suite of rooms vacated for us. One room for Mom and Dad, another one for the five children and a third for Ah Woo and Ah Lo. Ah Woo would use the communal kitchen to cook our meals.

But our visit at the Ko factory was short. After two weeks, Ah Woo complained to my parents, "It's so inconvenient for me to cook and take care of the children at the same time. It takes me twice as long to cook and carry the food to your rooms. And all these men around us is such a nuisance. If you don't want to go back to our old house, I will. All by myself."

Of course that wouldn't do. How could we manage without her, our chef and amah? Mom and Dad also felt cramped. Even though Uncle Ko meant well, we decided to take our chances and return to our house in Pasay. The adults pulled the wooden cart loaded with our belongings and us five children. Since Uncle Ko's factory was about a half hour from Pasay, we had to travel by Taft Avenue, the main street, and saw Japanese soldiers at work - digging tunnels for land mines and explosives on both sides of the road. We were told to keep our eyes down and not look at them.

Soon Uncle Wang and Uncle Sun, friends of our parents, joined us. Both about Dad's age, they came to Manila by themselves while their families remained in China. Having Uncle Wang in our home was certainly a treat. Each night we children would hurriedly wolf down our supper to cluster around him outside on the verandah. "Story time, story time," we chimed eagerly as we clung to his arms and made him sit down in the big rattan chair.

Uncle Wang, a born storyteller, entertained us with ghost stories and Chinese folktales. His stories became more eerie as the night darkened. We were both frightened and fascinated and begged for more as we huddled closer and closer to one another in the dark of the night.

When bedtime came we clung to each other as we made our way to our bedrooms. It was after story time that the adults, Dad, Uncle Wang and Uncle Sun had serious talks. A local carpenter was hired to put up a 10 by 10 foot frame, with a flat roof by the side of our garage. Bags and bags of sand were piled one upon the other on all sides of the shelter, leaving room at both ends to enter and exit. This was our air-raid shelter, with two rows of benches inside for our family.

A 10-foot by 4-foot foxhole was dug under our house. We could all crawl into the open area under the house, supported by the stilts and sit cross-legged on the cardboard-lined foxhole to avoid flying shells. All of our neighbors built air-raid shelters and foxholes as the war between the Japanese and the Americans escalated.

We started out staying in the air-raid shelter for an hour or two, but later lengthened it to four or more hours a day. The droning of the American B-29s overhead became more frequent. Those big silver birds dropped many bombs on strategic Japanese factories and barracks. We knew the Americans were coming to liberate us from the Japanese occupation and silently prayed for the safety of the American troops.

With the return of General Douglas MacArthur to the Philippines in 1944, fighting between the Americans and Japanese intensified. Long vigils in the air-raid shelters and foxholes, sirens blaring, and B-29s flying overhead were common. We didn't really experience the horrors and tragedy of war until we watched our home and our belongings burn.

The Day Our House Burned Down

In the spring of 1945, the retreating Japanese soldiers became desperate and frantic. They killed and burned as they retreated. Late one night the sky was as bright as day - glowing bright red and yellow. The rubber factory, two streets behind our home, was on fire. Ashes and globs of blazing red fire balls were flying in the smoky air. All around us I could smell and taste something sour, like vinegar or sulfur. We could hear explosions and gunshots from all directions. We children were so scared that we couldn't sleep until 3 a.m. Four hours later, we were rudely awakened.

"Get up, get up quick," Ah Woo shouted.

Instead of the usual breakfast of rice porridge with fried eggs and pickles, we were given a glass of powdered milk and a piece of plain bread.

"Get dressed. Bring your *baofu*.* Hurry to the air-raid shelter," Mom commanded.

For months now we each kept our *baofu* at our bedside. Inside mine was a pair of pants, two tops, two sets of underwear, two pairs of socks, a toothbrush, a comb, a red brocade box containing my bronze statues of Saints Peter and Paul, and a card with my name and address - all bundled and tied together with a big scarf.

Within minutes we were hustled into our air-raid shelter. "Why are we here now?" I asked, since I didn't hear any siren nor was there any sign of B-29s overhead.

That day was strange. I couldn't understand why I could see and

19

feel the worry and fear on the faces of Mom, Ah Woo and Ah Lo. Suddenly a neighbor ran over to us and blurted out, "Quick, quick! Leave the shelter! The Japanese soldiers have gone crazy. They're burning and killing everywhere. Run and hide in your neighbor's big home." He pointed to the Bocobo's house, next to ours. It was protected by a tall iron fence, about a foot taller than Dad, with a locked gate. Their red brick house was three stories high, with many rooms. We had known them since we first moved here, five years ago.

We ran from our backyard to the Bocobo's backyard through a side door. We went inside, headed down to the basement which was full of people. In the center of the room was a large table covered with food - sandwiches, cakes and fruit. What a treat! My stomach was aching and growling.

"Come, children, help yourselves. Eat, eat!" Mrs. Bocobo said.

I was the first in line and quickly piled some food on my plate. I was just beginning to eat when another neighbor came running down the basement, screaming to Mom,

"Look! Your house is on fire!"

"No, it couldn't be! We're just there!" I heard my mother shouting. I was so stunned that I dropped my plate of food and dashed up the stairs.

As I looked through the window, our home was indeed on fire. Smoke came from the windows, there was fire on the porch and shafts of red and blue flames everywhere. Soon, Mom, Ah Woo and Ah Lo and my siblings joined me as we stared in disbelief at our burning home. We sobbed and cried and kept shaking our heads.

"All gone, all gone - clothes, furniture, books, toys - everything," I said.

"But what about Puppy?" Mimi screamed as she suddenly

realized that her pet was tied to the porch last night.

"I must go and save Puppy," she cried.

Mom and Ah Woo grabbed her.

"Puppy will be all right," Mom comforted her. "She's a smart German Shepherd and will find some way of saving herself. You can't go out there. It's too dangerous."

It didn't take very long for our house, a wooden bungalow, to burn down. As we watched that awful scene, all kinds of thoughts and questions came to my mind. *Where are we to live now? Are we homeless? What is going to happen to us? And where are Dad, Uncle Wang and Uncle Sun?*

Suddenly the three men burst in. When Dad saw us, he rushed to hug Mom and each of us.

"I thought you were all dead and gone! When I didn't find you in the air-raid shelter, I went crazy!"

Dad was so choked up that he could barely talk. Until that moment I had never seen him cry. He kept sobbing and holding on to us.

"But Dad," I sobbed, "we lost everything!"

"No, not everything - we still have each other. It'll be all right. We can start all over again," he replied.

Later when things had calmed down, Dad told us his story.

"That morning when you were all in the air-raid shelter, the three of us went to the Tans to find out what was going on. We heard that the Americans had entered Manila and that the Japanese were retreating. In their anger and shame, the Japanese soldiers went crazy and began to burn and kill.

"Since the fence surrounding our house was low and our house was wooden and would burn, it was an easy target. Four Japanese soldiers, each with a bayonet and a can of gasoline, jumped over the fence and entered our yard. Now, mind you, Puppy was barking her head off. But she was chained so they ignored her. They poured gasoline on each corner of the porch and lit them with matches and set it on fire. Then they searched the house for people, with their bayonets drawn.

"We three were hiding in the foxhole. At first I wanted to rush out and ask them to spare us, since we're Chinese. But Uncle Sun, who understands Japanese very well, restrained me, saying, "No, you mustn't go. I just heard their leader saying, 'Shoot anyone you see.' These men are desperate and crazy."

Dad continued, "Finding no one in the house, the soldiers left. We came out of the foxhole right away. Thinking you're still in the air-raid shelter, I ran to look for you. When I didn't find you, I rushed over to the Tans, thinking you may be with them. No, you weren't there. I kept running up and down the street, asking everyone I met if they had seen you. There was a lot of shooting. Dead bodies everywhere. Several other houses were on fire. Finally, more than an hour later, someone told me that you were all at the Bocobos."

Uncle Sun came with a surprise for Mimi. He carried a bundle of black brown fur - Puppy. Although Puppy was chained to the porch, it was lucky that the hook in her chain broke a few days ago. So Dad used a piece of string to tie her chain to the porch. Puppy dove into the fire to look for us. It was then that Uncle Sun saw her and quickly called to her. Puppy had burns on her back and on her front paws. But she was so happy to see Mimi and all of us. In spite of her injury, she kept licking our faces and jumping on us. Fortunately, Mrs. Bocobo had some special ointment for burns. Mimi quickly applied that to

Puppy's back and paws.

In a few weeks Puppy was back to normal. But it took our family much longer to recover. Many of our neighbors brought us food, clothes, bedding and toys, too. While we were left with nothing, we were thankful to be alive and that no one in our family was hurt during this terrible war.

Suddenly we had become refugees. In retrospect, our family of eleven (five children, two amahs, Mom and Dad and uncles Wang and Sun) were fortunate to have escaped intact, although we lost everything we owned.

Dad kept saying, "We have each other and can start over again."

Sketch of our home

The Horrors of War

We were certainly among the fortunate ones. Many lost their lives. In retrospect, it was a good thing we moved back to our house in Pasay. We later heard that fighting was fiercest in the downtown area where Uncle Ko and his men stationed themselves.

The retreating Japanese soldiers ordered all people in that area to leave their homes and line up outside. The men and the women were separated. The soldiers took aim at the men, killing almost all of them. Uncle Ko escaped miraculously, but most of his men were lost.

Our friends, the Lims, lived in the same area. They had two teen-age sons and when they were ordered to line up, their dad had his sons stand behind him, so when he fell, he would fall on one who would pretend to be dead. That was how the father saved John, but John's brother, James, wasn't that lucky. He died with his father.

Then there was the Loke family tragedy. Uncle and Auntie Loke decided to invest their large fortune in diamonds. They told my parents that diamonds will always be valuable, and they're small and very easy to carry. So their entire wealth was kept locked in a small metal box.

One day when the crossfire and shelling between the Japanese and Americans was intense, Auntie Loke thought it safer to leave the house and seek shelter in the yard under a big tree. No sooner did she do that when a 45-caliber bullet hit her in the middle cutting her in two. When her daughter Mary Jane saw what happened, she ran to embrace her mother's body and she too was killed by a bullet. When Uncle Loke realized what had happened to his wife and daughter, he went berserk. He left the house in shock, and wandered up and down the neighborhood, holding his box of diamonds. We later learned that he was robbed and killed in the mayhem.

Although we were homeless and had lost everything, we were unharmed and Dad claimed we weren't quite destitute. He and uncles Wang and Sun owned a pharmaceutical warehouse which had a thriving business, including a stockpile of penicillin and other drugs which were very much in demand.

But when he and the uncles returned to the warehouse, they found it completely destroyed by fire. Even though all the goods and supplies in the warehouses had turned to cinders, Dad was still optimistic. He had prepared for rainy days and had converted all his earnings to the mighty U. S. Dollar secured in the steel safe in his office. The safe was still there, but when Dad opened it, the U.S. currencies had all turned to ashes. "All gone, all is lost," Dad lamented.

Many years later, while working as a librarian, I read somewhere that the U.S. Treasury Department had a method of identifying and reconstructing the "ashes" of burned currencies. But that was too late for us - Dad had disposed of the ashes and lost every dollar that he saved.

Mom was in shock. Everything was lost. We had nothing except the clothes on our backs. But wait, what about her personal jewelry? Didn't she put them in a glass jar and bury it in the backyard by the guava tree? She hurried to that spot and sure enough, her jewelry (heirlooms given to her by her parents and grandmother) was still intact.

In addition to our lives, we still had Mom's jewelry. Our entire family of eleven was safe and alive - definitely the greatest blessing.

Soon another miracle happened. When communications between Manila and China was established, Dad found out that his former employer, the Bank of Communications, had compensated him for the pay he missed during the war years.

However, we were still homeless. The Bocobos, our neighbors, insisted that our family of eleven be their house guests for a while.

Our stay with the Bocobos was pleasant. They had four children and their youngest daughter, Theresa, was my age as well as my classmate at St. Scholastica's, so Mimi and I felt right at home. Ah Woo was still our chef, and she still cooked our meals. Occasionally, we invited our hosts and their family to join us for dinner. They were delighted with Ah Woo's cooking.

One day, another neighbor came and reported, "The American Army is advancing. In fact, they're not far away, about an hour's walk from here. They have big guns and are counter-fighting the retreating Japanese. Many have sought safety with them. My family is going too. Maybe yours should." So Mom, Dad, uncles Wang and Sun and all of us went to seek protection from the Americans.

I remember that afternoon - we walked and walked for miles. Each of us carried our little *baofu*. We finally reached the American base where there were four or five big anti-aircraft guns. Oh, how glad we were to see the U.S. Marines - young men with golden hair and big smiles. We had to cover our ears each time they fired those guns, for the sound was frightening and deafening.

Night came. We were safe, but hungry. In her haste, Ah Woo had only brought a box of crackers - no water, no real food. Other families had food - rice, fish, hard-boiled eggs and more. We children were eyeing them with envy and hunger. Finally one family was kind enough to bring over a bowl of congee (rice soup) for us. The adults let the five of us children share it. It was delicious, although it was nothing more than thin rice porridge, spiked with a beaten egg and some soy sauce. This was the only time we felt hunger pains. I thought to myself, *Now I know what it is to be hungry, to go without food.* I promised myself, *I'll never waste any food on my plate in the future.*

Fortunately the weather in Manila was warm. We were all huddled together under the big guns, with just a thin blanket to cushion our bodies.

The next day, Dad, uncles Wang and Sun felt that to seek protection from the Americans wasn't going to work. We had no food or drink to sustain us. So back we walked - slowly and painfully - to our home. On our way, we passed some Japanese soldiers who appeared to be very nervous and angry.

"Keep your eyes down," Mom said.

"Don't look at them...just look at where you're going," Dad whispered. "We don't want to be the butt of their anger and desperation."

We were so glad to return to our temporary home with the Bocobos and to enjoy sleeping on regular beds and filling our tummies with hot food, even though produce and supplies were slim. At least we still had hot cooked rice and a delicious dish of crunchy vegetables stir-fried with bits of pork.

After World War II

The war was over. While we lost our home and everything we had, somehow we managed. After staying with the Bocobos for a month, Mom and Dad arranged to rent three rooms from Dr. Tan and his family. We kids were elated, for their children, Nora, Robert and the others were our dear friends. Each day, 10 of us (five Chiu children and five Tan children) played and invented many games and never had a dull moment.

It was at this time Mom started her first job, as teacher of Chinese literature and history at the Pasay Chinese School. That also became the school where Mimi, James, Francis and I attended. This was the first time we studied Chinese in Mandarin.* It was also at this time we kids used our official Chinese names. Mine was *Wen Huei*,* *Wen* for culture and *Huei* for wisdom. Little did I realize how valuable this year would be to my future mission and work.

I loved school and did well. My history teacher, Mr. Chua, in his early 40s, was kind and mild-mannered. Each time I scored high on a test, he would be all smiles and reward me with a new pencil or notebook. His attention made me proud.

Even though the Tans had a big house, their kitchen was, by modern standards, primitive. Cooking was done on a big stove with four burners with firewood as fuel. Since Ah Woo was still in charge of cooking our meals, we had to buy our own firewood.

One morning, Mrs. Yen, a neighbor down the street, asked if Mimi and I would like to join her to gather firewood. It sounded like a splendid idea. Although Mimi was not quite 12 and I was almost 10, we were anxious to help Ah Woo as well as surprise Mom and Dad. We readily agreed to her proposal and didn't mention a word to Mom, Dad, Ah Woo and Ah Lo.

After breakfast, we stole out of the house and joined Mrs. Yen at the end of the block. She had a wooden cart and we helped her push it down the street. We were heading toward Intramuros,* the famous Spanish City later known as Ghost City, which was completely burned by the retreating Japanese Imperial Army. Every inhabitant in that city was killed.

The trip took about an hour. As we pulled our eight by four foot wooden cart along Taft Avenue to Intramuros, we passed many half-burned buildings, saw lots of homeless people and corpses along the way. It was a scene of devastation and death. We tried to look the other way and not let the images upset us, but they were everywhere.

At our destination, Mrs. Yen showed us what to pick - charred pieces of wood detached from buildings and scattered everywhere. We were careful not to step on sharp metal or glass and were thankful we had worn our socks and shoes.

A few hours later, the cart was piled high with wood. We were so proud of ourselves. It took us another hour to arrive home. Mrs. Yen was very fair: she allowed us to share half of the load for our kitchen.

But no sooner did we step inside the Tan compound when Mom and Ah Woo ran to meet us. They questioned where we had gone, saying they were worried. They scolded us.

I said, "But, but we wanted to surprise you - we thought we were being helpful..."

My explanation and plea fell on deaf ears. Mom was furious and Ah Woo had to restrain her from spanking us. We later found out how dangerous it was to be at that place. Although Intramuros burned down, the remains of bullets, shards of shrapnel, broken glass and other hazardous materials were everywhere, and possibly even Japanese snipers.

We were totally oblivious of the danger and hazards that lurked there. We thanked God that we had returned home, safe and sound, unscathed.

Dad's 43rd birthday was on Dec. 2, 1945. Although it wasn't a particular milestone, Mom said it was time to celebrate, to invite joy and happiness into our lives. Together with Ah Woo, Ah Lo, Dr. and Mrs. Tan, Mom planned a big dinner party for Dad. It was an act of defiance to war, desolation and despair. Neighbors and friends were invited. The entire Tan house was decorated with bright-colored lanterns and flowers.

Ah Woo and Ah Lo and the Tan servants did the shopping, cooking, cleaning and preparations for the party. The children were told to stay out of the way. So we did.

Before dinner, we were told to wash up, change into our best clothes, and then greet our guests. I was excited to meet new and old friends, kids from different neighborhoods who had survived the war. When dinner was announced we headed into the dining room. In the center of the room stood a large oval table, filled with a variety of meats, fowls, vegetables, tofu and more. In the center was the piece de resistance, a large pig, roasted to succulent golden brown.

The succulent-smelling centerpiece immediately caught my attention. A roasted pig or *lechon** was the toast of any party in

Manila. Suddenly something inside me clicked. NO, NO, NO. It couldn't be my beloved pet Piggy, could it? I ran to Mom, "Is that Piggy on the table?"

Mom's face turned white. She looked at me and said in a soft voice,

"Yes, but we had no choice. Where could we find another pig and how could we afford one even if we did?"

That was enough. I dashed out of the dining room in tears, all the while feeling so sorry and sad for Piggy and myself. They killed my Piggy, my beautiful Piggy, my pet. Piggy had survived the war and the fire, only to be slaughtered as food.

I ran outside, refusing to eat anything that night, sitting on the wooden bench crying. Ah Woo tried to console me several times and left a plate of delicacies (not *lechon*, of course) for me. But I didn't touch anything, even Dad's birthday cake, which was a special treat.

Out in the dark I thought about the happy times I had with Piggy. One day in the summer of 1942, Ah Woo returned from the market with a three-pound little piglet, the runt of the lot, barely a week old. The moment I saw her, I was in love with her. She was a lovely, huggable piglet, and she was all mine. Although I was barely seven at that time, I felt motherly and named my baby, Piggy.

Piggy lived in the detached garage. Her bed was a large wicker basket, lined with an old blanket and sheet. Each day, before and after school, I fed her milk from a bottle, petted her and played with her. As she grew bigger, we had races together. Sometimes I would chase her and when I caught up with her, I would scoop her into my arms for a hug and an embrace. Soon, even Puppy, Mimi's German Shepherd, accepted Piggy as a member of the family.

When Piggy graduated from milk to solid food, Ah Woo made sure we set aside some of our food for her at each meal. As Piggy grew bigger, we added leftovers and scraps to her dish. Piggy was not fussy - she gulped down whatever she was given. After all, who, including Piggy, would not appreciate Ah Woo's cooking? She could even turn a plain turnip into gourmet fare.

Each night, Piggy, like a typical, small child, didn't want to leave us to go to bed. Puppy, would, as if by instinct, gently pull her tail and lead her home to the garage. As Puppy was dragging Piggy by the tail, Piggy would oink and squeal and complain loudly. Oh, how we kids laughed and clapped our hands as we witnessed this nightly ritual.

When the Japanese presence intensified, we built our air-raid shelter by the side of the garage and stored Dad's maroon Studebaker in the garage. Piggy's bed was moved to a corner of the back porch. Piggy didn't mind that at all. Because schools were closed, I had more time to play or sit with her.

When the retreating Japanese burned our house, Piggy hid in the bushes in our backyard. When we moved in with the Tans, Piggy tagged along.

As I sat on the bench in the backyard on that starry night with the moon full and bright, I offered a silent prayer to my Piggy. I wished her well and told her how sorry I was and how much I loved her.

Goodbye, Manila

In September 1946, Dad was offered a position at the United Nations Headquarters in New York City. We were all very excited, for that meant a new life in a new country, the United States of America. We were ready to leave Manila and this war-torn country. Mom was particularly happy that Ah Woo and Ah Lo would come with us to the U.S.

Before our departure for the U.S., Dad decided to take a side trip by himself to Hankow (now Wuhan), China to visit his uncle, his father's only brother.

"I must visit him," he told Mom. "He's over 80 and is old and frail. Who knows how much longer he has to live? He went through great trouble to support me in high school." Granduncle Chiu was Dad's last surviving relative since his own father died when Dad was very young.

A week after his arrival in Hankow, a telegram came for Mom:

"CANCEL PREVIOUS PLANS. HEAD FOR CANTON INSTEAD. HAVE BETTER JOB OFFER. LOVE, FRANK."

That was that. No discussion, no option. Since Dad, head and breadwinner of the family, made all the decisions, Mom and all of us had to obey.

When Dad stopped in Shanghai en route to Hankow, he connected with his old colleagues. After many dinners and discussions, they prevailed upon him to stay in China to help rebuild our war-torn country. Dad's sense of duty and patriotism prevailed and so our lives changed once again.

Ah Woo and Ah Lo, however, begged Mom to release them from their obligation to her. Post-war Manila was slowly regaining its economic stability and they knew that many of Mom's friends were anxious to hire them - Ah Woo for her culinary skills and Ah Lo for her housekeeping abilities. Mom had misgivings, but didn't have the heart to refuse them, although she had depended so much on them in Shanghai and Manila and through thick and thin. She knew she would be without a crutch, but hoped she could find others to replace them.

A tearful Ah Woo and Ah Lo saw us off as we sailed for China. Ah Woo cupped my face in her hands, hugged me tight and promised, "I'll come back to take care of you and your children."

That was the last time I would see my beloved amah.

Ah Woo
Ah Woo, my beloved amah

Two days before our big trip to Asia in 1997, I rushed to the bank, less than an hour before closing time. Albert and I were leaving the next day for a three and a half months' stay in Singapore.

In a private room I checked the contents of our safe deposit box. As I removed the papers and envelopes, I spotted a little pink plastic box, tucked in a corner. I opened it, not remembering what it contained, and found a 24-karat gold ring, barely large enough for my pinkie finger. It was a traditional Chinese design - two thin flaps that overlapped to fit a small finger. In the center of the bands was a heart and engraved inside were two Chinese characters. As I slipped it on my finger, I was back in my childhood.

It was a lazy summer day in Manila on July 25, 1945 when I

turned 10. World War II was just over. To me, it was a magical time of the year. Bright red and yellow hibiscus and white and purple orchids were in full bloom. The guava, banana, mango and coconut trees in our neighbor's backyard were heavy with ripe fruit and their fragrance filled the air. When the sun rose on the dot at 6 a.m., I was up. This was atypical for me, usually a late sleeper, especially during the summer. But today was different. It was my big day – my 10th birthday. I couldn't wait, especially when 10 of my best friends were invited to help me celebrate.

As soon as I jumped out of bed, I ran to greet Ah Woo, my amah, who was in the kitchen preparing our breakfast. Some mornings she would serve jook,* thin rice gruel, accompanied by small platters of shredded pork, thousand-year-old eggs, pickled cucumbers, you-tiao* and fermented bean cake. Other times she made a Western-style breakfast - bacon, fried eggs and toast. Each meal was a surprise. Ah Woo, the genius in the kitchen, was forever thinking up and creating dishes to please us. On this day, she was cooking noodles.

"Good morning, Ah Woo. Guess what's so special today?"

"Good morning, my pet. It's Wednesday, isn't it?"

"Yes, but what else? What's so special?" I asked.

"Oh, it's summer and it's July, the prettiest month of the year. The flowers are blooming, the bees are buzzing..."

"Yes, yes, but what else?"

Then with a mischievous twinkle in her eyes, Ah Woo said,

"And...and...it's the 10th birthday of my favorite girl."

"Right," I chimed, "What surprise do you have for me?"

Ah Woo was always much more than my amah. She was my grandma, my godmother, my nana, all rolled into one.

"Close your eyes. Don't peek. Now open your hand..."

I did as ordered and in my palm she placed the little pink box. I found the heart-shaped gold ring with my Chinese name, Wen Huei, (文慧) etched inside the heart.

"Oh, thank you, thank you, Ah Woo!"

I slipped the ring onto the fourth finger on my left hand. I raised my hand for Ah Woo to see. She smiled, seeing I was happy.

"Now, sit down and eat your long-life noodles!" she said, "Chang Ming Bai Sui.*" (May you have a long and happy life and live to be 100!)

I vaguely remember helping Mom and Ah Woo prepare for my party. Mom surprised me with a big chocolate cake which was hard to come by in those days, since many bakeries were still closed due to the war.

I held my hand at eye level looking at the ring.

Dear Ah Woo, where are you now?

She first came to our home in Shanghai, in 1935 when I was a week old. She was in her mid-20s and was mine alone until my number two brother, Francis, was born, four years later. Aside from caring for the two of us, she was responsible for shopping, cooking and feeding our family.

Another amah, Ah Lo, her aunt, took care of my older sister, Mimi, and our brother, James. Ah Lo did the washing and ironing for our family. Other chores were delegated to other servants. Ah Woo and Ah Lo stayed with us until 1940 and followed us when we moved from Shanghai to Manila. We weathered the war years together and finally parted in January 1947 when our family headed back to Hong Kong.

Both amahs were in great demand among our friends in Manila. My parents reluctantly agreed to let them both remain in the Philippines, so they could continue to earn more money.

"I will return to find you. I will retire in your home and take care of your little ones someday, for you are my family – you're my very own," a tearful Ah Woo promised me before we parted.

So we left them in Manila as we returned to Hong Kong. I remember after my high school graduation in 1952, I wrote to Ah Woo to tell her I was awarded one of the 20 government scholarships to the University of Hong Kong.

Within a week, Western Union brought me a surprise. Ah Woo had sent me a gift check for winning my scholarship.

"Mom, look. Ah Woo sent me HK$1,000!"

"That's kind of her," said Mom. "Of course we can't accept it - that's her life savings."

The check was returned to Ah Woo, but the love that came with it has stayed with me all my life, for she was truly a mother to me.

Once when a friend from Manila asked if he could do anything for me, I asked him to visit Ah Woo in the sanatorium, for by then she had been diagnosed with a form of dementia.

"Tell her I love her, I think of her often and pray for her all the time."

Now as I look back, I think she probably had Alzheimer's.

I'm sure my love of Chinese cooking and enjoyment of food came from her. She was a born chef, a gourmet's gourmet. She could orchestrate a 12-course Chinese banquet with ease. During the Japanese occupation in Manila, when produce and food supplies were scarce, Ah Woo somehow managed to produce delicious dishes for our family. I remember the time she used the inner core stem of a banana tree in a stir-fried dish and delighted us with its crunchy and sweet texture.

My first lesson in anatomy came when I studied a set of pig lungs Ah Woo hooked up to the kitchen faucet, to flush away the toxins and prepare it for the pork lung soup with watercress. In the Chinese way of cooking and eating, every part of the animal, whether it is from the land, sea or air, is used. Nothing is ever wasted, since the Chinese value both the texture and taste of the food. When each organ (innards) is well cleaned and prepared, it is amazing how good it tastes.

Mom, who hosted many banquets cooked by Ah Woo, watched and learned from her as well. Mom's skills were dormant until we moved to the United States later, in 1955. I in turn, learned from Mom. Since Ah Woo cooked our meals, I grew up near the kitchen and watched her cut and chop, inhaled the aromas, and was always the first to sample, and critique a new creation - crunchy freshly-fried shrimp balls, fried taro cakes, succulent and tender pork shoulder and more. This is where my appreciation of Chinese food took shape and became part of my early training as a gourmet and chef.

Ah Woo was the one who consoled and hugged me when my parents scolded or spanked me. She soothed bruises and hurt egos. She was there to nurse me when I burned with fever and had diphtheria and chicken pox. She was the first one with whom I shared my triumphs and prizes in school. She would goad me on, encourage me to study hard, prove to my parents and to the world that I was what she called, "the brilliant one, who will shine like the stars at night."

I held my hand at eye level looking at the ring.

Dear, dear Ah Woo, you promised you would retire and stay with me in your old age - but where are you now?

A knock at the door startled me. It was closing time and the bank clerk had to lock up. As I placed the ring on my little finger, I wanted to bask in the memory of Ah Woo a little longer.

Mom and Dad and their five children

2

Canton

The six of us, Mom and my four siblings and I were ready to leave Manila for Canton in January, 1947. Mom had bittersweet feelings. Not so much about Dad staying to do his duty in China, but about actually returning to Canton, her birthplace. She had not been back since 1928, the year she married Zhou. Now after 19 years, she was to return to her hometown and see her parents.

She was certainly a changed person, more mature and sure of herself. She had the courage to divorce Zhou when he was womanizing. Her parents must have been shocked at her action, but she didn't care. She did it anyway. Now in her mid-30s, she had come into her own with Frank and their five children.

In January, 1947, the six of us (Mom, Mimi, James, Francis, Maria and I) left Manila and sailed to Canton at the mouth of the Pearl River in southern China. Since Dad's position with Civil Air Transport was prestigious, while he was stationed in the North (in Beijing and Tianjin), his family was given a spacious flat in the heart of Shamian.* This was a dramatic change from our abode with the Tans in Manila after the war.

Shamian, a beautiful green island of 330 acres, is situated in the southern end of Canton. It is surrounded by a man-made moat and used to be the home of foreign diplomats and corporate CEOs. Its streets are wide, well-paved and lined with evergreens. We were certainly privileged to live on the third floor of a house on No. 4 *Bo Ai Lu* (Road of Brotherly Love).

Our flat was a traditional one. The living room faced the

stairway which opened up to two large rectangular rooms flanked by lots of windows and adjoining verandahs. The room to the right served as the bedroom for all seven of us, Mom and Dad, and us children. The room to the left served as the dining room, kitchen and servants' quarters, partitioned by folding screens. Adjoining the two big rooms at the rear was a large bathroom, complete with a tub, toilet, wash basin and cabinets, all paneled in white wood and porcelain.

As a girl of 11, I quickly adjusted to our new world. Although I missed my beloved Ah Woo, I was excited about our new life and the adventures ahead. Mimi and I were immediately enrolled in the only English school in Shamian, about a five minute walk from our home.

It was a one-room schoolhouse run by Sr. St. John of the order of the Immaculate Heart of Mary. I vividly remember Sr. St. John, a tall American nun in her early 40s with horn-rimmed glasses, a pleasant smile and tons of patience. Mimi and I were placed in Form I, equivalent to Grade VI in the U.S. Since we spoke and studied English in Manila, we had no problem adjusting to our new school and curriculum.

Sr. St. John had her hands full teaching 55 boys and girls, ranging from senior high to first grade. She started the day by calling names of the students in each grade in a systematic way. She started with Grade I, then Grade II and so on. Each grade received its specific assignments for the day, while the students turned in the homework completed the night before.

After she completed the rounds, she would go from desk to desk to supervise and help individual students who needed her attention. Fortunately Mimi and I breezed through our lessons. As newcomers, we were warmly welcomed by the younger ones as well as by our older classmates. Our main preoccupation during our stay in school that semester was to develop our social skills and make new friends.

Aside from a class in religion each day, we also learned the basic prayers, the Our Father, (*The Lord's Prayer*), *Hail Mary* and *Glory Be*. Mimi and I volunteered to sing for the choir at St. John's Church nearby. Surprisingly enough, we started to attend Mass every Sunday.

We knew the tunes and lyrics of a lot of popular songs, especially those of Doris Day, Nat King Cole and Frank Sinatra and made friends easily. Our older classmates were especially interested in our stories of the war and our narrow escape from the Japanese in Manila. We soon received invitations to their homes for teas and lunches. We were happy to be so warmly accepted and included by our older classmates.

Wednesdays and Saturdays were half days. It was customary for the older students to go dancing at teatime, 3 - 6 p.m. at the Grand Hotel downtown. Very soon Mimi and I were invited to tag along. One afternoon the band played *I'll Walk Alone*, one of our favorite songs. Without hesitation we sang it with all our hearts. This so charmed our schoolmates and the emcee that we were invited to sing on stage. This time our song was *You'll Never Know*. We sang it like professionals and curtsied to loud applause.

Yes, we'll never know what life would have been had we settled in the U.S. instead of China that year. As I look back on our first year in Canton after World War II, I realize that transitions and moves were not all that bad - especially for youngsters who were resilient and could readily adapt to new environment.

It was in Canton that we finally met Mom's parents, Grandma

Luk, *Pau Pau*,* 62, was still a beauty and Grandpa Luk, *Kung Kung*,* 65, was jovial, easy-going and ready to tell us stories.

During the next six months, *Pau Pau* and *Kung Kung* were perfect hosts and grandparents. They took us to restaurants and parks, to the Cantonese opera house and *Litchi Wan*,* the famous bay with an amazing array of small junks. It was great fun to sail down the Pearl River and enjoy the beautiful view and amenities such as the taste of the freshly caught live shrimp.

I remember we sat on the seats of the deck of the junk while two big bowls of boiling water, small porcelain bowls, spoons and plates, together with bottles of soy sauce and vinegar were placed on a long wooden table in the center. Then bamboo-woven baskets filled with live, jumping shrimp, no longer than 1-1/2 inches, were brought in. The diners had to grab the wriggling tail of the shrimp and dip the whole thing in the boiling water to cook it. When the grey shell of the shrimp turned orange-pink, it was ready to eat. We were shown how to break off the head and squeeze the succulent flesh of the tail into our mouths. This may sound barbaric, but it is what happened. Although this is a primitive way of cooking, the taste and texture of the live shrimp is absolutely delicious.

We were barely in Canton for a month when we celebrated our first Chinese New Year with pomp and circumstance. The Chinese New Year, also known as the Lunar New Year, is based on the waxing and waning of the moon. It follows that the holiday usually fluctuates between January 20 and February 20. With *Pau Pau* and *Kung Kung* in their natural habitat, this occasion was celebrated with much tradition and fanfare.

The amahs at *Pau Pau's* house were busy, hustling and bustling about, as they cleaned and swept floors and dusted everything. Since by tradition no cleaning could be done for two long weeks following the New Year, they had to be sure the house was immaculate. It was the custom to have all brooms and dusters hidden. Which household could afford to have its good luck swept away by these implements?

Scrolls of auspicious sayings written in beautiful calligraphy on red paper hung along doorways. These all portended good fortune, peace and happiness.

Harmony, Happiness and Blessings to the Entire Family
For All Seasons throughout the New Year*

Porcelain vases and dishes were unpacked and washed, all ready to grace the banquets and teas. The kitchen was a hub of frenzied activities. Weeks before the New Year, ducks, chickens, hams, pork and liver sausages hung from the rafters to dry and age.

Vegetables were washed, preserved, and stuffed into big brown urns to ferment. Taro cakes and turnip cakes, filled with bean paste, lotus seeds and meat were steamed and stored.

The non-ending stream of visiting relatives and friends needed to be pampered and fed. The gods smiled on a household that excelled in hospitality and provided such delicacies for its guests.

Defying *Pau Pau's* orders, I often snuck into the kitchen to inhale the heavenly aroma, to feast my eyes on the variety of foods, and to sample tidbits before they were served.

At *Pau Pau's* behest, the children were taken to the tailor for new clothes. Red and pink paisleys and flowered prints were the materials appropriate for girls, while the boys wore light blues and greens. Everything was red - red tablecloths, red napkins, red

47

candles. Red stood for happiness and prosperity and would ward off evil and misfortune.

On New Year's Eve, we dined on a 12-course vegetarian banquet. *Pau Pau,* a Buddhist, was insistent that her family eat a *chai** (vegetarian) dinner to welcome the New Year. What a feast! The duck, chicken, eel, shrimp, abalone and fish served were all made from soy beans to simulate the actual thing right down to the shape of the original. It wasn't until years later when I returned to Shanghai, my birthplace, in the early 1980s and dined at the Jade Buddha Temple that I remembered the delicious vegetarian banquet I had that memorable New Year's Eve of 1947 at *Pau Pau's* home.

A vegetarian banquet is labor intensive and requires a master chef to prepare it. With so many varieties of greens in the Chinese vegetable family, so many different kinds of mushrooms, fresh or dried, so many kinds of spices and sauces, it's no wonder that a true vegetarian banquet cost twice as much as that of any other banquets and the flavors are even more amazing.

After dinner we were ready for the highlight of the occasion - shopping for flowers. Street after street was lined with chrysanthemums, azaleas, camellias, peonies, narcissus, daffodils, gladioli, hyacinths and more. Young and old flocked to this market to pick flowers that would symbolize the year to come. I was very excited and pretended to be a butterfly, flitting from booth to booth to smell and touch the petals. I couldn't resist buying a bunch of azaleas, a handful of camellias and several daffodil bulbs.

"These are lovely," *Kung Kung,* the avid gardener, said. "But we want something more meaningful." He led me to a booth crowded with people. "*Kung Kung,* these are not flowers, these are just twigs," I said.

"Yes, child, they look like dried sticks. But here - do you see these tiny buds on them? In several days they will blossom and bloom and fill the room with their perfume and buds. Peach blossoms are the most precious flowers of all. The family that owns a flowering peach is truly blessed. Happiness, longevity and prosperity will reign in the household all year long."

We were allowed to stay up all night to play and snack to our heart's content.

At the stroke of midnight we lit firecrackers to chase away all demons and bad omens. By 2 a.m. my eyes drooped. Before I laid down, I reached for the red packets under my pillow. Yes, *laisees* (lucky money in small red envelopes)were already in place to ensure a happy and prosperous year. Not too far from my pillow was a golden tangerine with a sprig of bright green. Tangerines are specially prized for their shape and color, since they resemble gold coins and represent good fortune and happiness.

We woke up a few hours later, washed quickly and donned our new outfits. We came before *Kung Kung, Pau Pau,* and our parents to pay them our respects. With folded hands, we bowed our heads and wished them respectfully *san nin faai lok! san tai gin hong! maan si jyu ji!* (Cantonese), *xin nian kuai le! shen ti jian kang! wan shi ru yi!*(Mandarin), which translates to Happy New Year, Good health, Prosperity, and Blessings. After each greeting, we were given more *laisees.*

The dinner that night was wonderful - another 12-course banquet. This was the traditional high banquet, complete with shark fins, roast pig, bird nest, roast duck, chicken, fish and delicacies from land and sea. I remember it well.

The Lunar New Year is Thanksgiving, Christmas and New

Year all rolled into one. The children from a large household receive many packages of *laisees*, many of which are usually saved in the bank toward a college education. For us, newly returned from abroad, we used our "lucky" money to shop for gifts and things we wanted in our new city.

Hong Kong

After an eight-month stay in Canton, Mom decided, over Dad's protest, to send Mimi and me to study in Hong Kong. She prevailed on Granduncle Hotung to introduce us to a good English school, since entries to good schools in Hong Kong are difficult and essentially dependent on connections. Mom and Dad were Seventh-Day Adventists, but she knew the Catholic nuns had a good reputation for education and discipline and felt we could benefit from that.

St. Mary's was quite close to Auntie Nancy's (Mom's older sister) home, only a few minutes' walk and Auntie Nancy was willing to take us as boarders. At first she refused to be paid, but Mom insisted on giving her HK$250 each month for our room and board. This was to make sure that we wouldn't be treated as poor relations. It was Mom's hope that since Auntie Nancy's three children were grown, she might be happy to have us with her. This would give us a chance to know our only aunt and her us.

But Auntie Nancy never had time for us. She was too preoccupied with her social life -shopping, playing mahjong, going for dim sum with her friends, and taking care of her daughter, Pansy, who was pregnant with her first grandchild.

Her flat on Middle Road was spacious even though half of it was rented to a Japanese family. Auntie Nancy, a widow, needed the additional income to support her leisurely lifestyle. So the five of us, Auntie Nancy, Pansy and her husband, Chung, Mimi and I were crowded into one large bedroom. This was not unusual in Hong Kong, where every inch of space is precious and fully used. The dining room was converted into our living room and Auntie Nancy's eldest son, Robert, had his partitioned bedroom in that area as well. We shared the corridor and the kitchen with the Japanese family while the tiny maid's quarters belonged to Ah Suen.

That one large bedroom contained four beds, arranged at right angles to each other. Cousin Pansy and her husband had the large double bed, while Auntie Nancy, Mimi and I each had a single bed. Fortunately Mimi and I were able to store our suitcases under our beds. We all shared the communal bathroom stacked to the ceiling with cabinets to store toilet paper, towels, medicine, cosmetics and basic health items.

Living in Auntie Nancy's home was cramped, but we had no alternative. We had to manage. Here we were, two girls, aged 14 and 12, all by ourselves. Thank goodness Mimi and I had each other since we had little to no attention or care from Auntie Nancy. We had a roof over our heads, three meals a day, clean laundry, but no supervision.

Another advantage of Auntie Nancy's flat was its location. Middle Road was only a 20-minute walk to our school on Austin Road. The walk each morning and afternoon was our exercise for the day. Her flat was close to the main railway station by the tall Clock Tower, a landmark in Kowloon and to the Star Ferry pier, which could take us across the harbor to the Hong Kong side. It was also the main terminal for the double decker buses that ran to different parts of town - such as Shumshuipo, Kowloon Tong, and Lai Chi Kok.

Each afternoon when we returned from school, we immediately did our homework on the dining table before dinner. If we needed more time, we had to wait until the dishes were cleared after the evening meal. Very often we retreated to the kitchen to talk to Ah Suen, since she was the only one interested in our school and what was happening to us.

Actually she wasn't the only one interested in us. There were the good nuns at St. Mary's whom we got to know quite well during our five years there as well as our pastor, Fr. De Angelis.

St. Mary's was run by the Italian sisters of the order of Magdalene of Canossa. Magdalene, a rich, young noble woman from Verona, Italy, dedicated her life to helping the street children, the wounded, and the sick. At age 34, she founded a new religious order, the Canossian Daughters of Charity, which combined deep prayer life with active apostolate. The first group of Canossian missionaries reached Hong Kong in 1860, after an arduous journey of 48 days by sea. On October 2, 1988, Magdalene was canonized as a saint by Pope Paul II.

Those Canossian nuns, from various cities of Italy, had a good command of English and were very dedicated to their vocation. Although they didn't understand much Chinese, they were devoted to their students and opened their hearts to us. At St. Mary's, our minds were challenged and our hearts and souls were nourished and loved.

St. Mary's was one of the outstanding grant-in-aid schools in Hong Kong. In addition to the public and private schools, grant-in-aid schools had substantial government subsidies, but the governance and teaching were done independently by the nuns themselves. The main requisite was to maintain an educational standard of excellence. Strict inspection and rules were enforced and an assessment of student progress was made each year. Two main exams were held annually in Hong Kong. Student performance was graded and rewarded with a c (credit) or D (distinction) for excellence on the School Leaving Certificate Exam, the official graduating requirement for high school, the equivalent of an American high school diploma.

The Matriculation Exam was mandatory for students who wanted to qualify for college admission. Before they could take the exam, they had to attend another full year of studies. This was followed by a series of exams held on several consecutive days. The results were graded Pass or Failure, while exceptional scholarship received a (D) for distinction.

Both exams were held under strict circumstances. In the exam rooms, desks were spaced at least two feet apart. Students could only take with them their official exam permit which included their name with a black and white photo, and a pen. No paper of any kind was permitted.

Examiners, usually teachers from other school districts, patrolled the aisles. Talking was strictly prohibited. Any student caught talking was immediately disqualified. The rules and protocols were so strict and intimidating that many students panicked and were stressed out before sitting for these exams.

Hong Kong schools have half days on Wednesdays and Saturdays. Wednesday afternoons are visitation days with classmates, while on Saturday afternoons Mimi and I went to a movie at the Star Theater two blocks away. A single matinee ticket costing 75 cents was sufficient for the two of us to share a designated seat. The theater attendants knew us and since we were both petite, they allowed us to share a ticket. Maria Montez, Sabu, and Tarzan were our favorite movie stars. Reading novels, comics and short stories was my other hobby.

We looked forward to our long vacations at Christmas, Easter and summer. It was during these times that we'd take the five-hour train from the Star Ferry Terminal to Canton, to be with our family. We missed our parents and our siblings terribly and the friends we'd made at the Shamian school, especially the Tse family - Imelda and her brother Robert.

During my five years with the Canossian sisters, from Form II to Form VI, I had come to know many of the nuns well. Although they each differed in looks and personality, they were all loving and caring. They were my mothers away from home who gave me unconditional love. The warmth and love lacking in Auntie Nancy's home was made up for in abundance by the nuns. They knew that Mimi and I were boarding with relatives and went out of their way to lavish us with kindness.

Then there was Fr. Horace de Angelis, pastor of Rosary Church which was next to St. Mary's. He was a tall, robust man in his 50s, with thick glasses, a booming voice, and a big heart. His home town was Rome, Italy, but he had been in Hong Kong for more than 30 years and spoke excellent Cantonese. He took his pastoral work seriously and was known to be a caring shepherd to his parishioners and students at St. Mary's. When he found out that our parents were not in Hong Kong, he volunteered to be our guardian. He would review and sign our monthly report cards, and we would leave his office happy with a Kit-Kat bar in our pockets.

Mother Mary was the teacher of Form II. I still remember her fondly. She was gentle and kind and was good to Mimi and I. When I was promoted to Form III, Mother Emma was my teacher. She was a tall nun with a nose like a hawk's beak. But underneath that austere mien was a warm and loving heart. She invited us to stay after school each afternoon to learn and study catechism. We were two lonely sheep and readily lapped up all the attention we could get. So it was not surprising that we were both baptized by

Fr. de Angelis on Easter, 1949. When we told Mom of our desire to be Catholics, she didn't object.

After our baptism and confirmation, Mother Emma decided we were ready to be true soldiers of Christ. She enrolled us in the Legion of Mary,* an organization that started in Ireland where young and adult Catholics were recruited to be Mary's helpers. We were sent two by two to visit catechumens (future Catholics) and to the sick to perform works of mercy in hospitals, orphanages and old-age homes. Assignments were handed out during our weekly meetings after school. We took these assignments seriously and did our best to be disciplined and loyal soldiers of Mary.

Aside from our work with the Legion of Mary, we were involved in activities in our parish. Each Christmas, Fr. de Angelis secured financial backing from large corporations to pay for chefs to prepare food to feed hundreds of poor children. This was a Boxing Day (December 26) Activity. I remember how excited we were to be chosen to be instruments of love and service to those hungry children in Hong Kong.

Fr. de Angelis personally hand-picked 50 students from St. Mary's to help run this event which was supervised by our religious and lay teachers. It started at 9 a.m. with decorating and setting of tables, wrapping presents and preparing games. Hundreds of children were lined up to register for their number by 11 a.m. They played simple games before the dinner and prizes were awarded to the winners. Each child was a winner. All of them left with a Christmas present and a full tummy.

I recall one young boy of about 10, who carried his younger brother on his back. At dinner, the older boy refused to eat his portion. When I asked why, he said, "I'm saving my share for my mom at home."

"Eat. Eat your meal," I said. "I'll save another portion for you to take home to your mother." The dinner was a chicken and rice dish with healthy greens.

In late December of 1949, Mom and Dad and my four younger siblings moved from Canton to Hong Kong. Mimi and I now had our family with us and a real home. We lived in a rented third floor flat on Tong Mei Road in Shumshuipo. It had a dining/ living room, two bedrooms, a small kitchen, a bathroom and a verandah, spacious by Hong Kong standards, but for our family of eight plus two maids, it was certainly congested.

By adding glass panels, the spacious long verandah was converted into two bedrooms: one for Mimi and me, and the other for James and Francis. Mom and Dad shared their bedroom with my three younger siblings, Maria, Shirley (born in Canton in 1947) and George, born in Hong Kong in mid-January, 1950. The second bedroom served as a storage room and maid quarters. We had floor-to-ceiling closets for our clothes and belongings.

As occupants of the top floor, we shared the use of the open terrace with the other family that lived across the hall. We'd rush through supper most nights to "cool" off in the terrace on hot and humid evenings. The terrace also served as our living room when we had company. We could walk, talk and admire the view at the same time.

Quite a few boys came visiting at this time. Although Mimi was not quite 16 and I was 14, Mom was comfortable about this, since they came to visit us at home and she knew that we were all respectable and proper. Definitely there was no kissing and not even holding of hands. However, it was exasperating and embarrassing when four or five would all show up within half an hour of each other. There we were, all six or seven of us in our living room, staring and tongue-tied. Later on Frankie Ho, the son of my Confirmation godmother and our family doctor, became my steady boyfriend, but that didn't deter Conrad Kcomt and Joe Lee from visiting. Conrad was my dance teacher (waltzes, fox trot, rhumba and cha cha), while Joe taught me how to jitterbug. Hosting house dancing parties was a frequent occurrence during our days. Mimi and I were often invited to the parties at our friends' homes and we enjoyed dancing, chatting and singing.

Televisions weren't popular in Hong Kong at that time, but we had Redifussion, a local radio station which featured current news and hit songs which Mimi and I memorized and sang over and over again. It was a popular pastime for bobby soxers to write requests to Redifussion and dedicate songs to their friends. At supper time we hovered around our radio to find out if there were song requests for us or our friends. Mimi and I had pleasant voices and were often asked to sing at parties and gatherings.

Life at Tong Mei Road was simple and happy. In the summer of 1950, Dad secured a visa and immigrated to the U.S. to try new ventures. Mom entrusted him with most of our savings, which was substantial, since she had saved part of Dad's regular salary as well as his bonuses and travel compensations for the last three years. Dad agreed to send Mom a monthly sustenance and he would eventually arrange for us to join him in the U.S.

So Mom became our caretaker and sole parent. At last she was forced to pay attention to her seven children. Her social life had taken a different turn. She was no longer the glamorous *tai tai* with Ah Woo and Ah Lo behind the scenes to care for the children and the household. Although she still had maids to clean, wash and cook, they were not like Ah Woo and Ah Lo, who had been like family and had run the household. Without them Mom seemed lost, with no one to lean on.

She gradually substituted Mimi and me for Ah Woo and Ah Lo. Mimi helped with the care of the younger children, I was Mom's right hand, giving advice and doing chores outside the home, running errands, shopping and banking. She didn't mind that we were still adolescents, for she was a traditional Chinese mother - daughters were supposed to help the family in every possible way.

In fact, she treated us as her younger sisters. Since Mom kept her beauty and her youth, it was very easy for her to pass as our older sister. Each time one of our boyfriends took us out to a movie or a treat, Mom was invited to tag along. And she did. Mimi and I were so proud we had a young and fun-loving mother. She fitted right in, more teenager than mother. Now, as I look back, I realize she never quite understood her role as our mother.

When I was promoted to Form V, Mother Piera was my form mistress. Born in Milan, Italy, she spoke English perfectly and served on the HK Educational Board and the Board of Examiners - a double honor for St. Mary's. She was not only the brains of St. Mary's, she was also the most beautiful and gracious teacher we had. She was gentle and soft-spoken. Her glasses didn't hide her beautiful eyes and long lashes. It was at this time that our lives intertwined. She became my after-school French tutor, my mentor and my teacher.

She challenged me academically and spiritually and I would have leapt through hoops for her. Since I took French as my second language, Mother Piera would take time after school, twice a week, to help me with the language.

That year was crucial for me. I was due to take the School Leaving Certificate Exams. Although I studied hard, my test results were not as good as I had hoped. I ended up getting a Distinction in Religion and credit in English, French, History and Civics. Quite disappointing to me. But Mother Piera wasn't discouraged. She continued to urge me to study and try for the Matriculation Exam, which was Form VI.

Father Horace de Angelis
Fr. de Angelis, a hunter

Fr. de Angelis was the pastor who baptized Mimi and me in 1949. He was our guardian when we were boarders at Aunt Nancy's home, and instilled in me the joy of giving and serving, above all else.

In 1980 when I returned to Hong Kong after 25 years, one of the first persons I longed to see was Fr. Horace de Angelis. He was a father and a mentor to me during my high school years at St. Mary's. He was the one who signed Mimi's and my report cards each semester, the one who saved me from getting penicillin shots I didn't need and the one who encouraged me to always strive for the best in myself.

But Fr. de Angelis was no longer the pastor of Rosary Church in Kowloon. During his 40 some years of tenure, the parish was his fiefdom. He was their beloved father and shepherd. He had ruled it with love, power, loyalty and glory.

It didn't take long to locate him. He was living in a flat on Tai Tung Street, just above a Catholic elementary school in Yaumatei, Kowloon. This was a far cry from Rosary Church in Tsimshatsui. I was also able to get his phone number from the Catholic Center.

"Hello, is this Fr. de Angelis? I'm Elizabeth Chiu from St. Mary's. Remember me?"

"Of course, the two Chiu sisters, Deanna (later Deanna used her nickname Mimi more frequently) and Elizabeth."

I made an appointment to see him the next afternoon. I was visiting another friend in Shatin that morning, a good distance from his flat in Yaumatei. It was a hot, humid, August day with a temperature around 94 degrees Fahrenheit. Sweat dripped down my forehead and my back, but no matter, nothing would stop me from visiting Fr. de Angelis, the father-priest whom I respected and loved because he cared so much for his sheep.

Recalling his penchant for punctuality. I was 45 minutes early. I pressed the lift button for the sixth floor and saw him waiting for me as soon as the door opened. He was dressed in a white undershirt with short sleeves and a pair of black trousers. Still tall, this big man I once knew, looked beaten, depressed and lackluster. I recalled what Fr. Cronin once told me about his removal from Rosary Church, "He's an honest man, but out of tune with the times."

Probably true, but to me, Fr. de Angelis would always be a

62

father figure – authoritative, baroque, grand, a little pompous, but still loving and caring.

I can only imagine how it felt when he was ordered by his bishop to retire and leave the parish which he built single-handedly to what it is today. He was torn between his own desires and his vow of obedience. Here was a beaten man of the cloth, who was every inch human in feelings and sensitivity. And now at 82, after bouts with arthritis of the hips and back and other ailments, he was alone and depressed. "Behold the man..." (John 19:5, New American Bible)

I showed him a copy of my new cookbook, "The 15-Minute Chinese Gourmet," hot off the press. I pointed to the acknowledgment page and asked him to read it.

"Oh, I don't know these people," he protested.

"Just read on, Father, you may recognize a few."

He finally came to his name and inscription:

"To Fr. Horace de Angelis, for believing in the pursuit of excellence."

I caught the gleam of pride in his eyes - to be remembered and lauded for all his efforts and the fact that I had come across the ocean to seek him out after a quarter of a century.

He looked at some of our family photos, then I slipped him a personal check, a small token of all that he had done for me during my years at St. Mary's and more.

"What did I do for you?"

"Don't you remember?" I told him how he saved me from depression and rescued me when I thought I had TB.

"Did I really do that?"

"Yes, Father, and more."

We talked about the Boxing Day picnics for the poor children, the fund-raising bazaars, the different parochial activities that he initiated and organized. I told him all these had inculcated in me idealism and desire to make our world a better place.

He smiled to himself, possibly thinking that his years of service and love had not been in vain. He was still loved and appreciated and indeed, he could honestly admit, "I am the good shepherd, mine know me and I know mine." (John 10:14, New American Bible.)

A Dream Come True

I had always wanted to attend the university and earn a bachelor's degree. But I knew that as a girl, my chances of a college education were slim, since I had three brothers who, according to Chinese tradition, were to be educated first. If my parents hadn't lost their fortune in Manila during World War II, things could have been different, but, that was not the case.

Mom's plan for me was a good secretarial employment like Mimi's. After she graduated from St. Mary's, Mimi worked at several secretarial positions. Her last one, before her marriage, was with the Registrar of the University of Hong Kong (HKU).

That summer I was interviewed at Lane Crawford, a prestigious English firm. The interviewer was impressed with my spoken and written English and promised me a secretarial position if I would spend a year learning shorthand, typing, and other secretarial skills.

I finished high school at 16, but I didn't want to be a secretary. During an intimate talk with Mother Piera, I told her my deep yearning for higher education. She understood and encouraged me to enroll in Form VI, a preparatory Matriculation year and promised personally to tutor me in the subjects I selected - English, English Literature, History, Geography, French, and Religion. I agreed and kept this secret from Mom.

With Mother Piera's encouragement, I enrolled in Form VI. Students in Form VI were selected with care. St. Mary's had to uphold its high academic standard, only superior students were allowed to enroll. There were six in our class, so each of us received personal attention. I knew that I had to double my efforts in all subjects. This was an honor and obligation to fulfill Mother Piera's trust.

A week before Christmas break, Mother Piera and the other mothers at St. Mary's gave me a big surprise. They chose me to be the Angel of the School. This coveted prize was awarded to a favorite student. I wore a lovely, white organdy dress with a pair of wings attached to my back and a halo over my head. My task was to go from classroom to classroom to distribute the Christmas cards students sent to one another via the school mail. It was a thrill to be so important.

After Christmas, I plunged into preparing for the June Matriculation Exam. Who better than Mother Piera, who had served on the Hong Kong Examination Board, to teach me to study? Day after day she drilled me in spelling, literature, French, geography, history and religion - the subjects I was to be tested on. When the big day arrived I felt confident - poised like a samurai, ready for the battle.

All exams were in essay form. I wrote long essays for all subjects explaining the logic of my premises and arguments. Each exam lasted two hours, from 9-11 a.m., followed by a 15-minute break, then from 11:15 a.m. - 1:15 p.m. - two exams a day until all exams were completed.

The day before Matriculation, I visited Mother Piera. True to form, she gave me a great pep talk on how I must take time to study the question, and jot down key points of my essay on a work sheet provided by the examiners. She reminded me to first pray to the Holy Spirit for guidance and inspiration, and second, to give to Jose, the St. Mary's errand boy, the pointers I jotted down for my essay when he met me at break time so she could see if my logic and arguments were correct. I promised to do as she instructed and felt certain that I could handle it.

On the first exam, I followed Mother Piera's instructions to the letter. When I went outside at 11 a.m. to hand Jose my notes, Mother Piera sent a surprise. Jose handed me a shiny red apple (an expensive foreign import) and a thermos of hot chocolate. She wanted to make sure I was nourished in body and spirit for my second exam. I have never forgotten her care and thoughtfulness. The same regimen lasted for the three days of my six exams.

After that ordeal, I was very tired and developed a bad, constant cough. I didn't want to alarm Mom so I secretly went to consult Uncle Ho, our family doctor. After a thorough checkup, he said I had contracted tuberculosis and needed penicillin shots twice a week. Although he didn't charge me for the shots, I had to pay for the medicine, and it was expensive. I didn't have any money, since Mom didn't give us allowances, even though I gave her every penny I earned from my private tutoring. Besides, I didn't want Mom to know, nor did she have extra money. Fortunately a good friend, Vince Ng, came to the rescue and loaned me the money for the X-ray and the penicillin shots. While I didn't have a reaction to the shots, I developed an allergy to penicillin many years later.

One afternoon when I bumped into Fr. de Angeles, he noticed how pale I looked and asked what was wrong. He refused to believe I had TB. Without hesitation, he reached into his pocket, pulled out fifty dollars and said, "Get another X-ray and bring me the negatives. I'll ask my friend, Dr. Chen, the renowned radiologist, to have a look at them."

I did as I was told. When Fr. de Angelis told me that Dr. Chen examined the negatives and found only swollen cold glands, not TB, I was greatly relieved. Such was the concern my pastor showed me.

When the official results of the Matriculation Exam were posted in the Hong Kong Standard, the official government way of announcing the results, I was elated. I not only passed (since students were primarily graded Passed or Failed, in addition to Distinctions in particular subjects) but I had received a Distinction in Dictation, which is part of the English course. In that exam the examiner read certain passages and we wrote them down with the correct spelling, punctuation and paragraphs.

On a hot summer day in 1952, a week after the results were out and we kids were all at home, without air-condition and feeling restless amidst the sweltering heat, there was a knock at our door. I checked the peep-hole and was surprised to see Jose, the errand boy of St. Mary's.

Now, why would Jose come looking for me? I thought when I saw him. *Mother Piera or Mother Virginia, the principal, must have sent him here.*

Sure enough, I was right.

"Come quickly, Miss Chiu. Mother Piera wants to see you."

We didn't own a telephone at home. It was both expensive and difficult to get a permit for a phone at that time. As I rushed into in her office that afternoon, the smile on Mother Piera's beautiful face said it all.

"Oh, Elizabeth, wonderful news. No, a miracle! You've been selected to receive one of the top 20 scholarships from the Hong Kong Government - a full scholarship for four years to HKU's College of Liberal Arts."

My wish had come true. I had a full four-year scholarship! I pinched myself to make sure I wasn't dreaming. I hugged Mother Piera to thank her for being my teacher and mentor.

"But you did the hard work," she said. "Come. Let's go to the chapel and offer our thanks."

When I returned home, I was on cloud nine. But, I had a confession to make to Mom. On the bus home, I practiced my explanation. To my great surprise, Mom was happy for me. Now as I look back, I can understand why. All her life, she had yearned for a proper education, but never had the chance. Although her father was wise enough to allow the Chinese tutor to include her as a student with her brothers, she never went to college.

That summer of 1952 was the happiest one in my life. Not only was I given a clean bill of health, but I had a four-year government scholarship - $2500 per year for a total of $10,000. The $2,500 covered tuition, fees, and books, leaving a balance of $1,200 which was turned over to me in cash. I gladly gave that amount to Mom for our household use.

Since Dad was in the U.S. and had taken most of our savings, our family of eight (not including our maids) subsisted on the monthly allowance Dad wired home each month. Whatever money I made in tutoring, together with excess from my Government scholarship, supplemented our day to day living expenses. The extra dollars allowed Mom to buy better quality of meat and seafood, and also paid for new clothes and weekly movies.

During my birthday week in July, Mimi and I went to visit the mothers at St. Mary's. Mothers Piera, Virginia and Emma were assembled in the office.

Unabashed, I announced, "Mothers, today's my birthday. I just turned 17. What present do you have for me?"

They asked what I would like to have.

It so happened that a litter of German Shepherd puppies was the newest addition to the school. Those adorable, cuddly bundles of fur were snuggled nearby in a large wicker basket. Mimi and I stooped to pick one up. We were immediately hooked.

"Oh, can I have one of these?"

"Choose the one you want to take home," Mother Piera said.

We decided on a brown and white male and named him "Puppy" in memory of our other German Shepherd in Manila years ago. When we presented him to Mom, she didn't object. Puppy became a beloved member of our household until we left Hong Kong in August, 1955.

At Christmas, a package came from Dad. All of us crowded around the table as Mom opened the box. The package contained a black and white checkered dress, a sky blue printed dress, and a green wool coat - for me. Nothing for Mom and the others. Everyone, except me, was disappointed. I was ecstatic, but also embarrassed and sad. As I look back, I realize how jealous my siblings must have been. In retrospect I also realize that parenting isn't an easy job. One should be fair and loving to each child.

Mother Piera
Mother Piera, my teacher and my mentor

It was not until 1990 that I was able to keep my promise made ten years ago. Albert was scheduled to attend a biomedical meeting in Formia, a suburb of Rome. I accompanied him to that meeting, but left early to go to Milan.

This visit started with a promise I made when I spoke to my beloved teacher, Mother Piera, in Hong Kong, in 1980. She was about to return to her home in Italy and asked me to visit her there. Finally it was happening. I had just stepped off the train in the Milan station, with two heavy suitcases, not speaking a word of Italian. The place was packed with tourists, visitors, locals, and soldiers dressed in fatigues with their fingers on the trigger. So many people, and I was all alone.

I regretted I hadn't learned some basic Italian as Mother Piera suggested. That would have at least tied me over until I was picked up by the convent car. Here I was, in her city, not knowing which way to turn or when I would see her.

I hastily dialed her number, fed the coins into the phone slot, only to be told, time and again, something about the "numero" was wrong. What to do? I wanted to use the restroom, but couldn't, since I didn't see any elevators or escalators and my suitcases were too heavy to lug up the steep flight of stairs.

Fortunately I bumped into a young man, whom I surmised, by his looks, was English. He turned out to be Irish and we struck up a conversation. That made me feel better. Then the gelato man passed by and I purchased a cone from him. At least in licking the gelato, I felt comforted and less alone.

Each time a nun came by, I approached her and asked in my broken Italian, "Canossian? Madre Piera?" The replies were a shake of the head. After what seemed like an eternity, Sister Maria, a nun in her 40s, came by, smiled and greeted me.

"Ah, you must be Elizabeth, Mother Piera's student and friend." With that, she grabbed both my suitcases. I breathed a sigh of relief and followed her to her car.

The drive to the Canossian Convent in Milan was an adventure. Sister Maria was a wonderful guide. She pointed out the famous La Scala, the Milan Cathedral and Santa Maria delle Grazie, decorated with Leonardo da Vinci paintings.

We arrived at the convent, an L-shaped Renaissance style

palace of the 16th Century, not unlike one in a travel movie. I was taken to my room, the suite reserved for visiting prelates and priests. Then I was told that I would be eating with the sisters in their dining hall and would see Mother Piera in the morning.

Mother Piera, dear, beloved, beautiful Mother Piera. Yes, I have traveled half the world just to see you for one last time. How much do I owe you and love you? How much have you loved me? Let me harken back to the early years at St. Mary's.

I unpacked and sat down to reminisce: 1947, 1948, 1949, 1950, 1951 and 1952 - these years were like photo frames passing before my eyes.

Suddenly a gentle knock at my door roused me from my reverie.

"Dinner is served."

I followed Sister Maria to the dining room and sat with her and some 40 other sisters.

What an experience to be accepted as one of them. How things had changed. In the 1940s and 50s, the sisters were fully clothed in their habits - black and brown in the winter months, and fully-starched white cotton in the spring and summer. Their hair was tucked in a bonnet that framed their faces and students were never allowed to enter their private quarters.

Now, I saw their habits were simpler and more functional,

light grays and blues and with their heads covered with a light veil. The fact that I was actually eating with them in their dining room was also a new practice.

That evening, Sr. Angelina, the mother superior, came by and welcomed me formally to their convent. She said that she had lived in St. Mary's (my alma mater) in Hong Kong for two years and was particularly fond of fried rice. Saying that, she added hesitantly,

"Would you cook some fried rice for us tomorrow?" (This recipe can be found in pp. 318-319.)

Mother Piera, I was told, was feeling much better and would see me in the morning. Before I left on this trip, I had learned that Mother Piera was suffering from emphysema, diagnosed with acute pneumonia and given only six months to live. When I decided to accompany Albert to Italy, I had telephoned her from Detroit, giving the exact dates I would be in Milan. She was strong enough to come to the phone and I kept repeating,

"Wait for me. I'm coming to see you."

I knew that if the sick and dying have something to look forward to, they will postpone their death until it happens.

That night I slept restlessly. The room was actually a suite, with a living room and a full bath. It was at the tip of the L-shaped building. The nuns were housed in the other side of the L. I locked my door, kept all the lights on, fearing the ghosts of this old place might visit me. It felt eerie so I slept on my back with

74

the Bible on one side of my pillow and my rosary on the other.

In the morning, I dressed quickly, ate breakfast and waited to be taken to Mother Piera. When I saw her, soft and frail, seated in her wheelchair, I was overwhelmed. I bent down to hug her, saying, "Dear mother, teacher, mentor – I've found you at last."

It was a beautiful moment. I had kept my promise, made in 1980 when I first returned to Hong Kong after an absence of 25 years. She was constantly in my mind and heart all these years. When I was in Hong Kong that summer, I called St. Mary's, but was told to try Sacred Heart. The person I spoke to didn't know her. So I called Sacred Heart. I can't remember how many times I called. The line was either busy or kept ringing. On the last day of my visit, I finally got through and was able to connect with her. We spoke briefly and her parting request was,

"Elizabeth, come to Milan. Come to see me in Milan."

"Yes, yes, I will."

Now when she saw me, she too was overwhelmed. All she could say was, "Elizabeth, you're here. You're in Milan." But her voice was so soft I had to stoop and put my head next to hers to hear what she was saying. As I pushed her in her wheelchair, we talked and reminisced about the past, those happy days at St. Mary's. I gave her a copy of my new book, "The 15-minute Chinese Gourmet" and showed her where she was listed separately in the Acknowledgment, "For challenging my mind and spirit at St. Mary's." I detected the joy in her heart and the look of pride in her eyes.

Later that morning she showed me her art work - paintings, small sketches and bookmarks and gave me a bookmark to remember her by. She asked for my photo because she wanted to paint my portrait.

After two hours, I noticed she was tired and I reluctantly handed her back to the nurse and promised to visit the next morning before my departure. When I returned to my room, I couldn't help but compare Mother Piera to a gently stir-fried dish of fresh bamboo shoot with white mushrooms. The taste is delicately sweet and simple yet it embodies gentle flavors, drawn from nature's best.

The following morning we met and renewed our conversation. Then I embraced her tearfully for we both sensed that this would be good-bye until we would meet again in our Father's home.

On my return flight I detoured to Minneapolis to connect with Jonathon, my literary agent. I had several cookbook proposals to show him, but he was not enthused about them. He kept asking about my visit with Mother Piera. I was not about to write my memoir. The visit and events were too raw. I wasn't ready to share them with him or the world. They were locked in my heart and soul and frozen in time. Mother Piera died shortly after.

Someday I'd like to return to Milan to revisit that mother house and relive my memories of Mother Piera. Perhaps I will take some wild flowers to her grave and tell her once more how much I love her.

Yes, that will be another odyssey to undertake when I am in Italy.

The University of Hong Kong

While Dad was in the U.S., I attended the University of Hong Kong (HKU),* from 1952 to 1955. HKU, located on Pokfulum Road in Hong Kong, was THE university every boy or girl aspired to. With an enrollment of under 1,000 students, it was the "elite" of the elite. How privileged I felt to be one of the elites and have the opportunity to learn, to be challenged, and to excel.

I had just turned 17 and was having the time of my life. I chose English, French, History and Logic as my subjects during my freshman year. Since Mom wanted me at home, not at the dorm, I was a long-distance commuter, still the good Chinese daughter who had yet to learn to rebel or state my own wishes.

Each morning I left the house at 8 a.m. and took a bus to the Star Ferry Terminal. From there I caught a ferry from Kowloon to Hong Kong before boarding another bus that went directly to the University. The commute was about an hour. Fortunately I was able have a 9 a.m. class, allowing enough time to make it. My last class, Logic, ended at 4 p.m. I usually arrived home around 5 p.m.

For lunch, I could choose from several cafeterias - fried or soup noodles, rice with different toppings, *dim sum** or *jook* - all rather inexpensive. For $1.00, one could have a hearty meal.

The news of my government scholarship spread quickly. Within weeks, I was elected Freshman Class Representative for our class of 120. We were a motley group of young people from many places - Singapore, Malaya (now Malaysia), Macau, Taiwan and Hong Kong.

78

This way of life continued for three years. I enjoyed my studies and classmates. In my sophomore year I chose English, French, History and Psychology. As a junior I declared English (six papers) as my major and Philosophy my minor (three papers).

During my sophomore and junior years, I served as secretary to the Arts Society (in our Liberal Arts College), the Social Studies Society, and the United Nations Society. At the same time, the mothers at St. Mary's encouraged me to be the Curia Secretary, the governing arm of the Legion of Mary groups in HK. I was a little nervous, since the Curia was composed of CEOs and executives of large firms, while I was a young college student. But the good mothers helped and guided me, even editing my minutes and other official correspondence. At the same time I served as a regular member of the Legion of Mary group at Ricci Hall, an all-boys residential hall run by the Jesuit Fathers.

I had come to know Fr. Fergus Cronin, the Jesuit rector at Ricci Hall (men's dorm) who was my Logic instructor during my freshman year. I think he liked me because I aced his course. Later he was generous to me in many ways. Ricci Hall was quite liberal and its residents were free to invite women friends to lunch and dinner. I was a frequent guests at Ricci and thoroughly enjoyed the gourmet Continental fare served there.

In addition to these activities at HKU, I did private tutoring. One of my students was Cynthia Ng, who started out with the ABCs, later attended St. Mary's, and is now a physician in Canada. The wife of the French consul, who lived in a beautiful mansion at the Peak, the prime location in Hong Kong, was also my student. Each fortnight, I took the tram to her house, taught her conversational English for an hour, and was treated to afternoon tea of petit fours, chocolates, and hot tea.

As a matter of routine I gave all my earnings to Mom for our household use. Occasionally when I needed a few dollars I'd ask her for some. I didn't have much need for money nor was it my custom to shop much.

My junior year at HKU, 1954-1955, was exciting, at home and at the University. Our family was busy preparing for Mimi's marriage to Philip Gotuaco, third son of Auntie Aggie and Uncle John, dear friends of our parents from Manila. Philip just graduated in Civil Engineering at Notre Dame University in South Bend, IN. Mimi and Philip had started going steady "by mail," and Philip proposed in a long-distance phone call which was extravagantly expensive that summer.

Our whole family was involved in the wedding preparations. In addition to being the maid of honor and her chief assistant, I was the courier of "wife cakes" to our friends and relatives in Kowloon and Hong Kong.

The wedding on October 24 at St. Theresa's Church, Kowloon, was magnificent. Mimi, a radiant bride, married her true love, Philip.* While all six of us kids were in the bridal party, Dad couldn't come to give her away. If he left the U.S. for Hong Kong, even for this happy occasion, his return visa to the U.S. would be in jeopardy.

On the university front, I participated in many school events, including the lead in the stage play, *The Duchess of Malfi*. This was the first time Mrs. Mary Visick, our English professor, staged a play. Both Ida Cheung and I were vying for this part, but Mrs. Visick was non-committal. Ida, in her eagerness to get the role, went to beg Mrs. Visick for that part, saying that it had always been her dream to be an actress, whereas Elizabeth, she claimed, had no such aspirations. That didn't convince Mrs. Visick, who immediately decided to give me that starring role. The play was staged for two evenings to a packed house. Several of the boys I dated attended the performance and had a great time.

Then came a surprise.

In the early spring of 1954, Fr. Cronin received a foundation grant to send four HKU students to Madras, India, to the First Asian Pax Romana Seminar. I was one of the four chosen. Little did I know how this would affect my life and my future. The others were Albert King from the College of Engineering, David Woo from the College of Medicine, and Michael McDougall from the College of Architecture.

Fr. Cronin briefed us on the purpose and mission of the seminar. The intent of Pax Romana was to promote solid Christian values as well as to educate, inculcate and nurture future leaders who believed in world peace and cooperation among nations. Who better than young Catholic university students already typed as leaders of tomorrow, to carry the torch? It followed naturally that after the seminar we would return to Hong Kong to continue the mission and spread the good news.

Albert King, 20, was appointed leader of our delegation. Although he was the youngest of the three men, he was astute, organized, fair and decisive. On December 1, the four of us took off from Kai Tak Airport. After a brief stop at Bangkok, we landed in Calcutta and spent the night there before flying to Madras.

I continue to cherish this incident at the Great Eastern Hotel during our short stay in Calcutta. The Hotel, built during colonial times, still had its British trappings and etiquette. The four of us dined in the formal dining room, with fully-attired waiters in attendance. The six-course prix fixe dinner that evening was delicious: a soup, salad, entree, dessert, with bread and butter, coffee or tea, and chocolates. While I can't recall the other dishes, I distinctly remember the ox-tail soup (I now make a similar version of the soup when I can find fresh ox-tail in our supermarket.)

After we finished the meal, the waiter asked if I wanted anything else. I promptly replied, "Another bowl of ox-tail soup, please," to the utter amazement of my three male companions. It was not until many years later when reminiscing with Albert that I found out that while he loved the soup and would have desired more, he felt it was bad etiquette to request it after we had finished our full dinner.

The seminar was held at Loyola University with 75 delegates from 13 countries - Australia, Burma, Ceylon, Hong Kong, India, Indonesia, Iraq, Japan, Malaya, (now Malaysia), New Zealand, Pakistan, the Philippines and Thailand. Men and women were housed in separate dorms. I shared a big room with seven other delegates. Each of us had a bed and a dresser. It didn't take us long to bond. We were all friendly and eager to make new friends and to learn from one another.

Some details linger in my memory. Bolts of material of different textures, colors and designs, instead of dresses, were packed in the suitcases of the Indian girls. These were their saris. The smell of coconut was very strong in the air. It turned out some popular brands of shampoo and perfume among Indian women are made from coconut. Getting used to our meals wasn't easy, since most of the dishes were made with some form of curry - curry chicken, curry vegetables, curry rice. I had stomach problems after our second week. Campbell soups and visits to nearby Chinese restaurants saved me.

In the talks, training sessions and group discussions conducted by religious and lay teachers, we exchanged ideas and hopes for the future. On our free time we went shopping, sight-seeing, and attended concerts, plays and movies, including *White Christmas*, starring Bing Crosby. We even staged a pageant to re-enact the First Christmas.

Delegates from different countries were vying for this, but our Hong Kong delegation finally won the roles. Albert was Joseph and I was Mary. Our homesickness faded when we sang carols with one heart, especially the *Adestes Fidelis* in Latin. That Christmas Eve of 1954 was a memorable, holy and beautiful night.

As we parted, we promised to stay in touch and carry on the mission of Pax Romana. The following month, January 1955, the four of us founded the Catholic Society of HKU (KATSO). Albert was the president, I, the secretary, David, the treasurer, and Michael, a member-at-large. Fr. Cronin was our spiritual director. We drew up a simple mission statement - to uphold the ideals of truth, beauty and love, supported by faith and prayers.

When we returned from India and classes at HKU resumed, I missed Mimi. She and Philip moved to his home in Manila. Now I was Mom's right and left hand, responsible for tasks in our home, and outside.

At this time that HKU Student Union held its official election of officers for the coming year. Three candidates vied for the presidency and each selected his/her cabinet. Since I was picked by two candidates to serve as the External Relations Member, I knew my chances were very good. I won the position to represent the University at conferences and meetings in the Philippines, Australia, Malaya, Singapore and the U.S.

A Time of Change

In early May of 1955, a cable arrived from Dad in San Francisco. It read:

YOU CAN ALL COME TO THE U.S. UNDER THE NEW REFUGEE RELIEF ACT. START PREPARATIONS FOR AUGUST DEPARTURE. LOVE, FRANK.

While Mom and the rest of my family were overjoyed at the news, I was heartsick. I had been looking forward to my senior year at the University - filled with adventure, excitement and travel. I begged Mom to let me stay. I didn't want to leave HKU, my friends and several young men I was dating. She refused. I pleaded, but her mind was made up. This was my first encounter with her iron will. She had always been rather gentle, indecisive and easy-going. Hard as I tried, I couldn't make her budge.

Years later I realized that her reason for insisting I stay with the family was because she desperately needed my help. She had lost Ah Woo and Ah Lo in Manila, then Mimi left for Manila after her marriage. Mom knew she couldn't cope without me.

As the good Chinese daughter, I obeyed. The die was cast. For the next three months we worked to prepare for our departure to the U.S. - land of the Golden Mountain.*

When Mother Piera and Mother Virginia heard of our plans to migrate to the U.S., they too had mixed emotions. On one hand, I, their star pupil, wouldn't be able to graduate from HKU and take full advantage of my four-year scholarship. They would miss me very much, but in the end, they said my mother knew best and that

I must obey her.

In the past, each time I visited those good mothers, they insisted on giving me money for bus fare and books. I had refused their help before, but realizing their eagerness to help, I would occasionally accept. Now, knowing of our pending move, they wondered how they could help.

Mother Virginia and Mother Piera came up with a plan. One of the teachers at St. Mary's, a Mrs. Chow, had to take a two-month maternity leave from Form II (freshman year). They invited me to fill in for her and offered me the same pay. It was the first week in May. My classes at the university were over and we weren't scheduled to leave for the U.S. until August.

This was a good offer. While I had tutored many students and taught them English from scratch, taking charge of a class of 50, ranging in age from 13 to 18 year-olds was another matter. I hesitated, afraid I wouldn't do a good job, but Mother Virginia and Mother Piera assured me that they would be around to advise and help whenever I needed help.

In June and July, I served as a teacher at St. Mary's. I made sure I was properly dressed and groomed. Each morning I took time to make sure that I looked older than my 19 years - high heels, some make-up and hair properly styled. Many years later I met one of my former students in the U.S. She still remembered me as Miss Chiu and told me how much she and her classmates admired and respected me and were in awe of me. They all tried to emulate me in manner and style.

The income I received for my teaching went into the family coffers for necessities and new outfits for our trip.

Dad had arranged for free passage for the seven of us on Civil

Air Transport from Hong Kong to Tokyo. From Tokyo we could get free berths on one of the ships owned by his good friend, C. Y. Tung, to San Francisco. The arrangements seemed perfect - direct connections from Hong Kong to Tokyo, then Tokyo to San Francisco.

What Dad failed to anticipate was our 44 pieces of luggage - wooden crates, suitcases and boxes, big and small. Although we had given away our furniture and many household items, we still packed our clothes, books and lots of miscellaneous items. Mom said, and I agreed, that we had to bring these to our home in America for we couldn't afford to buy new things later.

Now, how could the seven of us with 44 pieces of luggage travel as freeloaders on Civil Air Transport and Uncle Tung's ship? Obviously, we would be accommodated on space-available basis and most probably the seven of us would be split up and travel separately. James was only 17 and Francis, a year younger. I thought both were too young to travel alone.

When I presented this scenario to Mom, she realized that Dad's plan wouldn't work. The only way for all of us to stay together was on a larger ocean liner. Seven third-class tickets on one of the President Liners added up to almost $3,000 U.S. Although Mom had $5,000 in U.S. currency with her, she was reluctant to spend it for our passage. We worried about what Dad would say. We knew he would be angry.

"It's okay, Mom," I assured her. "I'll tell Dad it was my decision. Since I've already finished my junior year, I'll work and pay you back after we settle in the U.S." We booked passage on the S.S. President Wilson and scheduled to leave Hong Kong on August 2 for our 18-day trip to San Francisco.

As our pending departure drew near, I had to attend many

rounds of lunches and dinners hosted by my classmates and friends. A special one was the dinner at Ricci Hall, given by Fr. Cronin. I vaguely remember my speech at the dinner, and it went something like this, "It's with a heavy heart that I leave Ricci, my home. Even though I don't live here, I'm here often enough for meals and events. I'll miss you all."

I was cheered by all the Ricci boys, much to my delight.

Fr. Fergus Cronin, SJ
Albert kissing Cardinal Spellman's ring
while a bespectacled Fr. Cronin watches

Whenever I think of Fr. Cronin, the tune and lyrics of "When Irish Eyes Are Smiling" keep resurging in my heart. He was a true Irishman, with his gentle mien, wry Irish humor and a big, big heart filled with wisdom and compassion.

When we could afford the time and money to travel to Europe in the mid-90s, Ireland was the second country (next to Italy, home of Mother Piera) that I wanted to visit. I wanted to experience the land of Fr. Cronin, sample and feel its air, its earth and its people.

Fr. Cronin was also the leprechaun that helped me find my pot of gold at the end of the rainbow – my husband. Albert's surname is actually "gold" in Chinese character, but his grandfather opted for King, instead of Jin which is the official spelling in Pinyin used in China today.

It was Fr. Cronin who handpicked Albert, David, Michael and me for the Pax Romana Seminar in India. Although I hardly knew Albert, since he was dating someone else and was polite and businesslike with me, we were aware of each other. In 1958, when Albert was immigrating to the U.S., he wrote to ask if he could stop by San Francisco and visit me since I was the only friend he knew on the West Coast.

Twenty five years later, in 1980, when Albert and I visited Fr. Cronin in Hong Kong, he remarked with a twinkle in his eye, that our marriage was the happiest result of the Pax Romana. We agreed, for it was in India that Albert and I first met and worked together and it was six years later that we courted and married in San Francisco. In India, we didn't realize that we were both cut from the same cloth, active in the Legion of Mary, and other Catholic activities. Both of us had the zeal for missionary work and took our faith seriously. We recently celebrated our Golden Anniversary and wished Fr. Cronin could have been with us. (Fr. Cronin died in 1990.) But his spirit lives on in our hearts.

I first met Fr. Cronin when I chose Logic as one of my subjects during my freshman year at HKU. I usually sat at the back of his class and would invariably doze off after listening to his monotone Irish voice. But I studied the required text, completed all the assignments and was elated to receive an Excellent as my final grade.

After that Fr. Cronin and I became good friends, but it

wasn't until later that I realized what a true friend he was.

During my sophomore and junior years at the University, I frequently visited Ricci Hall, the residence for male students where he served as rector. Although it was not a co-ed dorm, girls were welcome for lunch and dinner as invited guests. Besides, Ricci Hall was the center for many meetings, so Fr. Cronin and I often bumped into each other there.

It was during one of these meetings that he noticed my pallor. "What's bothering you, Elizabeth?" he asked. I told him I was worried because Dad's monthly check for our family seldom arrived on time. He asked how much we needed. Once I told him, he went to his office and brought back a check for that amount. He said to pay him back when Dad's check arrived. As Ricci Hall's rector, he had access to some funds. Each month from then on, he always made sure we had enough to live on.

After Fr. Cronin chose me to be one of the Pax Romana delegates, he made sure I had enough pocket money. All our expenses, including airfare and hotel, were paid for. In addition, I also received a generous sum as pocket money which I used to purchase a beautiful lavender sari and other gifts, including a small hand-carved boat of wood for him. I didn't realize, until later, that I was the only one who received the allowance.

After we returned in January, 1955, we formed the Catholic Society of the University of Hong Kong (known as KATSO*) with Albert as the president and me as secretary.

David was the treasurer and Michael, a member-at-large. Fr. Cronin was our spiritual director.

We organized religious discussions, mini-retreats, picnics and dinners for the students. In June 1955, Albert graduated from engineering and in August 1955 I left Hong Kong with my family. Fifty years later, Michael Lau, an old HKU classmate, asked Albert and I to write about the beginning of KATSO and participate in its golden jubilee. The two of us, together with our son, Albert Jr., made a special trip to Hong Kong to celebrate that occasion. Our other son, Tom, couldn't make it.

In 1988, when I returned to Hong Kong to do research for my third cookbook, I made sure I visited Fr. Cronin again. This time he was the one who introduced me to Lectio Divina, that is, meditating on a passage from Scriptures or a religious book.

Fr. Cronin mentored many students at HKU. In the mid-80s, a few of them got together and bought him a first class around-the-world ticket. He managed a visit with us in our home in Detroit. He reconnected with Albert, met our sons and also enjoyed my home cooking.

I acknowledged him in the introduction to The 15-Minute Chinese Gourmet: "For introducing me to Albert, logic and India."

I didn't realize then that he was an O.B.E (Order of the British Empire.) and J.D. (Juris Doctor) until I came across his business card later. He never preached, but he showed us by his humility, wisdom and kindness that he was the true Christian shepherd.

3

Hello, America

Our photo in the San Francisco Examiner

August 2, 1955. The band was playing, the streamers were flying, there was much hustle and bustle about. Presently the two large chimneys of SS. President Wilson belched out several sonic roars, signals to visitors on board that it was time to leave, for the gangplank would soon be hoisted up.

Mom, the kids and I were standing on the lower deck waving goodbye to relatives and friends. The strains of *Harbor Lights* brought tears to my eyes. I waved to my friends until they were almost out of sight.

My heart ached. I didn't want to leave Hong Kong, HKU, my classes, and my friends, but I had no choice. Mom commanded. I didn't know what life would be like in America.

Because we had third class tickets, our room on the lower deck was crammed with 40 beds without a window or air conditioning. It was awful. The lounge, where we congregated for snacks and games, had benches along the wall and was practically deserted by 10 p.m. That became our bedroom. At 9 p.m., the seven of us would lug our pillows and covers to the lounge and sit and wait until the benches were unoccupied. After several nights, Lee Yuen, the purser, accepted our presence there, as did the other passengers. We claimed squatters' rights and slept comfortably in the air-conditioned lounge for the rest of our journey.

Some 50 students bound for various colleges in the U.S. were on board. In no time we made friends and I organized a student group, shared stories as well as our dreams and plans for the future. We published a newsletter and performed a skit (imagining what life would be in the U.S. for us in the future) on the last evening on board, much to the delight of Mr. Lee and the other passengers.

The food on board was quite good since the cooks were all Chinese. We had a choice of either Chinese or Western fare or a little of both. Aside from the three meals, tea was complete with petit fours, cookies and finger sandwiches, while late evening snacks included porridge or *jook*, soup noodles and some *dim sum*. Since none of my family was seasick, all of us except Mom enjoyed every moment of our trip.

I didn't know how lonely and depressed she was until months later. She blamed me for being too busy organizing events than to be with her. I hadn't realize she had lost her social charm and didn't connect with anyone of her age group. She was the wife of a diplomat during her first two trips to America. On this, her third trip, she was the mother of six children and we were all immigrating to live in America for good.

On August 20, we sighted land and the Golden Gate Bridge, the symbol of the Land of the Golden Mountain. We had arrived. We were in San Francisco, California. When our ship docked outside San Francisco Bay, we were all on deck, eager to drink in the colors and excitement of our arrival. Then we saw a speedboat approaching. There was Dad on board together with the U.S. Immigration Inspectors and Customs. What a wonderful welcome.

He had told his story to the Port Authorities - his separation from his family for five long years and how, at last, we were coming to join him. A reporter from the San Francisco Examiner tagged along. The next day our picture and story were featured in the paper. I was wearing a pink hand-knitted sweater top over a linen skirt with hand-painted designs of Hong Kong - reminders of the land we had just left.

Our temporary home on 33rd Avenue in the Richmond District in San Francisco was different from our flat in Kowloon. It was more spacious and airy, but so was everything else. This world looked strange and new too. Although we spoke English fluently, we felt like fish out of water. I was lonely, without friends and without the challenge of my HKU studies.

Within a week, Dad registered me with the Kelly Girl Agency. He returned home one evening proudly announcing that I had a job.

"You've been accepted as a clerk in the largest bank in California - the Bank of America. You start tomorrow."

This was great news for I was eager to work to make good on

my promise to pay back the $3,000 we spent for the seven third-class tickets on the SS.President Wilson.

The next morning, wearing a dark blue, linen suit with a pale blue, silk blouse, Dad drove me to the bank, located at the corner of Powell and Market Streets. That building still stands today. It's a prominent tourist landmark and the terminal for the Powell-Market Cable Car. I reported to the supervisor of the Trust Department at 8 a.m. and started to work immediately, duplicating copies of trusts.

The monstrous duplicating machine was housed in a room on the third floor. It consisted of two giant rollers, spinning nonstop. My job was to take a batch of trusts, feed them through the rollers, one page at a time, neatly in a row. Duplicate copies were assembled and filed in the correct sequence, then stapled and stacked. Hour after hour. Page after page. I went around the machine to keep feeding it. What a chore to feed paper into that hungry monster, eight hours a day, five days a week. It certainly wasn't my idea of a challenging occupation.

I consoled myself. *This is just temporary, things will improve. I should be grateful that I have the chance to work, earn money and help my family...*

During coffee breaks, I sat in the staff lounge, where I became acquainted with the vending machines and coffee. For a dime I could get a good-sized cup of coffee with sugar and cream. I didn't make any friends, although I smiled at some of the people whose faces I recognized. I became shy, quiet and reticent, very different from my HKU days. For lunch I brown-bagged, a custom Dad taught me. On my first day of work, I packed a baloney sandwich and a quart of homogenized milk.

Dad told us, "When in Rome, do as the Romans do. When in

the States, do what the Americans do. You're now an American and must discard your Chinese ways and adopt American customs and habits." To him, we all appeared skinny and sickly-looking. So he bought many gallons of regular milk and dozens of fresh oranges to make us healthy. At that time, we could get 10 dozen Sunkist from a truck parked in Chinatown for only a buck.

But drinking so much milk at one time nauseated me. In Hong Kong we were accustomed to a glass of milk a day. It was never fresh milk, which was quite expensive. Instead, it was made out of KLIM powder or it was canned milk. We didn't eat cheese either. Cheese was a far cry from the shrimp or pork fried rice, chicken or beef chow mien or *ho fun* (flat rice noodles) I was accustomed to having for lunch in Hong Kong. Just the thought of which made me nostalgic for Hong Kong.

My first paycheck issued exactly two weeks later was the reward. It was no more than $70 and change, since I was paid $1.50 an hour while Uncle Sam and the Kelly Agency took a big chunk. But I earned it and felt as proud as a war hero bringing home a medal. I gave my check to Dad as the first installment on my loan. From then on, whenever I felt depressed or sad, I would just think of payday and that cheered me up.

My one-hour lunch break gave me time for a short walk outside the office and I frequently visited Woolworth 5 and 10-cents store across the street. I enjoyed looking at its window displays and its showcases with knick-knacks of all kinds. Although I didn't have the money to buy much, I learned a lot about the tastes and habits of the people of our new country. There was a large display of housewares, as well as inexpensive custom jewelry - earrings, brooches, bracelets and necklaces and a variety of make-up.

During our office Christmas party, we exchanged presents with our co-workers. Each of us drew a name for the person we were to give a gift. I remember wrapping a beautiful Chinese silk scarf for Sally, the office receptionist. While I placed it in a box, I just wrapped it with some brown paper without ribbons. In return, I received a small box, exquisitely wrapped, which contained a shining Christmas brooch like one I had seen at Woolworth's.

Dad also found part-time jobs for James and Francis as busboys in restaurants in Chinatown. They, too, gave their paychecks to him.

Although I was gainfully employed and fulfilling my promise to pay back the loan, I was depressed. What a change of lifestyle and environment from Hong Kong. Instead of being an active student, I was a bank clerk with a dull job and no friends.

However, word about us spread in the Chinese community and soon young men came calling. There was a shortage of Chinese girls in the Bay Area. But, none of our visitors interested me. They were either too old or too stuffy, and some were ABCs, American-born Chinese, like bananas, yellow outside and white inside as we used to say - too Americanized for my liking.

Our First Christmas

O ur first Christmas in the U.S. was the first time our whole family (except Mimi now living in Manila) was together to celebrate the birth of the Christ Child. We were invited to a party at the luxurious home of Mr. and Mrs. Chen in Sausalito. They were dear friends of our Auntie Mary Szeto (a good friend of Dad's) in the city across the Bay.

I wore a deep blue *qi pao** embroidered with a dragon and phoenix in gold sequins.

Even Mom commented. "The dress looks good on you. Make sure you put some color on your cheeks and lips."

Dad drove us to the party in his blue DeSoto. This was our maiden ride across the Golden Gate Bridge and it was breathtaking. The lights of the San Francisco skyline glistened like diamonds in the evening sky.

Our hosts were Betty and T. Y. Chen. Their home, built of wood and glass, looked like something out of a magazine. The guests included quite a few young people. A tall and rather handsome Chinese American man from Honolulu, Jim Lee, stood out. We danced and talked and he took lots of pictures of me with his Rolleiflex.

Two days later he came to see me at work, treated me to lunch, and gave me a stack of photos he had taken of me. He returned day after day and we went out for lunch. I no longer needed to brown-bag. We saw several movies, walked and talked and later I invited him home to visit with my family.

At the end of the second week, before he was to return to Honolulu, he asked, "What do you think of me? I mean, how do you like me?"

I was dumbfounded. *What a direct way of asking such a delicate question,* I mused.

"Well, you're nice and friendly, but I hardly know you. We just met three weeks ago."

"But, but I'm leaving tomorrow morning and before I go, I want to know how you feel," he insisted.

"I d-o-n't know - I c-a-n't answer that question," I stammered.

"You must know how I feel. I'm crazy about you. I had a long talk with my folks last night and told them I've found the girl of my dreams. They gave me a thumbs up. Please, Elizabeth, would you consider marrying me?"

I started to laugh nervously. I wasn't laughing at him, but at his proposal. My reaction must have struck him as cruel. I apologized and told him that marriage was too serious a matter to rush into.

We parted abruptly. That night, I turned over Jim's proposal in my mind. *Yes, it was flattering that he wanted to marry me. But I'm not sure. I hardly know him or his family...*

Four weeks went by without a word from him. One afternoon when I returned home from work, my younger brother George ran to greet me.

"Second sister, guess what came in the mail for you!"

"What came?" I asked and ran to follow him.

There, on the living room floor, were two big canvas bags marked, PROPERTY OF THE U.S. POST OFFICE.

"What are these?" I inquired.

"See for yourself," Mom said. By this time, she had joined us in the living room.

I opened one bag and pulled out a stack of letters, stamped, canceled and addressed to me at our home address. I ripped one open and read,

Dear Elizabeth,

I saw your lovely photo and ad in the Honolulu Star. I'm so glad you are looking for a boyfriend. I hope you'll pick me. I'm 21, a midshipman serving in the U.S. Navy in Honolulu. My family lives in Boston. After my discharge from the service in a year, I plan to study law at Boston University. Please write as soon as you can and tell me more about yourself. I'd love to have an autographed photo of you. I can't wait.

(signed) John Kline

Hundreds more letters were similar in content - lonely servicemen in the Army, the Navy, the Marines, even the Air Force, all hungry for a girlfriend. Some were downright blunt and intimidating. I was furious and hurt. I felt violated - almost like being raped. Who in the world would do such a thing to me? Who would have put an ad and my photo in the *Honolulu Star*? All fingers pointed to Jim Lee, of course.

Anyway, I didn't bother to open or read any more of those letters. I incinerated them all, since each one would add salt to my wound.

About a month later, Jim Lee appeared at my work place. I greeted him cordially, lunched with him, and went out of my way to be extra kind. Not a word was mentioned about the letters and the ad in the *Honolulu Star*.

Jim stayed cool too, but I could sense the curiosity and the many questions he wanted to ask. I simply pretended nothing ever happened. We said our goodbyes and he left without knowing what happened. Touche! My revenge was sweet.

My Mentor

Me, a USF Graduate

That Christmas at the Chens completely reversed the direction of my life. Mr. Chen called me the following January and offered me a full time position at his import/export firm as bookkeeper of accounts receivable. The pay was double my bank salary and he assured me that he and his office manager, Ted, would help me learn my job.

I couldn't refuse. Here at last was the golden opportunity in this land of milk and honey. My duties as a bookkeeper weren't that difficult. Although I had no training in accounting, I learned how to use the NCR machine that posted invoices to the different accounts. China Dry Goods was an import and export firm of non-perishable decorative items for the home, kitchen and office. I was delighted with its merchandise and spent a small part of my paycheck each month buying knick-knacks for myself and my family.

Mr. Chen, 60, was a robust, rotund man with a big heart and a pleasant smile. He reminded me of my *Kung Kung*. While he was busy with many phone calls and appointments, he nevertheless found time to talk with me in his office. Our weekly chats would range from my family, to my work, to my dreams, and vision for the future. He was a good listener. Once I shared with him the circumstances of our immigration to the U.S., my promise to pay back the loan of our passage and my yearning to finish my college degree. This was also a wish of Dad's and he kept reminding me that I had to finish my last year in college someday. I found out, months later, how kind and generous Mr. Chen was.

One day he asked me how I enjoyed my work at his firm. I told him that I had familiarized myself with the accounts and that by noon, I was able to take care of the entire backlog of the previous day.

He was quiet for a moment, then he said, "Well, Elizabeth, that's great. Now, how about if I pay you the same salary and let you out by 1 p.m., when your work is done for the day? That way, you can register at a college and finish your bachelor's degree."

I didn't know what to say. After all, Mr. Chen had been more than generous. He had given me two raises in six months and now this offer? I hesitated, but he was adamant. "Yes, you must finish your degree and I will be more than happy to help you." End of discussion.

When Ted, my supervisor, heard the news, he was distressed. I later learned that he immediately reminded Mr. Chen that such favoritism would demoralize the rest of the staff. But Mr. Chen had his arguments ready and his word was law.

I wasted no time and went shopping for possibilities at various colleges and universities in the Bay Area. Lone Mountain, a girl's college, offered me a work-study scholarship, 20 hours work each week for free tuition. Then there was the Jesuit University of San Francisco (USF). I applied for a scholarship and was granted one by the president of the University.

I enrolled at the liberal arts college at USF and signed up for six classes, five from 6:30 to 9:30 p.m., Monday through Friday, and 9 a.m. to noon on Saturday, for a total of 18 credits in English and Philosophy. Fortunately, USF gave me full credit for my three years at HKU and I was a senior with English as my major, with philosophy and theology my minor. I would complete my Bachelor of Science in English in two semesters, needing only 36 units to graduate.

At this time I was dating Tony Kho, my brother-in-law's best friend. I met Tony during my junior year at HKU when he stopped by Hong Kong on his way to visit his family in Singapore. After our arrival in the U.S., Tony came to visit. He had returned to California to finish his M.Sc. in Chemical Engineering at the University of California in Berkeley.

But Dad forewarned me, "Stop seeing Tony. He has epilepsy. You don't want to date a man that's sick."

Epilepsy made little difference to me. Instead of shunning him, I was sympathetic. And the more I got to know Tony, the greater was my admiration and love for him. To me, he was a Renaissance man. Although a Chemical Engineering major, he was well versed in the classics and loved Shakespeare, Keats,

Shelley, and Byron, some of my favorite authors. His knowledge of classical music and art was broad, and it was he who introduced me to Broadway musicals. After we saw *My Fair Lady*, I was hooked.

Besides, Tony was not only kind and considerate, but sincere and thoughtful - qualities I admired in a man.

I started my classes at USF that fall. While I literally worked only half time, I was a full-time student. Since Tony was my daily chauffeur, my work and study were much easier. He picked me up when I left China Dry Goods at 1 p.m., drove me to USF where we would get a quick bite, then accompanied me to the USF library until classes started. While I was in class, he worked in the library for his classes in the U.C. graduate program.

Gradually, Tony's epilepsy worsened and his dizzy spells began. As a precautionary measure he showed me what to do in case of an attack. He kept wooden tongue depressors in the glove compartment of his car as well as the names and phone numbers of his doctors at the U.C. Berkeley Hospital. To appease his folks at home, he purchased a round trip ticket to Singapore in mid-January.

Around Thanksgiving he suggested that we take a day off for shopping in downtown San Francisco. As he drove, I looked at the stores and the crowds on Market Street. Suddenly I realized the car was weaving. I looked at Tony. He was having a seizure. I tried not to panic and told myself to be calm. Although I didn't know how to drive, I knew that the only way to stop the car was to pull out the ignition key. I reached for a tongue depressor and hastily inserted it into his mouth. By this time, two of the wheels of our car were wedged in the rails of the Market Street tram. Deafening sirens of police cars came from every direction.

"Show me his driver's license," demanded one policeman.

I found an expired license in Tony's wallet. Fortunately his passport and plane ticket were also in his coat pocket. I showed them to the officers and that pacified them for the time being.

"Please call for an ambulance," I pleaded.

"No, No, NO!" Tony shouted. He had come out of his seizure.

"My girlfriend will get a taxi and take me to my doctor in Berkeley."

The officers agreed to his request, provided he would allow them to tow his car away and promise he would no longer drive. Phew. What a narrow escape.

Tony's doctor prescribed a stronger dose of medication and wanted to hospitalize him right away. But Tony argued, and promised that he would fly home soon and see his family neurosurgeon in Singapore.

Tony wanted me to accompany him to Singapore. I refused. I couldn't miss my work and classes. Besides, I had promised Dad (and myself) that I would complete my bachelor's degree that June. It was my secret plan that after I graduated, I would teach, earn a living, and even support Tony if I had to. I never confided my plan to him since I didn't want to hurt his pride.

It was with sad hearts that we parted at the airport in late November, 1956. After he left, I was on my own. I managed to take the buses to and from classes and plunged, heart and soul, into my studies. I often cried myself to sleep at night. I had no one to talk to or confide in.

Months dragged by. Working during the day and going to classes at night by bus was tiring and lonely. But, I persevered,

I lived for my studies. After finals, I was elated to learn I would graduate Magna Cum Laude.

Mom and Dad were ecstatic. They bought me a beautiful graduation dress of my choice, a white taffeta and net, and threw a big dinner party for me at home. Dad even went to the kitchen to cook his specialty, Smoked Fish, Shanghai style. It was not until many years later when I had to cook all our meals in Detroit that I discovered how time-consuming and involved that Smoked Fish recipe was.

By now, Tony's letters came less often. Eventually he stopped writing altogether. One night I had this horrible dream. His grandmother, the dowager of the clan, parents, uncle and aunts were all assembled in the living room of their big mansion in Singapore and were looking me over. I felt like a caged monkey in the zoo, being ogled and examined from head to toe. One aunt exclaimed loudly, "I know why a pretty girl like her would marry you, Tony. For your money."

Another one said sarcastically, "Without question. Why would a healthy young woman want to marry you - a sickly man?"

I woke up hurting and believing that Tony's family really thought I loved him for his money and family position in Singapore.

The month after graduation was hard. I was at a crossroad and didn't know what to do next. But I attended Mass daily at Star of the Sea, a church close to our home to find the strength, courage and determination to carry on. I resigned from Mr. Chen's firm for I felt I needed a change of venue. Saying goodbye to him was hard, but he told me he understood and that it was alright.

Star of the Sea

That summer I worked full time at Levi Strauss Headquarters on Montgomery Street. My responsibilities included typing invoices and checking on accounts receivable. When September came, I was hired as a fulltime teacher for the fourth grade at the Star of the Sea Catholic School.

While attending daily mass at Star of the Sea Church, I had come to know Sr. Miriam, a friendly young nun. We would often linger after mass to chat. Later she suggested that I apply for the teaching vacancy in her school.

My interview with Sr. Mary, the principal, went well. My USF degree (with a minor in Philosophy and Theology) and Sr. Miriam's recommendation helped. But I expressed trepidation. Although I had two months' teaching experience at St. Mary's in Hong Kong and had tutored many others on a one-to-one basis, I was a neophyte in the U.S., without any education courses.

"Don't worry, my dear," Sr. Mary said. "Sr. Miriam and I will be around to help you anytime."

My year as a fourth grade teacher was an adventure I'll always remember. The pay was $3,000 for 10 months. I was in charge of 53 boys and girls between the ages of nine and ten with reading levels ranging from the third to the twelfth grade.

Teachers at the Star of the Sea were responsible for teaching all subjects, except gym. I taught religion, English, math, social studies, art and music. Since I was a fresh college graduate, I adapted some of my college syllabi to the fourth grade level. In religion, for example, our class studied and discussed the Holy Trinity. To Sr. Mary and Sr. Miriam's surprise, my students were equal to the challenge. Their short essays on the Trinity were simple, clear, well done and were bound in folders for display at our Parents/Teacher Day.

For reading I divided the class into three groups - upper, middle and lower. My experience in the one-room school in Canton, China, gave me insight on how to help and manage each group. Since I didn't play the piano, I used my love of singing and my musical ear to my best advantage. My little ones were taught popular songs, such as *Getting to Know You, You Are My Sunshine* and *Don't Fence Me In*. Their response was so positive that for the Christmas pageant schoolwide, they sang and acted out *Getting to Know You* to thunderous applause.

My students were often assigned to write short essays. So each evening, I had to read and critique them.

Decorating our classroom was one of my responsibilities. Since my colleagues changed their room decor each month, I had to do the same, but found this job not only time-consuming but stressful, since I had little experience with art. Fortunately, Sr. Miriam came to my rescue by introducing me to an arts and craft store where I could purchase many ready-made stickers and posters.

Star of the Sea parish was composed of middle income families of Irish, German, Portuguese and Italian stock. The parents were kind and assured me that I had their full support. I was asked, in no uncertain terms, to let them know if one of their children gave me any trouble. This made my job easier.

It didn't take long to spot the trouble makers. Take the case of Willy. He appeared to be a slow learner and was disruptive in class. One day I asked him to stay after school to erase my blackboard, a job coveted by all students. To my surprise, Willy's attitude changed and he quickly opened up. He told me he lived alone with his mother and older brother. His brother was an A student in the Fifth Grade and always had their mother's attention. This made Willy feel unloved. He considered himself the slow and stupid. Once I understood his problem and went out of my way to give him more attention, his attitude improved and his grades soared.

The first semester sped by. Evenings were spent with a big stack of papers to read, grade and critique. On weekends I prepared daily lesson plans. I loved my work and my kids, all 53 of them. I also enjoyed the friendship of their parents as well as support from Sr. Miriam, whose fifth grade classroom was across the hall from mine.

I still lived at home, and was happy to give $100 (half of my take home pay) to Mom for my room and board, while I spent the rest on incidentals for my class and treats for my siblings.

In mid-February, I came down with a bad cold. I thought staying home to rest for a day or two would cure it. Not so. My cold persisted and turned into pneumonia. Fortunately, Dad's insurance from New York Life covered my one-week stay in the hospital. My doctor ordered a full month's rest. My students and their parents sent flowers, candies, get-well notes and cards. When I returned to class a month later, a large poster "WELCOME BACK, MISS CHIU, WE MISSED YOU" hung in my classroom. Ah, such were the joys of a fourth-grade parochial school teacher.

June came too quickly and it was the end of the school year. I prepared final report cards and certificates of merits, as well as a performance in the school's Closing Day ceremonies. My class did a small skit on the Holy Trinity, a subject we had spent months discussing and writing about.

All in all, it was a wonderful year. Sr. Mary, the principal, was pleased with my performance and told me so. I was happy, but decided to pursue a master's in English at the University of California in Berkeley (U.C.).

When I told Mom of my plans for a graduate degree, she had mixed emotions. This meant that I wouldn't be working and helping with the family finances. Dad, on the other hand, was elated and encouraged me to go for my dream. Mom finally gave in, on one condition, that I live at home and commute to classes each day.

Attending U.C., Berkeley

The summer of 1958 brought many changes. We moved to a larger and cheaper fourth-floor flat at the corner of Leavenworth and Washington. It had three bedrooms, two full baths, a large living room, a dining room, and a fully equipped kitchen. An old-fashioned elevator took us up to our home. We were given the use of three extra rooms in the basement, one housed the washer and dryer, the second we used for storage, and the third became a guest room.

Our building was four blocks from Grant Avenue in the heart of Chinatown where Mom worked, and Shirley and George attended school. The landmark cable car, Powell and Leavenworth, stopped at our corner, as well as several buses.

Before starting on my summer job, I decided to take my first vacation. I went to New York to reconnect with Michael McDougall. He was one of the three other students who attended the Pax Romana Seminar with me in India in 1954. Michael was like the big brother I never had. He took care of me when I had stomach trouble from too much curry and when I was homesick during that Christmas in Madras, my first time away from home. We kept in touch sporadically after I left Hong Kong in 1955. He happened to call during the month I broke up with Tony and it was comforting to hear his voice. After Michael earned his master's in architecture in London, he was offered a fellowship to study city planning at Cornell University, in Ithaca, NY.

I boarded at the New York YWCA while Michael stayed at the YMCA, a block away. We toured and took in the sights of the Big Apple, tried several famous Jewish delis and enjoyed the food in Chinatown. When we parted he promised to come to San Francisco in September to look for a job. I also went on to Chicago to attend a Catholic Students' Conference. It was there that I met Mary Ann Lou (now Sr. Mary Ann, SDSH), a famous breast cancer surgeon and former head of the Cardinal Tien Hospital in Taipei. Sr. Mary Ann and I are still good friends and we see each other every time I visit Taipei.

After my return, I started on my summer job at an insurance company. At this time Albert King wrote that he was immigrating to the U.S. Since I was the only friend he had in San Francisco, he asked if he could be our house guest for a week. Mom remembered him well as the wholesome young man who helped me with my visa for India. She said he was welcome to stay in our guest room in the basement.

Albert stayed with us for a week. Although he and I, together with Michael and David, founded the Chinese Catholic Society at HKU (KATSO), my relationship with Albert had been rather formal and proper. What a surprise to find him so much at ease with my family, especially with my younger siblings. Since I didn't take time off from work, Albert was left at home with the kids on their summer break. We were together in the evenings.

I invited him to accompany me to several events that week. One was a reception for Archbishop Yu Pin, (then the Bishop of Taiwan) hosted at my alma mater, USF. Many Chinese priests, nuns and young Catholics were present.

"Who's that handsome young man with you?" inquired Fr. Thomas Liang, a priest who was instrumental in 1954 in obtaining my scholarship to a college for women in the Bay Area. Unfortunately I couldn't use it since the U.S. Consulate in Hong

Kong refused to issue me a visa. I had met Fr. Liang when I came to the U.S. in 1955 and found him to be a good, empathic listener.

"Albert's just an acquaintance from Hong Kong," I replied.

"Does he have a girlfriend?"

"I don't know," I answered.

"Well, if he doesn't, I'd like to introduce a few young ladies to him."

"Go ahead. He's not mine."

"But on second thought, I think I'd like to reserve him for you." He said with a funny grin.

"Don't you dare!"

Roland Chan, a former HKU classmate of ours, hosted a dinner party at Stanford that weekend. All I remember was that we had dinner, chatted much about the good old days at HKU and took a few Polaroid shots. When Albert and I returned to my home, it was bittersweet. I didn't realize until he was about to leave how much I had enjoyed his company. Returning home with him was pleasant.

It was now the third week in July and my birthday was approaching. In past years, Mom let me invite my girlfriends for dinner at home. We would eat, chat and have a lot of fun. It didn't take Albert long to learn of my pending birthday. Maria, Shirley and George kept begging him to prolong his stay, at least for my birthday. He politely refused, saying he had to visit the cousins who sponsored him as a permanent resident in Pittsburgh before classes start at Wayne State University (WSU) in Detroit.

He had received a graduate assistantship in Engineering Mechanics at WSU. On the eve of his departure, he gave me a cute birthday card with a fluffy cat on the cover together with a copy of *A Life of Christ*. In return I gave him a copy of *The Imitation of Christ*. After we said goodnight, I was surprised that my eyes were moist. Mom noticed and remarked, "I told you not to meet Michael in New York."

I didn't reply, but went to my bedroom with mixed emotions. The next morning Albert got up early to accompany me to mass. We were at Old St. Mary's, a beautiful cathedral built in the 1800s which still retained its former glory and magnificence. Before I boarded the California cable car for work, I told him that this was the church I would choose for my wedding someday. I hinted to him that Michael was coming in September and that we had plans for marriage sometime later.

Albert left and Michael came to San Francisco. Before Michael's arrival, Mom suggested that he rent an apartment nearby. That way, we could see each other every day and he could have dinner with us. "What's an extra pair of chopsticks," Mom said.

Michael and I thought this was an excellent idea. He found a job in an architectural firm on Montgomery Street and an apartment two blocks from us. He came for dinner each evening and we got to know each other.

In September I officially enrolled for a M.A. degree in English at the University of California, Berkeley (U.C.). I carpooled with several American born Chinese. As a full-time student, I found the requirements and standard for English at U.C. rigorous. Since U.C. was a state university, I didn't have to pay any tuition as a bona fide Californian. Sixty-five dollars were sufficient to cover incidental fees in addition to my books. This enabled me to audit as many courses as I could manage in one semester and I took full advantage of that.

A typical day began with reveille at 7 a.m., carpool at 7:30, classes at 9, carpool at 4 p.m. and home an hour later. The months went by quickly. Michael was absorbed in his new job and I with my classes. We had time to talk and share our views, beliefs and hopes for the future. I continued to lead our Legion of Mary group at the St. Mary's Chinese Mission. Hard as I tried, I couldn't convince Michael to join me in this activity.

He hinted that he would buy me an engagement ring after he was settled. First he had to furnish his apartment, buy a good stereo, and outfit himself with several Brooks Brothers suits. I accepted his terms and waited.

At this time, Fr. Liang, whom I had come to know quite well, was living in Berkeley and was chaplain to many U. C. students. He knew of Michael's arrival and was anxious to meet him. We agreed on a date and Fr. Liang treated us to an Italian meal downtown. It was a pleasant dinner, or at least that was what I thought. Imagine my chagrin a week later when Fr. Liang told me in no uncertain terms, "If you insist on marrying Michael, you can count me out. I won't officiate at your wedding."

"Why? How can you be so prejudiced against him? Is it because he's not Chinese? You met him once and have already drawn your conclusions?"

"Trust me. I know. Don't ask me why or how. I just know that he is NOT the right man for you."

Fr. Liang's opinion of Michael shook me up. Fr. Liang was my spiritual director in whom I had confided my feelings and had many discussions about issues and problems. What was I supposed to do, jilt Michael when he had made such effort to come to the

Bay Area to be near me? I couldn't do that to him - it was unfair. No, I decided, I will show Fr. Liang that Michael is a good man and the right one for me. I could be stubborn too. *I'll show him yet*, I vowed.

Weeks went by and then months, Michael no longer mentioned an engagement ring and I was too proud to beg for one. I waited for him to make the move. Seeing each other every day took the glitter and excitement out of our courtship. But I accepted that as normal. *After all, life cannot always be exciting and fun*, I consoled myself.

Soon it was the Christmas season. It was a tradition in our family for all the kids and Mom to go shopping for presents for one another a week before Christmas. On that particular Saturday, Mom took a day off from work and Michael came punctually at 10 a.m. as agreed. But with just two bathrooms in the house, it was not until noon that the seven of us were dressed and ready to go shopping.

Michael was furious. He showed his temper right in front of Mom and all of us. There I was, caught in the middle. I was embarrassed and angry at Michael for his impatience and temper, and angry at my family for their tardiness.

"You just go ahead and side with Michael," shouted Mom. "He's selfish and inconsiderate. If that's the man you must marry, I'll have nothing to do with you. You can stop calling me Mom!"

I bowed my head and left with Michael, fuming.

"Why did you have to explode in front of my mother?" I asked. "Yes, I know, we were two hours late, but, see what you have done?" I shouted.

He was penitent, but the damage was done.

The following days were unpleasant. When Michael and I were together, we didn't have much to say. Anger and disappointment were still welling inside me. Anger at what had happened, disappointment that Michael wasn't as mature as I thought him to be. I realized that seeing and being with him each day wasn't such a good idea after all. We had started to take each other for granted. Gone were common courtesies.

He stayed away from us for a week. Around Christmas he returned for dinners, but the atmosphere had changed. Mom and the kids were cordial, but the feeling of one, big, happy family was gone.

I realized that was why Mom had suggested that Michael come to dinner each evening. She wanted us to see each other as we were, with no frills and pretense. And she had succeeded. We no longer had much in common. Our interests and our ways of thinking were different. *Did I really want to spend the rest of my life with him?* Doubts started to plague me.

Michael brought Christmas presents for everyone - a beautiful silk scarf for Mom, a shirt for Dad, toys and books for my siblings. A white angora turtleneck sweater, identical to the one featured on the cover of *Vogue*, was his present for me. No diamond ring. It was just as well for I already had a plan for the first week in January when classes resumed at U.C.

Instead of attending classes, I went to the U.C. Student Health Center and told the counselor that I was having a nervous breakdown and needed to check myself into the U.C. Hospital for a good rest. Fortunately, hospitalization and medication were free for full-time students. On the third day, the attending physician came. After a thorough checkup, he said, "Look here, young lady. You don't have a nervous breakdown. I need to discharge you tomorrow."

In the meantime, Mom secretly contacted Fr. Liang and told him what was happening. He waited outside the hospital main entrance on the afternoon of my discharge and insisted on taking me to his parish house where we "would have a long, long talk." I had no choice but to comply.

I didn't know Fr. Liang was an experienced therapist. He handed me a big, yellow pad and asked me to write out the pros and cons of my relationship with Michael. After he reviewed my answers he analyzed each item, point by point.

"Do you know how much a therapist charges for this kind of counseling?" I shook my head for I had never been to see one.

"If we don't resolve your dilemma this time, you're heading for trouble." We continued. He asked me questions, and demanded honest answers.

"But he came all this way to be with me. I feel so responsible," I argued.

"Well, he took a chance. How can you blame yourself for that?"

After hours of talk and tears, he asked, "If Michael were the last man on earth, would you marry him?"

Finally I saw the light and answered with a quick "NO." I stayed overnight in the parish guest room and returned home after breakfast. Mom had told Michael I was with my friend Linda Loke in Berkeley.

I braced myself for a clean break with Michael. We talked amicably and I told him I had done a lot of soul searching and decided we were not really that compatible. He was completely surprised. I had never seen him cry and for a brief moment I went limp. But, I couldn't, and wouldn't, renege on the promise to myself and to Fr. Liang. Although our breakup was hard, it was better to do it now rather than later.

"I'll buy you the engagement ring," he said.

"Please don't. It's no use. I no longer love you, Michael."

"But Liz, you gotta give me another chance. I'll do anything you want. I'll even join the Legion of Mary for you."

That afternoon Fr. Liang paid us a surprise visit.

"Please, Fr. Liang, talk to Liz. Convince her to change her mind," Michael implored.

"Michael," Fr. Liang replied, "Let her go. She's not the right girl for you. You're a talented and successful man of the world with a bright future. I'm sure there are many other girls for you. Let her go."

A crestfallen Michael left my house that afternoon. Fr. Liang tarried a bit longer. Before he left, he asked, "Shall I write to Albert and tell him about your breakup?"

"No, definitely not."

I needed time to process these emotions. Even though I no longer loved Michael, there was the bittersweet feeling of loss. I needed time to heal.

Albert

Albert arriving in the U.S. in 1958

The next day the postman brought a letter from Albert. It was brief, asking if I had any job leads in Berkeley for his dad, a political science professor who was coming to join him in the U.S. The P.S. was the key that opened the door to the future. "Have you and Michael set a wedding date? Do give me some advance notice so I can save up my pennies for a gift."

I replied with a short note assuring him that I would inquire about job opportunities for his father. My ending line was, "Michael and I have just broken up. No wedding plans."

Albert replied with a three-page long letter detailing the classes, work and life he was leading in Detroit. That was the beginning of our letter-writing friendship. When I returned to Berkeley the following week, I confronted Fr. Liang and asked if he had anything to do with Albert's letter.

"To be perfectly honest, the idea did cross my mind. On second thought, I felt it better to leave matters in God's hands. Now, doesn't this show you how the Good Lord cares and works things out?" he said.

I rolled my eyes and gave him a funny look. In the depth of my heart I was wondering the same thing.

At first Albert's letters came weekly. Then twice a week, then daily. He found Special Delivery, a service in the U.S. Post Office. For 30 cents extra, a letter was guaranteed to be delivered the next day. We wrote to each other about our thoughts, our philosophy of life, our hopes, our views of the world, and of God, our families and ourselves. I have saved every letter he wrote, and he mine. Someday, I'll write a book about our love affair.

Albert's daily letters became longer and longer. My response to his fervor and devotion was the same. I was becoming more attached to him all the time and finally, I was in love.

I had 10 and 11 a.m. classes that semester, then a two-hour break, until 2 p.m. I used the break time to walk to Newman Hall for noon Mass. Albert was also a daily communicant. The spiritual bond between us deepened our friendship and enhanced our courtship.

One day after Mass, I heard an inner voice, *Expect a special message from Albert today.* I was surprised and pleased that my intuitive voice was involved in our relationship. Deep down I was hoping our friendship would take a more romantic turn.

Sure enough, Albert's letter that evening included a formal

123

proposal of marriage. I knew beyond a reasonable doubt that he was the right man for me. He was the one I always dreamed of marrying - a man with principles, strong religious faith, intelligent, kind, gentle and considerate. We shared similar family backgrounds. Both his college euducated parents were from Shanghai too.

I accepted his proposal whole-heartedly, so did Mom and Dad. Dad was particularly overjoyed to discover that he and Albert's parents shared many mutual friends in Hong Kong and Shanghai.

Two weeks later, my intuitive voice told me that I would receive another surprise when I got home that evening. Sure enough, a package from Albert was waiting for me on our breakfast table. After opening box after box, I found a diamond ring inside a small velvet case - my engagement ring. The diamond was set in white gold, flanked by three smaller diamonds on either side in the design of a branch. Later Albert showed me the matching wedding band. He explained that he chose that set because they reminded him of the vine and the branches mentioned in the New Testament. (John: 15:5). Our love was founded in His love, a marriage made in heaven.

Now, more than 40 years later, I'm still wearing the same set of rings. Although Albert has bought me bigger diamonds, he still wants me to wear the original set.

I was in seventh heaven, happy and content. So was Fr. Liang, for he had long known that Albert and I were made for each other.

Albert managed to get an interview with IBM in San Jose for a job that following summer. We were formally engaged on August 29, 1959, with a Mass at Sts. Peter and Paul Church, with

Fr. Liang officiating. Our wedding was set for June 18, 1960, at Old St. Mary's Church.

Albert also came in time to attend the prestigious Asilomar Conference which I chaired. The theme I chose was *Is Life Worth Living*. Over 200 students from Berkeley, Stanford and other neighboring colleges came. An executive committee and a newsletter committee were hastily organized.

My leadership at this conference also precipitated three lucrative offers from different sources - to be the secretary of the third party of China, the Democratic Socialist Party; to attend law school with all expenses paid and be trained for the foreign office for the Republic of China (Taiwan); to attend graduate school at Fordham University on a full scholarship and be trained as a student leader for the U.S. Catholic Church. All three offers were very tempting, but I was already engaged to be married to Albert. I politely declined and told them that I had chosen to be a wife and mother instead.

Aside from the Asilomar Conference, I was also very active in campus life at U.C. Berkeley. I emceed all the Chinese events, including fashion shows, talent skits and others and made many friends, including Linda Loke and her siblings. These occasions gave me opportunities to develop my speaking and leadership abilities.

It was also at this time that Fr. Liang urged me to find my own place to live. This came as a surprise. He pointed out that since my wedding was less than a year away, it would be wise for me to prepare Mom for our gradual separation.

"Move to Berkeley and rent a room in a boarding house," he said. "Then you can gradually sever your ties and her dependence on you."

Moving to live in Berkeley was a wise idea, but I didn't have any money to pay for it. In fact, I didn't even have a savings account of my own. I had paid Dad in full for the $3,000 we paid for our passage on the SS. President Wilson. The earnings I made from China Dry Goods, Star of the Sea and other summer jobs were all turned over to Mom for our household use. My parents didn't have to ask, I offered it voluntarily, for I was properly brought up as a good Chinese daughter.

Mom wasn't enthused about the idea, but I told her truthfully that I needed more time for class work since the daily commute was tiring. She finally capitulated and even offered me a monthly subsidy of $80. That came in handy, for my room rent was $90 a month, and I still needed money for books, groceries and incidentals. Fr. Liang went a step further. He found a benefactor who was willing to give me a monthly loan of $100. I promised to return the full amount within two years.

I signed a lease for a room within walking distance to classes. It had a single bed, dresser, desk and chair. I brought my own bedding and other necessities. I was elated to find several Chinese students in the house. We all shared bathrooms and a kitchen.

It was here that I started to cook for myself. I was Mom's sous chef during the years I lived at home and my responsibilities included cooking rice from scratch (rice cookers were not available then), preparing the vegetables and other ingredients as well as marinating the meat or seafood. Mom planned the menu, did most of the shopping, and the final cooking. In Berkeley, however, I was my own chef.

It didn't take me long to master some dishes. As a child I had watched Ah Woo plan, cook and orchestrate dinners and banquets. The sound of her chopping and cutting, the heavenly aroma of her creative efforts, and the different textures of the ingredients she prepared were deeply ingrained in my heart and soul. At last, I could experiment and succeeded quite well. Mom was generous and provided me with fresh vegetables and other ingredients whenever I needed them.

Since my engagement, I had time on weekends to cook. I usually planned seven entrees, one for each day of the week. Word got out and soon housemates and friends stopped by to see what I had whipped up. I had to label my food to prevent borrowing.

One day I was surprised to receive a check for $500 from Albert with a note. "Please open a bank account in your name. This is meant for our wedding expenses. More checks will be sent to you in the future." I knew Albert's graduate assistant pay was modest, but I didn't know that he wouldn't even spend a dime for a cup of coffee for himself. He saved every penny for us.

In spring I found my perfect bridal gown with a princess waistline and a full train, delicately decorated with seed pearls. I selected bouquets of roses for my bridesmaids and butterfly orchids for myself, and a venue for the reception. Albert's parents in Hong Kong offered to print our wedding invitations in Chinese and English. At last I was to be married at my favorite church - Old St. Mary's. It is located at 660 California Street, at the entrance to the San Francisco Chinatown. It was built and dedicated as the cathedral of San Francisco on December 24, 1894. A fire destroyed it in April 18, 1906 but it was rebuilt and rededicated three years later. To this day it graces the city of San Francisco and has a world-renowned choir.

Our Wedding

Liz and Albert at Victory Hall, San Francisco

Albert came to San Francisco a week before the wedding. He drove from Detroit in his 1954 Ford, covering over 2,000 miles in 50 hours. He was young and in love. I remember that night he arrived. I was looking out our window, hoping to spot his blue Ford. At 11:30 p.m., I heard the sound of a noisy muffler, looked out and there was he was. Joy. Joy. My bridegroom had arrived.

In the week ahead, I briefed Albert on the wedding preparations. He agreed with all my choices and was happy with the details. Our service, scheduled at 10:30 a.m. was the first of seven weddings that day.

On June 18, 1960, I woke at dawn and started preparations.

Auntie Mary Szeto, a close family friend, helped me with my gown, headpiece and make-up. By 9:30 a.m. I was ready, so was my family. Albert, in our basement guest room, was waiting, I was told.

Mom, Dad and I rode in a borrowed white T-bird decorated with white and pink Kleenex carnations and dragging a pair of old shoes and several tin cans for good luck. Albert and his best man, David Woo, and my other siblings left earlier in other cars.

We arrived at the church promptly by 10 a.m. as instructed so we wouldn't delay the other weddings. No sooner had the three of us alight from the car did Dad suddenly remember that he had left the top for our wedding cake at home. Before we could stop him, he took off.

Since we had to wait for Dad and had time, I hurried to the side altar of the church where a beautiful statue of our Blessed Mother stood. It was to her I often prayed and sat in her presence to think things through whenever I was confused or distressed. It was at her altar that I had offered the long-stem yellow roses Albert once sent to me. I couldn't enjoy them since I was scheduled for a retreat that weekend. Today, however, I offered her my gratitude for her loving care, and for bringing Albert and me together.

It was 10:30 a.m. The entire bridal party was present: June Chang, my maid of honor and my bridesmaids, Bernice Woong, Anna Ching, my sisters Maria and Shirley, and the little flower girl, Denise Chan. Albert and his best man David Woo, and the groomsmen, Joseph Ku, my brothers James and Francis, and Collin Quock, were ready and waiting. Fr. Thomas Liang was the officiating priest, assisted by two altar boys, my brother George and his friend, Clifford Louie. Everyone was present, except Dad.

Father Donald of Old St. Mary's was frantic. "Where's your

father? We can't have him hold up the line. There're six weddings following yours. We've got to start. Choose another relative to give you away."

I wouldn't budge. I couldn't deprive Dad of that honor. He had waited so long for this moment. He wasn't in Hong Kong when Mimi was married so mine was the first official family wedding in which he participated. I calmly consoled Fr. Donald, "My Dad will be here any minute now."

Finally he appeared. The organ started to play Purcell's *Trumpet Voluntary* and the bridal procession began.

Fr. Liang celebrated our Nuptial Mass and many of our guests received the Eucharist with us, including 53 of my former fourth-grade students and their parents from Star of the Sea School. My original intention was to invite them to the wedding ceremony, but not to the reception. Instead, 53 candy baskets were prepared for them. But before the recessional, one of the ushers announced from the podium that the reception site had been changed from St. Mary's Chinese School Auditorium to Victory Hall. All were invited and welcome.

When Dad realized that we had over 500 guests, instead of the 250 we anticipated, he quickly consulted Rachel Chun, a friend and fellow volunteer from St. Mary's Chinese Church. Dad and Rachel managed to secure Victory Hall which was two blocks away from Old St. Mary's. Fortunately, Rachel, an experienced organizer, recruited enough help from many of my friends from the Legion of Mary to put everything in place.

Our nuptial mass took about 50 minutes. Because there were six other weddings following ours, there wasn't time for photo shots inside the church. Besides, taking photos during Mass was strictly forbidden at that time. Fortunately a non-Christian friend who didn't know any better, took a few candid shots. His Polaroid pictures together with those from our official photographer were all the momentos we had. No sooner did we come down the aisle as newlyweds, then we and our guests were politely shooed outside the church. It was pandemonium and we later discovered that many of our wedding gifts were lost - mixed in with the other weddings.

When Albert and I arrived at Victory Hall for our reception, the tables were beautifully decorated and filled with food: Fried Rice, Seafood Chow Mien, Roast Pork, Roast Duck, salad, bread, many varieties of cold cuts, fruits and of course, a wedding cake. The piece de resistance was a whole Roast Pig, a must in a Chinese wedding, traditional symbol of the bride's virginity. The succulence of its meat and skin can't be overstated.

There was not only enough food for all the guests present, but for another 200. It was a grand party, filled with joy and laughter, conversation and good wishes. I was so happy to see my "little ones" from Star of the Sea School, although they were almost as tall as I was. Many of our distant relatives and friends were present too.

At around 3 p.m. Albert and I finally left the party, but not before we were showered with rice. Our chauffeur drove us to the Huntington Hotel on Nob Hill. No sooner did we check into our room and change into regular clothes when we both felt light-headed, tired and famished. We hadn't eaten all day. We hurried to the hotel coffee shop and wolfed down a club sandwich. By then it was 5 p.m. We decided to retire to our room and rest, instead of keeping my promise to visit Sr. Miriam and the other nuns at Star of the Sea School. It wasn't until weeks later, when I called to apologize to Sr. Miriam, that I found out what we missed. The good nuns at Star of the Sea had prepared a reception for us. They had waited and waited and were deeply disappointed. To this day I regret not making the side trip for we would have experienced the same joy Maria, in the movie *The Sound of Music*, did when she visited the convent after her wedding.

After a night's stay at the Huntington, we drove on to Carmel by the Sea. Back then Carmel was just a village, not the cosmopolitan resort it is today. I loved it because it was quaint and quiet, alongside the Pacific Ocean. We stayed in a small cabin and were delighted to find it was named Elizabeth. During that same week, Mom, Dad, my younger siblings and David, our best man, were also in Carmel. They gave us the address of their cabin and told us to visit if we had time. We did, for our cabin was just 10 minutes away. We ended up spending almost our entire honeymoon with them.

After our honeymoon we returned to my parents' apartment for a few days before moving to San Jose. That summer I became a full-time housewife. When Albert was at work at IBM, I prepared meals and decorated our little apartment. Then there were thank-you notes to write. Weekends were usually spent in San Francisco with my folks. They had just purchased their first home on Granville Way, near Portola Drive.

The lease for our San Jose apartment was from June to the end of August. By mid-August, however, I found I was pregnant in spite of the fact that we were both naive about sex. We consulted Fr. Liang and he gave us a medical book with helpful information. My dream was to have a dozen sons and Albert went along with it.

When Mom learned that I was expecting, she suggested we move in with them so she could cook for us. I was having morning sickness and couldn't cook. We agreed, so Albert commuted daily to San Jose in mid-August. It was at this time that Albert's younger brother, James, arrived in San Francisco from Hong Kong. He had just completed high school and was ready to start his undergraduate program in engineering at WSU. Fortunately, my parents had an extra room and James was welcome.

One morning in late August, I started to hemorrhage. Albert had already left for work, so Mom and James rushed me to St. Francis Hospital in a taxi. I had a miscarriage, with a D&C following. Although we weren't able to baptize our baby, we named him Peter. The attending physician at the hospital said, "You must let your body rest - no more babies for a while."

In September Albert had to return to Wayne State to complete his master's in biomechanics. Since I had barely recovered from my miscarriage and was scheduled to take the oral for my master's in English at U.C. in late October, I remained in San Francisco. It was good that James could accompany Albert on the drive back to Detroit. Albert's car hauled a trailer full of stuff - our wedding presents, my books and personal belongings.

For a M.A. in English at U.C., I had the option of writing a thesis or taking a two-hour oral comprehensive exam. I chose the latter and could also pick two of the three professors on my committee. Dr. Wayne Shumaker and Dr. James Sledd, my two favorites, were available. The third one, the chair, Dr. Charles Muscatine, a Chaucerian scholar, was assigned by the department.

I read and studied and used all my study aids, from Chaucer to the 20th Century, American and British authors and writers. Finally the big day came. After a good breakfast I left with promises of prayers from Albert, Mom and Dad and the family.

I paused for a silent prayer before knocking at the door of Professor Muscantine's office. Fortunately both Drs. Shumaker and Sledd were present and welcomed me with a warm handshake.

Professor Muscatine was less friendly, since I had only audited one of his courses. We didn't know each other personally.

The questions started - I was calm and organized. The questions were connected with each other, then fanned out to join others - on and on for two full hours.

I believed I answered all the questions, although at one point, my opinion on Chaucer differed from that of Dr. Muscatine. When the two hours were up, I was asked to leave the room and return within half an hour. Those 30 minutes seemed like an eternity since my academic fate was hanging in the balance.

The final moment came for the verdict. I have passed and have earned a M.A. in English from the University of California, Berkeley!

Now I couldn't wait to pack and fly to Detroit to join Albert and James at our new home at 740 Hazelwood, close to Wayne State University.

4

Detroit, Here I Come

I was full of dreams and hopes for a beautiful life, like the happy ending in many fairy tales. I wanted to resume homemaking and become a mother. On November 19, I flew to Detroit - to my husband, my new home and a new city.

I had never visited Detroit, but Albert had been touting its virtues. "It's the fifth largest city in the U.S., the home of automobiles and Michigan is the land of a 1,000 lakes," he said, knowing how much I love fish. Now, with 1,000 lakes, there must be lots of pickerel, perch and other fish, I reasoned. Wrong. In the 60s, fish markets in Detroit were few and far between, as was the case with Chinese grocery stores and restaurants.

I could hardly wait to see my own home at 740 Hazelwood. Our small apartment, on the fourth floor, was serviced by an elevator. It had one bedroom. James slept in the Murphy bed in the living room which doubled as our dining area. Our bedroom had a double bed and dresser. A small dinette set with four chairs stood in the living/dining area with two sofas. A refrigerator, and a gas stove with four burners were in the kitchen, along with several cupboards. We used wooden crates and large cardboard detergent boxes, covered with decorative wall paper, as storage bins for our books and knick-knacks.

For the first two months I was excited. I brightened and beautified our home with pictures and Chinese artifacts, mostly wedding gifts. I consulted Chinese cookbooks for appetizing dishes to cook for the three of us.

Since Albert was a graduate assistant, we had to watch our

budget. After paying $99 for the rent, we barely had enough for food and gas. The $75 a month that Albert's mother insisted on giving us to cover James's share was put to good use.

But Detroit wasn't San Francisco and there was only one Chinese grocery store in the area, Wah Lee, on Cass Avenue near Wayne State. Its stock of Chinese ingredients was limited, so was its supply of fresh Chinese produce. But I managed to get by with what we had since my mother sent us provisions from time to time. My cooking soon became my hobby and obsession. I loved feeling free and creative.

Our apartment complex had 40 units, 10 on each floor. While we didn't get to know the other tenants, we got on quite well with the caretaker, Mrs. Jenny Christiansen. She was a tall, motherly woman from Sweden, pleasant and affectionate. She was helpful, knowledgeable, and was always willing to offer suggestions and advice. She taught me how to sew, and her sewing machine was always available for my use.

Since I didn't know how to drive, and buses here, unlike San Francisco, were not that convenient, I looked forward to weekends when Albert and James would take me shopping at the grocery store and at Wah Lee.

For Thanksgiving we were invited to Professor and Mrs. Herbert Lissner's home. He was Albert's department head, teacher and mentor. It was he who offered Albert a fellowship when he applied from Hong Kong in the spring of 1958. Usually assistantships were awarded at least a year in advance. When Albert applied, he received offers from Wayne State and University of Iowa.

It was providential that Albert chose Wayne State University (WSU). Professor Lissner, in collaboration with Dr.

Steve Gurdjian, a neurosurgeon, were the pioneers in Impact Biomechanics, a new discipline. They were the professionals who dropped steel balls onto human skulls to study the mechanism of skull fractures in 1939.

Thanksgiving at the Lissners was my first foray into a Midwest American home. Our hosts were gracious and kind. Although we didn't particularly relish the overcooked turkey, we enjoyed the accompaniments - baked yam, green bean casserole, pumpkin and pecan pies, cranberry sauce, and mashed potatoes.

On our first Christmas we sent sizable *laisees* (red envelopes filled with cash or checks) to our parents in San Francisco and Hong Kong, so little was left to spend on ourselves. We gave James a pair of leather gloves and we bought special Hallmark cards for each other. To this day, giving cards for birthdays, anniversaries and Christmas has become a tradition for Albert and me. We were like Jim and Della in O. Henry's *The Gift of the Magi*. We had each other and that was enough.

Our monthly budget included $100 for phone bills since Mom always reversed the charges for our weekly conversations. She missed me terribly. During our hour-long chit-chats, she would detail everything from what she cooked that week to her work, Dad's temper and my siblings' progress in school. I didn't have the heart to stop or cut short these calls, and Albert understood. Long distance calls were expensive then, before the use of undersea cables and fiber optics. Thanks to Albert's cousin, Dr. Charles Kao, the 2009 Physics Nobel winner, who pioneered the use of optic fibers, the industry was revolutionized and international and domestic calls became more affordable.

I was away from my parents, my five younger siblings, and all my friends. Detroit didn't have the network of buses, cable cars and trams that San Francisco had. I was cooped up in our small apartment and we didn't even own a TV. I read novels and cookbooks voraciously. I didn't have the wherewithal to travel around the city, nor did we have the financial means to indulge in hobbies or entertainment.

But we did manage to go to the movies at the Fox and Fisher theaters.* Tuesday nights were our movie nights. New features began at midnight. For 50 cents apiece, we ended up seeing six movies at one shot. We continued this even during the latter months of my second pregnancy. I remember how difficult it was for me to get up to leave my seat after sitting for nearly nine hours watching six movies nonstop. Afterwards I spent days trying to figure out the plots since the six movies were shown one after another. No wonder Albert Jr. is an avid movie fan, since he was exposed to them before he was born.

Aside from the movies, we also found poker a challenging pastime. Albert, James and I, with the Liu brothers, Young King and Lun King, played cards well past midnight on weekends. We called our game Probability Seminar and this got Albert and James out of trouble when their professors learned that it was their weekend preoccupation. They believed the King brothers were serious students who spent their weekends studying math. Later on, when the number of poker players extended to several of Albert's and James' male classmates, I was excluded. Male chauvinism prevailed.

Albert worked on his doctoral degree in biomechanics and was a full-time teaching assistant. James, an undergraduate, carried a full load in engineering classes and worked part-time in the department. Consequently, both were busy studying and working, I was a bored housewife with time on my hands. Since

138

my miscarriage in September, the physician advised me to rest before another pregnancy. I had to keep busy and decided to seek some form of employment.

In February I was offered a fulltime job as library aide at the Hamtramck Public Library. Beatrice Adamski and her library staff made me feel completely at home. I learned about Polish culture and food and wished I could speak Polish. They, in turn, were curious about my Chinese heritage and background. When a patron asked if I spoke Polish, I shook my head and replied, "How I wish I could." It was here that I learned to enjoy Polish kielbasa, cabbage rolls and paczki and more. Many years later when we visited Warsaw and Krakow I recalled my time at the Hamtramck Public Library.

Baby Albert

Our little Koala Bear, Albert Jr.

In the spring of 1961 I was pregnant. When I started spotting, Albert took me to Henry Ford Hospital where I met Dr. Eli Igna, an obstetrician. Dr. Igna and I had a long association and to this day I am grateful for his attentive care.

We had wanted a large family and were anxious to keep the baby. I resigned from the Hamtramck Public Library in July so I could rest. But I couldn't stay in bed all the time. Who would do the housework, especially the cooking? Neither Albert nor James could cook, and even when they tried, the food was hardly edible. I tried, more trouble. I was rushed to the Henry Ford Emergency, then stayed there on the obstetrics floor for three days. Dr. Igna said I should stay off my feet.

But, a week of bad cooking made me try again to prepare meals. For a short while I was able to stand, then I had to rush to emergency. This time Dr. Igna kept me for five days. His prescription was the same, but sterner.

Albert and James again tried hard to cook, but with little success. Hunger got the better of us. I had to get up to prepare meals. On October 8, I returned to Ford Hospital. Dr. Igna performed a C-section the next day. Albert Jr. was born, weighing 3 lbs.13 ozs. He was eight weeks early and looked like a small chicken. But he was alive and he was ours.

When Albert came to visit me in the hospital after my surgery, the first thing I asked was if he had sent the telegram to his parents in Hong Kong. He assured me he did, for this was crucial, since Albert Jr. was not only our first child, but the first son of the first son of the first son, for three generations of the King family. That made him truly special.

There is a strange twist to this birthdate. Albert's paternal grandfather lived in Shanghai, about 10,000 miles from Detroit. He was pushing 85, and still in fairly good health. In 1961, the "bamboo curtain" between Mainland China and Hong Kong made communications by mail slow.

Much later, my mother-in-law told me about how Albert Jr.'s Great Grandpa woke up laughing one morning. When asked why, he said, "I had the most wonderful dream. I've seen the face of my grandson's son. Now I know our family line is intact. I can rest in peace." This was long before the telegram was sent. Great Grandpa King died a few months after Albert Jr. was born. My in-laws pinpointed the exact date of his dream, October 9, the day Albert Jr. was born.

It was not until Albert Jr. reached a full five pounds and could return home with us that I learned that his dad had waited for a week before he cabled Hong Kong. That was upon the advice of both the obstetrician and pediatrician since baby Albert teetered between life and death during his first week. He had pneumonia, then jaundice and was running a fever. These affected his baby teeth which were brown without enamel until they were replaced by a permanent set.

At the maternity ward, I had the care and attention of many student nurses. One, in particular, stood out: Susan Durling. She was the typical American girl, with long blond hair, a beautiful dimpled smile, kind, courteous and eager to help. She washed and styled my hair, manicured my nails and made me feel loved. Susan and I are still in touch.

We didn't even have time to worry about our hospital bills before Albert Sr. received the coveted Boris A. Bakmetiff Award for Fluid Mechanics. Professor Lissner had submitted his name and paper for that nationwide competition which was an honor to Wayne State and to Albert. The award included a prize of $3,000, a handsome sum to us. We almost added Boris to Albert Jr.'s middle name, thinking that we might have to use the entire sum to pay our hospital bills. But God was good and kind. The student insurance at Wayne State covered 90 per cent of it. Our share was only $300.

Albert Jr. was hospitalized for five weeks so I couldn't hold him until he weighed at least five pounds. All I could do was peer at him through the window of the incubator room and send him my love and prayers.

When I returned home two weeks later, Albert had moved us from the fourth floor to the basement of our apartment building. The rent was $5 cheaper and there was more space. We reduced

James' monthly payment for his room and board to $70. Now we had two large bedrooms, a large living room with an adjoining kitchen, and a large bathroom. The only drawback was the heating and cooling ducts that hung overhead. In the winter, our apartment was close to 80-degrees Fahrenheit, while in the summer, it was cool and comfortable. The furnishings were about the same as before.

I was home, but our baby was still in the hospital. We went to see him each day and prepared for his homecoming. Baby clothes, furniture and a crib were brought over by friends and neighbors, including Grandma Helen Warner, a 75-year-old lady who lived in a house across the street from us. We met on the street and became friends. Grandma Warner and our manager, Mrs. Christensen, remained my trusted advisers for years.

Mom didn't come to help. She said she couldn't take time off from her job in sales at the Royal Cathay, a wholesale Chinese gift shop in Chinatown. But as I look back, I realized that she really didn't know how to care for babies. She had depended on Ah Woo and Ah Lo to raise her children.

After five weeks, Albert Jr. was big enough to come home. I had been trained how to feed and handle him in advance. I charted his daily weight gain by the ounce. Dr. Philip Howard, the pediatrician, said that when he reached five full pounds, he was ready to come home. He slowly gained weight day by day. A week before his discharge, I was allowed to hold him with wearing a clean hospital gown, a surgical mask, and sanitized hands. He was so tiny, my precious little one.

How can I describe my feelings at holding my baby - my first born? I felt a joy and gratitude that were beyond words. Indeed, a baby is a miracle, a gift from Above, especially when he's your very own.

In mid-November we brought him home. Albert, James and I went to the Preemie Room to take our "koala bear" home. The name koala came because I was very fond of Australia's famous koala bears and was given a stuffed one before I left San Francisco. When my sister Shirley learned of my pregnancy, she sent me a cute postcard with the following inscription: "Mama and Papa Bears waiting for their koala bear."

He was bottle-fed since I couldn't nurse him. I remember the bottles and nipples that we had to wash and sterilize each day, as well as the diapers. In those days disposable diapers weren't readily available nor affordable. A diaper service was also out of the question. But Papa helped with the washing of bottles and diapers. We used the washer and dryer in the apartment complex since we didn't own a set ourselves. A new Kenmore refrigerator for his formula was our only luxury.

Preemies take much longer to drink their milk. During the first month I had to feed our koala bear every three hours, and it took an hour and a half for him to finish his four-ounce formula. So I was feeding him every hour and a half. I had no time for anything else but caring for him. During feeding time, I rested and relaxed. As I look back, those days were great days for bonding and cuddling. All the housework could wait, including the cooking. That was when the casseroles and dishes brought over by friends and neighbors were especially welcome.

Although Albert and I still didn't have money to buy presents for each other, this Christmas was different. We had our gift - our pride and joy - little Albert. We didn't need anything else. How proud I was to sign our Christmas cards with "Albert and Liz and our little koala bear."

Little Albert continued to grow and blossom. Soon he weighed six pounds, then seven, then eight. He slept in a crib at the foot of our bed. Each morning when he woke up, he would just sit quietly and play and wait to be picked up and fed. When I picked him up he was all smiles and so cuddly! I wished I had sent his photo to Gerber for its poster baby.

At one of his monthly checkups Dr. Howard recommended a circumcision to prevent infection. How my heart ached when I saw the blood and bandage on his little penis after the procedure was complete.

Life then was regular and simple. In spring I took him out in his perambulator along Hazelwood. It was easy to make friends with other mothers who were also walking their babies.

That summer, Albert Sr. took classes at Illinois Institute of Technology (IIT) in Chicago. It was an adventure for all of us, except James, who had to stay behind for his summer job at WSU. We loaded our old Ford with necessities, mostly little Albert's stuff, and drove to Chicago.

It was a welcome change. Our apartment on campus was larger and more modern than our Detroit home. Chicago had a good Chinatown where I could stock up on groceries and foodstuffs.

We were overjoyed when Catherine and Bob Chou, dear friends who had left Detroit for IBM in Poughkeepsie, NY, over a year ago, came to spend the Fourth of July weekend with us. The day before their arrival, I spent hours cooking Shanghai Pork with Bamboo and Mushroom, Cantonese Buddha's Delight (a medley of at least 10 vegetables and mushrooms), and cut and marinated beef and seafood for stir-fried dishes.

It was wonderful to welcome them to our apartment. Catherine was enamored with little Albert. She and Bob were childless, and after years of trying to have a baby, they decided to adopt once they were settled in California. After a big dinner, we were anxious to show them the beautiful campus. We debated whether we should take little Albert's stroller along.

Catherine said we could take turns carrying him. That proved to be a crucial decision. It was dusk, the sky was getting dark as Albert and Bob led the way while Catherine and I, carrying little Albert, followed. Suddenly something hit my right thigh. It felt like a baseball, but we didn't see any kids playing baseball. I lifted my skirt and saw a hole in my thigh. It stung and I felt something was lodged there. I handed the baby to Catherine and called Albert.

Albert rushed me to a nearby hospital, while Catherine and Bob stayed with the baby. As soon as we reported my bullet wound to the information desk, they insisted I wait for the police. A bullet wound was a felony and the Chicago cops had to check it out. When they learned that we were with our friends, the Chous, they sent two police officers to our apartment to interrogate them. It was only after they had interrogated all four of us, separately, that I was properly admitted to the hospital, about two and a half hours later.

Afterwards, I was wheeled into the operating room and the surgeon removed a 45-caliber bullet from my thigh. By then, the bullet had tunneled through my thigh to my kneecap. I still have the scars on my right thigh from this freak accident.

When the surgeon showed me the bullet, I asked if I could keep it as a souvenir. Afterall, it was lodged in my body for a few hours. "No," he said, "That bullet belongs to the police and they need to check it out. You're certainly a lucky lady. If that bullet had hit you elsewhere, you'd be in big trouble."

Catherine and Bob were so sorry they couldn't stay longer. Their moving van was due in California very soon. Fortunately, several young families at IIT offered to care for little Albert when they heard of my accident. I felt relieved since Papa (Albert Sr.) wasn't too handy with babies.

"You should have seen what happened to one soldier when he was hit by a 45-caliber bullet. His torso split into two!" said the husband of my hospital roommate. "Some freak must have shot the bullet into the air to celebrate July 4. That bullet just ricocheted and ricocheted then it came down and hit you," he added. No matter, I was thankful that it hit me where it did.

Albert called several times a day to assure me that all was well with little Albert. But I wanted to go home. On the fourth day, I begged my attending physician to sign my release. "I just need to get home to my little baby," I pleaded. He finally gave his consent. I dressed hurriedly and flagged a taxi to our apartment. Albert was surprised when he saw me and had to pay the cab driver. Little Albert was fine, but he no longer recognized me. He even cried when I held him. I was crushed - my baby didn't know me! He was in the care of strangers for four long days. Poor dear, he must have thought that his mama had abandoned him.

"Chicago is certainly a dangerous city!" Dad exclaimed when he heard about my accident. That was an understatement. For years later, I wouldn't go anywhere near Chicago, especially during the July 4th celebration.

We returned to Detroit at the end of August. On Oct. 9, 1962, little Albert's first birthday, I baked a butter cake with white frosting and put a big red candle in the center. The delight in little

Albert's eyes was unforgettable. We sang Happy Birthday to him and showed him how to blow out the candle. What joy and fun.

In January, Dad paid us a visit by himself. We were so glad to see him and for the first time, he and I had the opportunity to talk and reconnect. He enjoyed the baby and was so tender with him. While he was here, Albert Jr was baptized. David Woo, our best man, was the godfather. The baptism was at our church - the Blessed Sacrament Cathedral.

Baby Thomas

Baby Thomas at two-days old

Soon I started to have morning sickness and proudly announced to Albert and the family that I was pregnant again. I went for regular checkups with Dr. Igna and didn't have any problems with spotting or bleeding. My due date for a C-section was in early September.

In June, Shirley Cheung, James' girl friend from Hong Kong, arrived from Arkansas. The love they had for each other in Hong Kong had survived the years of separation. They had a simple engagement and were kind enough to wait until I had given birth to our second child before they married.

It was serendipitous that I reconnected with an old classmate at St. Mary's, Vivian Lee. Her husband, Ronald Lee, was a student at Wayne State and had lived across the hall from Albert. One day in May 1960, Vivian and Ron were in Albert's apartment and saw a framed photo of me on Albert's desk. "Why, that's Elizabeth Chiu, my dear friend from St. Mary's," Vivian exclaimed.

That was how we reconnected after many years, but soon we had to part again. The Lees were moving to Seattle where Ron had a job at Boeing. I couldn't let Vivian leave without a long visit with me. We scheduled our get together for August 3. Vivian came early that morning and we had fun reminiscing about the years at St. Mary's and our classmates. I served a simple lunch of soup noodles with toppings. After I put Albert Jr. down for his nap, we had tea and more chit chat. We were like two birds who couldn't stop chirping. Finally Ron came for Vivian and we said our farewells.

That August 3 was a scorching, hot day. Fortunately we didn't feel the heat so much in our basement with its overhead air-conditioning ducts. But I needed a shower and so did little Albert. In a whim, I decided to shower with him in my arms. Within 15 minutes, we both felt refreshed. But suddenly I started to get cramps. The pains grew sharper and sharper. I called Albert at work and asked him to rush home. I knew I wasn't due until next month, but why this pain?

Albert came home and rushed me to Henry Ford Hospital. This time I was taken straight to the obstetrics ward while father and son waited. Dr. Igna was summoned immediately. All I could remember was that when I started to bleed, Dr. Igna started the C-section. I wasn't too heavily sedated and heard Dr. Igna shouting, as he pulled the baby out of my womb, "He's a little blue. Quick, let me clear his mouth!" I heard a loud cry. *Thank*

God, my baby is alive. Then I lost consciousness.

When I came to, Dr. Igna was in my room. I had not yet held my newborn.

"No more babies," he announced. "Did you know you had a ruptured uterus? First, placenta previa and now this. I can't let you kill yourself," he said.

I was heartbroken. What about cheaper by the dozen? That dream was shattered. I had just turned 28 and didn't know any better. After Dr. Igna left, I cried. When I had the chance to hold my baby, I was grateful that he was perfect and so cute, with 10 toes and 10 fingers, and a crop of black hair. As I fed Tom his bottle and held and caressed him, I was so thankful that he was alive and well and that I had at least two sons. Tom, AKA, Thomas Ignatius, was named after my beloved Father Liang. I owed him so much. Albert and I agreed on the first name and Tom had his dad's middle name, Ignatius. His nickname was Yogi Bear, named after the famous Yogi Berra of the New York Yankees.

Our Yogi Bear weighed seven pounds six ounces, almost twice as big as his brother and looked more like Albert's side of the family. He was darker than Albert Jr. who had a fair complexion. The two brothers are different in personalities and tastes. As a baby, Tom had a healthy appetite and was always hungry. He drank his formula in a flash and pooped just as often. He was a much easier baby to take care of. *Could it be because I was a more experienced Mom?* I wondered.

My stay at Ford Hospital was 10 days. Shirley, James' fiancee, offered to take care of little Albert. She wanted to do it gratis, but we insisted on paying her. She had little Albert for a month during my hospitalization and after my return home. With a brand new baby, many adjustments had to be made. When I returned home with little Tom in my arms, Albert Jr. ran to meet me and insisted on being carried. I hastily handed Tom to Shirley while I cuddled my little boy. He did miss me this time and didn't forget his mama.

I had my hands full with two boys 22 months apart. Life at Hazelwood was a continuous round of feeding, diapering, washing, cooking and caring for the home. I was so busy that I didn't have time to be lonely.

That was also the year that Albert's immediate family, his mom, dad and youngest brother Gordon, immigrated to the U.S. San Francisco was their first port of call. They liked the city so much that they decided to make their home there. My parents took them under their wing and made their move to the U.S. much easier.

Six weeks later, we celebrated the wedding of James and Shirley. They had waited until I had recovered from my delivery. I gave Shirley a bridal shower. Poor dear, she didn't understand the meaning of a bridal shower and thought it meant dunking her in a tub full of water. I did fill our bathtub with water that day to prolong the joke.

Shirley wore my wedding gown. Although she is five feet six, three inches taller than I am, she fitted into the full skirt. I was so proud - she was the third bride who wore my wedding dress. The second one was Frances Liu, younger sister of Lun King Liu, Albert's former roommate.

Detroit, 1964-1966

James and Shirley rented an apartment two minutes away from us. That was comforting, since they were our only close relatives in town. Their help with our little ones and the household chores was welcome. How I wish Mom could have come and given me a hand. She never offered and I never asked.

The summer of 1964, Albert, our boys and I went to San Francisco to visit both sides of the family. Although we had been there two years prior with little Albert, this was the first time we showed off Tom. I couldn't wait to meet my husband's family. His dad had come to Detroit for James' wedding, but not his mother and younger brother. It didn't take me long to be completely at ease with them, since I spoke their dialect, Shanghainese. Besides, his mother, Helen, had no daughters - another plus in my favor.

We stayed with my parents at their home in Granville Way. It was good to be in San Francisco again, to enjoy Mom's cooking and sample many new Chinese restaurants. We returned home after a month with my younger sister, Maria.

Mom suggested Maria could help me with my boys. "She's very handy around the house and with little ones," Mom said.

Maria was in her early 20s. She had meningitis when she was about eight years old and was under intensive nursing care for a year. We were so proud that she managed to graduate from Galileo High School in San Francisco. Maria was good-natured, soft-spoken, and very helpful. After graduation, she remained at home and took care of most of the chores when Mom was at work. I was delighted to have an extra pair of hands to help me, especially someone I could trust.

Maria considered herself the "ugly duckling" in the family. While Mimi and Shirley were considered pretty, and I smart, she felt left out. That wasn't true, but her self-esteem was low and she was often depressed. I was too naive and busy at that time to realize that Maria needed my attention and love just as much as my children did.

With Maria's help at home, I was able to find a part-time job to supplement our income. After taking an introductory library course, followed by two more, I decided to get a master's degree in library science. The University of Michigan (U.M.) had an extension degree course at Rackham Center, close to WSU. Fortunately it offered many library science classes. I took two night courses each semester while Albert Sr. babysat.

In the early winter of 1965, I worked part-time as a library aide at the main branch of the Detroit Public Library (DPL) near WSU. I was assigned to the Children's Department, located in a brand new wing on Cass Avenue. My hours were from 5-9 p.m., Tuesdays, Wednesdays and Thursdays, and from 9 a.m. to 5 p.m. on Saturdays. Not the most desirable hours, but beggars couldn't be choosers. Aside from the additional income, the job gave me time outside the house where I could enjoy a different world, meet people and return home refreshed to resume being a wife and mother.

My responsibilities consisted of helping patrons find books, answering telephone questions, and assisting with storytelling on Saturday mornings. I particularly enjoyed storytelling, for as a child I loved fairy and folk tales and planned to share them with my own children, Albert Jr., 3-1/2, Tom, 2. A fabulous collection of picture books and books for older children of all ages was housed in the DPL Children's Department.

My one handicap was not knowing how to drive. I didn't need to drive in Hong Kong and didn't drive during my five years in the Bay Area. When I arrived in Detroit, Albert said I didn't need to drive, since he would chauffeur me everywhere. We only had one car and after witnessing too many grizzly accidents as part of his job at WSU, he was definitely against the idea of me driving.

However, since my working hours were different from his, it was imperative that I learn to drive. At first Albert wanted to teach me, but his Ford had a stick shift, which for a novice is twice as hard to learn. After two lessons I refused to let him teach me anymore. It was difficult for me to step on the clutch and keep the engine running. I almost drove his car into the Detroit River during our second lesson.

"Yes, I know I'm stupid and clumsy," I muttered with tears streaming down my cheeks. "You don't have to say it, I see it in your eyes." I walked away, humiliated and angry. Yes, it's true. I've been told that it's always disastrous to learn driving from one's spouse. It almost cost us our marriage.

I enrolled in a commercial driving course and got my driver's license in two months. For a long time I didn't want to drive on the expressway. As a neophyte, it was hard to know when to merge, pick up speed, and change lanes. Just seeing cars whizzing by was enough to rattle my brain. However, it took me twice as long to drive on surface streets. We bought our second car, a used beige Mercury for $300.

It was at this time that we lost our dear Professor Herbert Lissner. He had a weak heart and was hospitalized after a mild attack. He ignored the warnings of his cardiologist and returned to work after two weeks. A more serious heart attack followed and he died within a week. Albert was devastated - he had lost his professor, mentor and doctoral advisor all at once. Professor Lissner was only 56. Albert was one of the pall bearers at his funeral.

With Prof. Lissner gone, Albert chose Professor Charles Perry to be his advisor. When Professor Perry left WSU after a year, Professor Larry Patrick, director of the Bioengineering Lab, became Albert's new doctoral advisor. Life slowly resumed.

Years later, Albert had to jump through hoops to establish the Lissner Memorial Lecture and Medal as an ASME (American Society of Mechanical Engineering) section-wide event. It was 10 years later that Albert (Prof. Lissner's only doctoral student) was a recipient of the Lissner medal.

Under the guidance of Professor Patrick, Albert finished his doctoral thesis on blood flow and received his Ph.D. We could finally see light at the end of the tunnel. The six years he spent studying, researching and writing had come to an end. I helped with some of his research and with the typing of his dissertation. I also learned to do computer calculations, although at that time, we used cumbersome computer cards. Once I dropped a box of these cards and had to spend hours organizing them.

The graduation ceremony at Cobo Hall on June 9, 1966 stands out in my memory. Albert looked absolutely regal in his black, doctoral cap and gown, with three wide gold stripes on his flowing sleeves. I wore an aqua Thai silk *qi pao* with matching jacket, which Mom had ordered for me in Hong Kong. The photo we took with Professor and Mrs. Patrick on that happy occasion was precious. What a relief, after six long, arduous years, Albert's study was finally completed. Now on to new horizons.

We were ready to move out of our basement apartment. We

went house hunting and discovered some areas were unfriendly and unreceptive to minorities. In the suburb, Dearborn Heights, we found a small brick ranch with three bedrooms, a living room with a small dining nook, a kitchen and a full bath. It had a full basement that was partially finished, with a parquet tile floor and cement walls. That served well as a play area for our boys in the winter as well as a storage area.

If we assumed its present mortgage, our monthly payment would be $85, $10 less than our rent for our Hazelwood basement apartment. There was a catch - we had to come up with $10,000 to assume the G.I. loan for the house. That $10,000 was a huge sum. While we liked the house and the neighborhood, we didn't have the money for the down payment. We had $2,000 in our savings account, but that was used to subsidize his parents' move from Hong Kong to the U.S. We were too proud to ask my parents for a loan.

During lunch one day Albert casually mentioned our house hunting experience to Professor Patrick.

"How much did you say the GI loan was?" he asked.

"$10,000," Albert replied.

Without a second thought, Professor Patrick took out his checkbook and wrote a check for that amount. He handed this to Albert with a big smile, "Here's the loan and you can take your time to pay back. Go ahead and buy the house."

Miracle of miracles. We couldn't contain our joy and gratitude at such generosity. It took us two years to pay off our debt to the Patricks. To mark this event, they even treated us to a "burn the mortgage" dinner at Stouffer's, their favorite restaurant. Professor Patrick passed away in 2006, but Albert acknowledged his kindness on many public occasions.

In mid-May, 1966, we moved into our first home on 6221 Amboy Street in Dearborn Heights. It was unfurnished except for a stove and refrigerator. Since we didn't have much savings, we didn't shop for new furniture. Instead we bought a second-hand futon bed which doubled as a sofa during the day and our bed at night, a used Formica dinette with four chairs, and a used washer and dryer. Albert Jr. and Tom continued to use their six-year old cribs as beds. We managed quite well for the first year.

A year later, friends of ours, Julia and T. S. Chang, were relocating to Seattle, WA. They offered to lend us their double bed with matching dresser and night stands. After 12 months we sent them a check for $250 per their request. We were also able to afford single beds for our boys.

Next we encouraged Maria to find a job elsewhere. She was single, young, and entitled to have her own space and be with her friends. Although we would miss her, she would benefit from the move. At first she was desolate. But when she found a teaching job at a nursery school and made friends at the Evangeline House where she was staying, she was happy. Later I had to beg her to come home for Thanksgiving and Christmas.

Now that Albert had his doctorate, I wanted to complete my master's in library science. This would give me an edge in job hunting. I was thankful that the University of Michigan (U-M) gave me some credits for the English courses in my M.A. from U.C., Berkeley. After completing all the courses Rackham had to offer, I spent a summer in residence in Ann Arbor to complete the degree requirement.

Ann Arbor is a good 60 miles and a full hour's drive from Detroit. We sublet a furnished apartment on E. William and

Liberty streets, close to campus. During those eight weeks, I plunged into my studies. In order to get an extra hour of sleep on weekends, we scotch-taped newspapers to the glass windows in our apartment so our boys wouldn't wake us up at the crack of dawn.

As a full-time student and mom, I had to do a lot of juggling. But Albert pitched in. He dropped off the boys in a nearby nursery school each morning before taking me to the library. In the late afternoon I walked to the boys' nursery school, picked them up and returned to our apartment. We had to leave our second car at our house in Dearborn Heights since finding parking in Ann Arbor was hopeless.

One of my required courses was storytelling - my favorite subject. I had to write a long paper on the history of children's books. Since the children's department at the Detroit Main Library was the best place to do my research, I had no choice but to work there. I still recall spending the entire day there doing research before rushing to take the Greyhound Bus back to Ann Arbor. Albert had a meeting to attend that evening and couldn't drive me back.

The Greyhound bus was late and I was worried to death. We didn't have cell phones then and it was well over an hour before I reached the boys' nursery school. It was impossible to catch a taxi so I ran from the bus station to their school, clutching my school bag and two little toy Greyhound buses. Fortunately, the teacher's aide was with them. The three of them sat on the school steps. Tears glistened in my boys' eyes. I rushed to hug them and told them, "So sorry, my bus was late and I was so worried." I thanked the aide and handed my sons their toys.

I didn't disappoint Albert or myself. I passed my courses

and was invited to join the honor society. But, I was too busy and didn't bother to fill out the application. While U-M waived my foreign language requirement, I was still obliged to take a test in French translation. Imagine my amazement when the assigned passage for translation was no other than Thomas Grey's *Elegy Written in a Country Churchyard*. This poem was among those I had to memorize during my classes at St. Mary's in Hong Kong. Because I knew the poem word by word, I had to search very hard for synonyms instead of using the actual words in the poem.

In late August we returned to our Amboy Street home. Albert Jr. was now ready for kindergarten in Wellever School nearby. Tom attended Real Life Nursery. Before the semester started, we took our first family vacation by ourselves. In the past we always had Mom in tow and these were three-day or long weekends at college campuses where Albert attended meetings.

This time the four of us went to Boston to visit our dear friends David (our best man) and Pat Woo and their family. David was a general surgeon at the Massachusetts General Hospital. Pat was a homemaker and cared for their children, Ben, Amy and a baby. Ben and Amy were about Albert Jr.'s and Tom's age. I fell in love with them - they were so beautiful, combining Chinese and Irish-American backgrounds.

The Woos lived in a large wooden ranch in Lowell, not far from Boston. I was surprised to find their children had so few toys. When I visited the famous Filene's department store, I couldn't resist buying a beautiful doll with blond hair for Amy and a big construction truck for Ben. I also bought a set of handmade wooden miniature Christmas dolls for our family. To this day I treasure these dolls and remember that special visit to Boston.

Since David was like a brother to Albert and we were almost

family, David had no qualms sending me to the kitchen. "Show Pat how to cook your Shanghai Red-cooked Pork," he asked. This is a favorite at our house too and in many Shanghai households. (Recipe on pp.314-315.)

Professor and Mrs. Larry Patrick

1967-1968 - Years of Simple Blessings

In September of 1967 I was hired as a full-time librarian at Henry Ford Community College (HFCC) in Dearborn, about six miles from our home and a 10-minute drive even at peak time.

For my interview with Mr. Avram Rosenthal and his staff for the position of circulation librarian, I wore a slim, navy blue linen dress accentuated with a fuchsia yoke, one of my more flattering outfits. I was 32, eager, articulate, and with the proper credentials. The pay at HFCC was four times my part-time salary at the Detroit Public Library, and the schedule was phenomenal. Librarians had the same status as the college teachers and were members of the Teachers' Union. We worked from September to June with the entire summer off, two weeks off for Christmas and the New Year, 10 days for Easter, in addition to the other public holidays. Then we were granted three weeks of sick days and five business days. This was ideal for me, a young mother with young children.

At the college, my boss, Mr. Avram Rosenthal (Skip), full-time colleagues and the many secretaries and student assistants brought color and many challenges to my life. Margaret McHenry and Thomas Quinn were the reference librarians, with Mary Frances Ray, book selection, Ida Murry, cataloguing, and Ken Walters, audio-visual. I was the circulation librarian. A clear line was drawn between professional librarians and clerical staff.

To this day, I am in close touch with Mary Frances, one of my closest friends, as well as with Pat Doline and Jane Geisler, and former student assistants, Paul Huff and Donna Micallef.

Life was hectic for me as librarian, mother and wife. When I returned home from work, I was quite tired. But I had the boys, a husband, and a house to take care of, plus shopping, cooking, washing, and cleaning. However, I was young and soon learned to multi-task.

As assistant professor in Biomechanics, Albert was very involved with teaching and research. At first I would have dinner on the table by 6:30 p.m. The boys needed playtime after dinner, before their bath and bedtime. Hard as he tried, Albert couldn't make it in time to have dinner with us. So dinner time was shifted to 7 p.m., then 7:30 p.m. but that still didn't help. The final solution was for me to eat with the boys at the regular time, then keep Papa's dinner warm until he returned which could be anytime between 8 and 11 p.m.

These were, however, much better hours than those we had in Hazelwood when Albert was a doctoral student and teaching assistant. Professor Lissner, although kind, was a hard taskmaster. He insisted that Albert make all his experimental instruments which were labor-intensive and time-consuming. Often Albert had no choice but to be in the lab until midnight or later.

One winter night Albert wasn't home when I awoke at 3 a.m. I was so worried I telephoned him at work to no avail. Then I telephoned the police and inquired if there were any accidents on the road.

"Ma'am, did you look outside your window?" the policeman asked.

"Why? What does that have to do with my husband?" I inquired.

"Just look out and you'll know what I mean."

We were living in the basement apartment with low windows. When I looked, all I could see was snow. I didn't realize that we had just had a big, snow storm. When Albert was ready to leave the lab at 2 a.m., the snow was piled so high that the door to the outside wouldn't budge. He didn't want to call and wake me up so he slept in his chair. He was so tired that he didn't hear the phone ring when I called.

My daily routine was reveille at 7 a.m., breakfast before 8 a.m., and leave the house by 8:30. During that time, I would be dressed and ready for work and have the boys dressed and ready for school. Then Papa would drop Albert Jr. off at kindergarten and Tom at his nursery school. Since Albert Jr.'s school was out before I was home, a neighborhood high school boy was hired to pick him up and stay with him until my return. I would pick Tom up on my way home. Before starting dinner, we talked about their day, and played together. Dinner was about 6:30. After clearing the table, the three of us would play for another 45 minutes, then bath time and bedtime for the boys at 8:30 p.m.

Weekends were hectic, for we usually did the grocery shopping together, then rushed home to prepare and cook and clean. Once a week, we all attended mass and ate out at either Howard Johnson or Big Boy. The menu for the entire week had to be planned. Sometimes I cooked dishes that could be served more than once; other times, I would cut and marinate the ingredients for cooking later.

Albert Jr. and Tom had their own bedrooms. Albert's was across from ours, while Tom's faced the bathroom and was beside ours. Fortunately our neighborhood consisted mostly of families with young children, so the boys had many playmates and we gave many parties for them - birthdays, Halloween, Christmas and Easter.

Several neighborhood mothers came to see me one afternoon. They expressed concern, "Our children told us that you kept pigs in your basement. Is that true?"

"Pigs? Oh, you mean guinea pigs? Yes, we do have two of these little critters in our basement. Would you like to come in and have a look?"

They were very embarrassed and apologetic. When they left, I had a good laugh and called Pa immediately.

"Can you imagine what our neighbors thought of us? They thought that we Chinese actually keep pigs in our basement."

In September, 1968, Dad (Albert Sr.'s father) was offered a job teaching political science at Macomb Community College, about an hour's drive east from us. We were so glad he decided to come to Michigan for this gave us a chance to get to know him better.

He rented an apartment near campus and lived by himself. Albert's mother remained in San Francisco because she had a good job at Cokesbury Publishing House and wanted to be near Francis (Gordon), their youngest son, who was attending U.C. Berkeley. They planned eventually to move to Michigan, but not until Dad had received his tenure at the college. Anyway, we were here as were James and Shirley.

We alternated our Saturday visits with James and Shirley and this worked out well. While Dad insisted on cooking dinner for us, we would bring him groceries and knick-knacks for his apartment. And he enjoyed playing with his grandsons too. Dad was quite a cook, since he was responsible for the cooking in San Francisco.

His menu included Stir-fried Baby Shrimp with Peas, Eggs with Tomatoes, Shanghai Red-Cooked Pork and more.

Actually Dad had impressive credentials. He was among the scholars sent from China to the U.S. in the early 20s. After China lost to the Allied Powers during the Boxer Rebellion,* China had to pay a hefty indemnity to all the countries in the coalition. The U.S. was the only country that converted her share into scholarships to American universities for China's brightest and best. Britain later followed her example. Dad was fortunate to be one of the beneficiaries. He received a master's in political science from U-M, then went on to Harvard graduate school and later to the London School of Economics. He was so proud to have something in common with President Kennedy. They both studied with Professor Harold Laski in London. Even with two master's degrees, Dad didn't have a Ph.D., which is a prerequisite for teaching at a large college or university.

But his expertise, scholarship and gentle personality were most welcome at Macomb Community College where he inspired many young students in his classes. From September to December, we alternated with James for visits. Saturdays were extra special when the four of us drove to Warren to see him, enjoy his cooking and see the joy in his eyes as he played and bantered with our boys, his first two grandchildren.

"Tell me, Tom, who's your favorite? Grandma or me?"

"Oh, I like you both equally," Tom replied.

"But you have to pick just one," Grandpa said.

"No, I can't. I have to pick both of you."

The week before Christmas, Mom and Francis came to visit and so did Uncle S. Y. King, Dad's cousin, from Vancouver.

Uncle S.Y. had just retired from HKU as its dean of engineering, Albert's former department. As a student at HKU, Albert had the opportunity to know Uncle S.Y. very well. Here's a standing joke that Albert loves to relate to his friends and colleagues.

Albert's B. Sc. diploma from HKU was signed by two Kings: Professor S. Y. King, dean of engineering, and by Gordon King, the English chancellor of the University. When Albert first applied for a fellowship at Wayne State University and showed them his credentials, he was asked,

"Is this a family university? How come all three of you are Kings?"

Christmas dinner at our home that year was a happy time. We managed to sit 10 in our small dining room: Mom, Dad, Uncle S.Y., Francis, James, Shirley and the four of us. I went out of my way to make the meal a celebration. Here's the menu:

Appetizers: Sesame Sirloin Meatballs

Chicken on Skewers

Soup: Steamed Chicken Soup with Conpoy

(dried scallops) and Black Mushrooms

Entrees: Pepper Steak

Curry Chicken with Onions and Potatoes

Scallops and Shrimp with Hoisin Sauce

Mandarin Roast Duck

Shanghai Red-cooked Pork

Sweet Sugar Snap Peas

Tofu with Mushrooms in Oyster Sauce

Steamed Whole Pickerel

Starches: Steamed White Rice

Cold-tossed Noodles

Sweet Endings: Almond Fruit Float

Fresh Fruit

Petit Fours

Chocolates.

It was certainly a feast and we toasted each other and thanked God for all our blessings. It had been a blessed and happy year. After waiting five years Dad was gainfully employed. He was happy and fulfilled. (See Recipe Section for some of these dishes, pp.305-320.)

1969 - A Death and A Wedding

After the New Year, Francis returned to San Francisco, and Uncle S.Y. to Vancouver. Mom remained in Michigan. She took a six-month leave of absence from her job to be with her husband and see how well she could adjust to living permanently in Warren instead of San Francisco. She got her driver's license before she came for she wanted to drive Dad to work each day.

It was a cold winter with lots of snow. After our big celebration, I came down with the flu and was bedridden for two weeks. Early in the morning on January 9 (this date is long affixed in my memory), Albert called from work to tell me that he had an urgent call from Macomb Hospital - his parents were involved in a serious car accident and he should come immediately.

Albert asked if anyone was killed or injured, but the caller wouldn't say.

After he hung up, fear and apprehension followed. I prayed and asked for strength and guidance, but I had the premonition that Dad was already dead, since he always sat in the passenger's front seat. Sure enough, after Albert reached the hospital, he called.

"Dad's dead. I just identified his body in the morgue. Mom's hysterical and wants to die. She's seriously injured with a fractured femur and wrist on her right side and needs immediate surgery. Start making arrangements for Dad's funeral. I'll be back after I calm Mom down. Also call James and Francis."

I couldn't believe what he said. Tears streamed down my cheeks. *Dad is dead? And Mom injured? Why, it was barely two weeks ago that we had such a happy family reunion and*

169

celebration. Now this? What was I to do? How do I make funeral arrangements? The only funeral I'd attended in the U.S. was that of Professor Lissner. I had no idea what to do or where to start.

I dialed Mary Frances, my colleague and dear friend at Henry Ford Community College.

"Liz, I'm so sorry. Try to stay calm. I'll come over after work and go over some details with you," she said.

She came to the house around 4:30 p.m. We sat down with a pad and started to list the calls I needed to make:

1. To the priest at our parish, St. Mel's, regarding the funeral Mass.

2. Ask him to recommend a funeral home.

3. Go to the funeral home to pick a casket and make the funeral arrangements.

4. Order flowers for the church and funeral home.

5. Buy a plot in a nearby cemetery.

I called James and found out that he had a bad cold and fever. He said he would go along with whatever arrangements we made and that he would call several of our close friends. One of them was Don Van Kirk who later called me and offered to help. He had just buried his father and would share his experience with us.

I spoke to our assistant pastor, Fr. Francis, since our regular pastor was away. Fr. Francis was most accommodating although Dad was not a parishioner. The fact that Albert and I were was good enough for him. It was coincidental that the following Saturday at St. Mel's Church was available for a funeral Mass. Fr. Francis recommended John Santieu and Sons in our area. I called and made an appointment.

But who was to call Francis in San Francisco? Who was to break the news to him? Neither of his brothers wanted that assignment, so the burden fell on me. I said a silent prayer and picked up the phone.

"Francis, I have sad news to tell you. Your dad died this morning from a car accident and Mom's injured and hospitalized."

"What? Who was driving the car?" were his first questions.

"Your mom," I said. "She's hysterical and injured, though not that seriously. Can you fly here as soon as possible?" Phew...I had crossed that hurdle.

Afterwards, Don Van Kirk, Albert and I went to the Santieu Funeral Home. Mr. Santieu helped us select a handsome cherry wood casket in the middle price range. Albert signed the papers and authorized the funeral home to pick up Dad's body and prepare it for burial. Then to the florist, and finally to Dad's apartment to get some things for Mom and a decent suit for Dad for his burial.

The attendees at the funeral Mass included our immediate family, a few neighbors, and a dozen of Dad's colleagues and students from Macomb Community College (MCC). To this day, Dad's three sons and four grandchildren have contributed to MCC for a scholarship in honor of Dad's memory.

We were surprised to see several Chinese acquaintances from the Metro Detroit area, a handful of Albert's and James' friends and my colleagues. We didn't host a lunch or reception, but thanked all for their kindness and for coming. After that, the seven of us - James, Shirley, Francis, Albert, Albert Jr., Tom and I - accompanied the coffin to St. Hedwig Cemetery where we saw the lowering of Dad's casket to the ground. It was indeed sad to say goodbye to him. He was just 65.

After the burial, I went to visit Mom in the hospital.

"Was the funeral done well?" she asked, knowing that I could only visit her after we had taken care of the funeral for Dad. "Were there many flowers?"

"Yes, it was beautiful. Fr. Francis gave an eloquent eulogy and over 50 were present at the Mass."

I don't imagine anyone can fathom her feelings. When Mom and Dad were rushed to the hospital by ambulance, Mom was hysterical and kept weeping and mumbling, "I killed him, I killed him. It's all my fault. I want to die, I want to die."

This was what happened as we later reconstructed the scenario. It was on Monday morning when Mom was driving Dad to his classes at the college. It had snowed heavily the night before. Although the snow stopped in the morning, there were many icy spots on the two lane road. Mom realized that and was extra careful and rather nervous.

At one point, Dad told her, "You're veering too close to the center, steer closer to the curb."

She did just that and tried to steer the car closer to the curb. Suddenly, without warning, her car hit a bank of black ice. The car swerved and turned into the oncoming lane of traffic. Just then another car coming the other way couldn't brake in time to avoid hitting her car head on. Mom tried to straighten her car, but it was too late. Another oncoming car drove smack into her right side, hit Dad and killed him. She was injured, hurting and hysterical. Someone immediately called 911. The ambulance and the police came immediately, but it was already too late.

Mom remained in the hospital for a week after her operation

to have a pin put in her femur. Needless to say, she was inconsolable. Fortunately, Francis flew in the next day and was with her all along. As the youngest of her three sons, 19 and single, he was the apple of her eye. She knew she had to live for him.

After her discharge I insisted that she and Francis stay with us, for I could at least cook and pamper them for a while. They remained with us for three months before returning to their home in San Francisco. Mom resumed her editorial job at Cokesbury, but tore up her driver's license and vowed never to drive again. Francis returned to his classes at U.C. Berkeley, a sadder but more mature young man.

We ordered a special headstone for Dad with the inscription "Blessed are the meek, for they shall inherit the land." (Christ's Sermon on the Mount, *The New Testament: Matthew 5.5*) That epitaph fit him very well, for Dad was indeed a gentle and compassionate soul.

That summer, my sister Maria met her true love, Tjong Lie. He is from Indonesia and worked as an engineer at Ford Motor Company. They dated for a few months before he proposed. Maria was a beautiful bride and the wedding was simple but elegant. While I couldn't be her maid of honor since I was still in mourning for Albert's father, we sisters had fun shopping for the bridal gown, hairpiece, bridal bouquet and flowers for the church. Mom and Dad and several of my siblings came for the happy occasion. We ended with a lavish banquet in a nearby Chinese restaurant.

1970 - A Harrowing Year

It was a snowy day on January 9, 1970. Albert left for work early and I followed him half an hour later. I hugged Albert Jr. and Tom, and dropped them off to school on my way to work. Traffic on Ford Road between Beech Daly and Evergreen was bumper to bumper. It was like a big parking lot as cars inched along. I reminded myself to be extra careful and alert on that slippery road.

About two miles from our home, on Ford Road just before Evergreen, I saw a station wagon neatly piled on top of another car.

I thought to myself, *Oh, that's why there's this tie-up - here's the accident. Gee, didn't think the police were able to pile that car so neatly on top of the other, in order to clear the other lane for traffic.*

Since the heater in my car was out of order, I kept cleaning my fogged-up window with a towel to get better vision. Suddenly, there was a tap at my window. Thinking it was the police, I lowered the window on my left side and was surprised to see Albert.

"What are you doing here?" I asked.

"Did you see my car?"

"What car?" I asked.

"Didn't you see the station wagon on top of my green Buick?"

Before I could react, he climbed into the passenger seat

beside me and asked me to pull into a side road.

Ford Road was icy so he was driving slowly, when suddenly, he saw a car sliding on the opposite side of the road. As it slid, it flew across the median and landed smack on top of his car. Fortunately he had enough experience with traffic investigations to know that he had to slide down instantly in his seat to avoid the impact.

Thank God his reflexes were that fast.

Then he pushed open the door on the driver's side and got out as fast as he could in case of a fire.

It was a close call. Three of the four wheels of the station wagon straddled his car, facing the opposite way. The driver of the station wagon managed to jump down, but was hysterical, thinking he had killed the other driver. Albert quickly went over to assure him that he was unhurt.

The police came minutes later and asked both to fill out an accident report. Very soon, however, Albert spotted my car on the right lane (since the left lane was blocked and all traffic were diverted to that lane), tapped on my window and got in beside me.

Together we completed the police report. The other driver suffered a small nick on his forehead and was bleeding a little. He was still shaken up. He showed us his report, but dated it January 9, 1969. When I noticed this, I crossed off the year and filled in 1970.

Strangely, January 9, 1969 was Dad's fatal accident and this one occurred at the same time, the same day, the same month, a year later. How eerie! What a strange coincidence! Just thinking about it gave me goose bumps.

After the police reports were completed, the other driver

insisted on giving us his business card. He was the manager of a sporting goods store and invited us to visit his store where we could get a big discount on our purchases. (Weeks later, Albert bought himself a pair of Adidas at that sporting goods store.)

Albert sat with me as I drove to my college to report the accident and asked for the day off. Our next stop was our insurance company.

"Was your car totaled?" asked the agent.

"Yes and totally unsalvageable," Albert replied.

After I drove Albert to Wayne State, I made a detour before returning home, to stop at Dad's grave, to thank him for keeping his son safe from harm.

A month later, during a weekend retreat, I took time to go through the entire process of grieving and planning. *What if Albert was killed that day? I'd be a widow with two young sons. What'd I do? Where'd I go?* It was only after I went through the motions of grieving and loss that I could be at peace.

When we went to the police pound to retrieve Albert's belongings, we discovered that the door on the passenger side of his Buick was totally inoperable. Fortunately, Albert got out on his side without any difficulty. Thank God for the protective windshield which shattered into a thousand pieces but didn't splinter.

We never told his mother about the accident. We drilled and reminded Albert Jr. and Tom not to mention a word to her, for fear of opening up old wounds. When we were with her in San Francisco the following year, Tom accidently mentioned his dad's blue Oldsmobile. After that scary accident, I insisted that Albert get a bigger car with two strong cross beams.

"An Oldsmobile?" asked Mom Helen. Fortunately little Tom was very quick and alert and quickly added, "I mean Dad's green Buick."

A week after the accident, I noticed that my monthly period suddenly stopped. Was I pregnant? It couldn't be, since we had been very careful to avoid pregnancy. Dr. Igna kept reminding me, "No more babies." Besides, I had been meticulously charting my body rhythm each month. After an appointment with Dr. Igna, he assured me that I was with child.

It was during this time that my friend Agnes Lee came to visit. She had just lost her youngest child and needed to share her pain and sorrow. Her baby daughter was quite blue at delivery and barely lived for a year. She couldn't lift up her head at six months and later caught pneumonia and died. As I listened to Agnes' story, my heart ached for her. I realized what a big cross it is for a mother to care for a child with Down syndrome.

That summer, the four of us went to California to be with our families. I was already more than six months pregnant, and had a very pronounced tummy. This time I was quite certain that my baby was a girl. I had gained much weight and was very full in my behind. When I was pregnant with Albert Jr. and Tom, my tummy was more pointed in the front and I felt light and lithe during both pregnancies.

Our first stop was Los Angeles where Albert had to attend a professional meeting. The boys and I enjoyed visiting the San Diego Zoo, Sea World, Knott's Berry Farm, and other attractions.

One evening I attended an official dinner reception with Albert. I was dressed in an elegant A-line organza dress with large black and yellow floral print which partially concealed my pregnancy. Dr. J. Lighthill, an authority in fluid mechanics from

Cambridge, was the guest speaker. After his much-applauded speech, Professor Lighthill sat down to dinner. As luck would have it, Albert and I sat facing him on the other side of the table. As our eyes met, I smiled to be courteous. But he kept ogling at me, much to my embarrassment. Then he started to squint. I thought he must have caught something in his eye.

After dinner we socialized with other guests. Then Professor Lighthill approached me and loudly recited Lord Byron's poem, *"She walks in beauty like the night."*

Oh my gosh, I thought to myself. *Is he daft or drunk? He's actually reciting love poetry to me - a very pregnant woman!*

After Los Angeles, we drove to San Francisco to visit my folks. At this time, Albert Jr. was 9 and Tom was 7, old enough to have fun with their relatives. We were busy - visits with the King side of the family as well as enjoying my parents and siblings.

On August 4, we celebrated Tom's seventh birthday. Mom and I had fun cooking the dinner for 20 and it was a delicious occasion for all.

This is when we met Francis' (Albert's youngest brother) fiancee, Lucy Lam. Lucy was a graduate student at U.C. Berkeley. Francis and Lucy were very much in love and were busy planning their wedding, scheduled for Labor Day in September.

But much as we wanted to, we couldn't stay for their big celebration. Albert insisted that we stick to our original plan of returning to Detroit right after Tom's birthday. I was almost eight months pregnant, and although I didn't spot or bleed during this pregnancy, we couldn't take the risk. We must return to Detroit and be near my doctor.

I resumed my bi-weekly visits with Dr. Igna, and was assured that all was well. He tentatively scheduled a C-section in early September.

As a type-A racehorse, forever-on-the-go, I had much to do. Aside from preparing for my baby's arrival - our house needed a thorough cleaning, and Albert Jr. and Tom had to be ready for school. On top of this, I had also planned a small dinner party - one last "fling" before I settled down to being a full-time mom again.

I delivered my baby girl on August 15, 1970. When I fainted twice at home, an ambulance was summoned to take me immediately to Dr. Igna at Henry Ford Hospital. I still recall the events. As the ambulance attendants carried the gurney with me half conscious, we left before I could hug my two boys. I saw the fear in their eyes. They were huddled together on a sofa in the living room. While I wanted to assure them that I would be alright and would come back to them soon, I didn't speak.

During the ride in the ambulance, I was aware that my baby was no longer kicking. I was alone in the back of the ambulance with an attendant, while Albert, in his moment of stress, had rushed to sit in front with the driver.

When Dr. Igna delivered my daughter hours later, she was all blue and didn't cry as newborns do. Although mildly sedated, I caught a glimpse of her dark hair and tiny face. She had her eyes closed, and looked so much like her brother Tom. Even in my drowsiness, I remembered to ask one of the nurses to baptize her with the name Helen Rowena Maria, after her two grandmothers and our Blessed Mother.

As I look back, had Helen Rowena Maria lived, she would be in her 30s today - my little girl - a woman. *What would she be like? Would she be married now with a home and children of her own? Would we be close, mother and daughter?* I look at the many women about her age I can see a bit of her in them.

Now I ask myself - why didn't we have a funeral or memorial service? Did I have a closure to my grief and loss? Did I give myself time and space to mourn and be normal again? Was this part of my depression, my big, black hole? I don't know.

During dinner one night in November, 2001, I recounted this incident to Tom. As I recalled the loss, I uncovered more feelings.

Now, 32 years later, as these memories and feelings return, how I wish they had allowed me to hold her, even for a little while. After all I was her mom and carried her inside me for eight months. She was my baby girl, the girl I always wanted and never had. Had I grieved over her death and my loss? I didn't.

Now, I know that Helen Rowena Maria is my little angel in heaven, loaned to me only for seconds, born on August 15, 1970, the Feast of Our Lady's Assumption. Could it be coincidental that our granddaughter, Kenny, was born on August 13? And why is it that I now have some adopted daughters - nieces named Sherri, Lisa, Beth and Alyssa? And what about my young friends - Dawn, Elaine, Jessie, Kathleen and Karen, all about her age, had she lived? These are the mysteries that I don't have answers for.

Even writing about my loss eases my pain. Finally, at last, I have some form of closure.

I had lost my baby. Fortunately I was in the gynecology ward, not obstetrics. Several days later I learned that to save my life, Dr. Igna, performed a partial hysterectomy on me. It was to make sure that I would no longer endanger my life with other pregnancies.

Without a little one in my arms, I was devastated. Albert tried to cheer me up with flowers and cards and carry-outs from my favorite Chinese restaurant, Golden Dragon, the only decent Chinese restaurant near Wayne State at that time. But I was inconsolable.

When I could walk more steadily on my feet, I ventured to the public phone booth on my floor to call my mother. I wanted to hear her voice, get some sympathy, affirmation and love. At that moment, I became the child, the daughter, and wanted my "mama."

After asking how she was, I said, "You know, you're the first one I'm calling since my admission to the hospital. Albert must have told you that we lost our baby girl."

"I'm okay. But your sister Shirley isn't. She's finally come to her senses and is divorcing Jay, that good-for-nothing bum. Will you invite her to come to Michigan with her little girl?"

Then she went on and on about Shirley. Not a word inquiring about my health, my feelings and my loss. As I held the phone to my ear, tears streamed down my face. Why did I telephone her? I needed her empathy, her love, but what do I get? Not one kind word of caring. Her insensitivity pierced me to the bone.

I returned home after 10 days and was overjoyed to be with my little ones again. And I was thankful that Shirley (James' wife) cared for them like a surrogate mother. Even though their dad brought them for visits to the hospital, this was much better. When I apologized to them for not being able to hug them when I was hurriedly wheeled out of the house to the ambulance, they understood. They said it was okay. They were glad I was at home again. Such wisdom from my little men.

A week later, my sister Shirley and her four-year-old daughter, Sherri, came from San Francisco to stay with us. Shirley's divorce wasn't a surprise, for she had confided in me that summer when we were in San Francisco. She could no longer tolerate living with his mother and family under one roof. Jay wouldn't change and he wasn't the man she thought he was. She made me promise to keep this to myself, not a word to Mom. He had threatened to contest Sherri's custody if Mom interfered.

I bit my tongue every time Mom pushed me to talk to Shirley and advise her to divorce Jay. My reply was always, "Let's just trust in God's providence - all will be well in good time."

It was very hard to maintain my composure, especially when Mom would retaliate and lash back at me, accuse me of being "heartless" and unfeeling toward my baby sister. I knew I couldn't win. In our Chinese culture, the elder sister is the caretaker of younger siblings and is held responsible for their happiness and welfare.

Having Shirley and Sherri with us was a joy. Sherri was a real doll and it certainly was a change to have a girl at our house. She was cuddly and so affectionate. Albert Jr. adjusted well to her, but Tom was quite jealous. If Sherri sat on my lap, he wanted to sit there too. When I bought the same toy for each of them, he would ask, "How come Sherri gets one too? She's not one of us." I had to explain, "She's your cousin and our houseguest. We have to share and be nice to her."

Within the week, Shirley applied for a secretarial position at the Ford Motor Headquarters in Dearborn. With her typing skills, beauty and charm, she was hired on the spot. Within a week, she and a handsome Caucasian engineer, Bill Hopeman, started to date. We liked Bill instantly. He was polite, courteous, thoughtful and kind - everything we admired in a man. He proposed within a year. Shirley and Bill were married by a Justice of Peace before Christmas 1971 and went to New York for their honeymoon.

Little Sherri stayed with us in their absence and although I went out of my way to give her special attention and love, she missed her mama. When a postcard of King Kong came from her Mom, she was inconsolable and cried herself to sleep with the postcard tucked under her pillow.

Poor child, she was deeply attached to her mother, and rightly so, for Shirley was a loving and caring mother. It made me realize that even at 35, I needed love and affirmation from my mother too. I suppose one never outgrows that need, no matter at what age.

When Shirley and Bill returned from their honeymoon, Sherri had a family again and soon Bill legally adopted her. We were happy for now we were surrounded by more relatives - James and Shirley, Maria and Tjong, and now, Bill, Shirley and Sherri.

Sherri and her cousin Tom

The Chinese Room at WSU

5

New Horizons

With no hope of more babies, I turned my attention and energy to other things. Our financial situation improved. This was my fourth year at HFCC and the salary I made helped. We could afford to entertain and reciprocate many of the dinners we were treated to. I cooked for our friends every other week. Soon our social circle grew larger and our boys met many other Chinese children.

The Chinese population in Greater Detroit at this time was only a few thousand. There was no Chinese language school for children. Paul and Julia Tai, Bill and Mary Mao, Bob and Lily Lo, Rev. and Mrs. Yap, Mr. and Mrs. J. T. Yang, and Albert and I were the families that founded the first Chinese language school in Michigan - the Chinese Cultural Center (CCC). We rented the Good Shepherd Church in Westland as our school on Saturdays. (Now there are over 30 Chinese schools in the metropolitan area.)

Every other Saturday afternoon, from 2 to 5 p. m., Chinese classes were held at the Good Shepherd Church. We improvised our own syllabus and all of us were there to help. The children learned to read and write Chinese, using Putonghua (Mandarin) pronunciation, and were taught Chinese culture and history too. We celebrated the festivals, especially the Chinese New Year, and were able to offer a class in Chinese folk dancing.

Lily Lo, Mary Mao, Julia Tai and I called ourselves "the four musketeers." We took turns having potlucks at our homes. While the children played together, the parents had fun too.

Our CCC experiment went well. Every other Saturday, Albert

185

and I took our sons to their Mandarin classes. Soon other families joined us - C.Y. and Shirley Chang, Charles and Terry Wang, Silas and Helen Cheuk, Francis and Lucy Yang, John and Theresa Shen and others. Shirley Chang was officially hired as a teacher and the six founding couples worked with her to devise a curriculum. We divided the children into two groups: 10-15 year-olds, and 10 and under. We finally had our identity and our children were learning Chinese language and culture.

This was also the year that other Chinese Americans, whether they were ABC's (American-born Chinese), Chinese from Hong Kong or Chinese from Taiwan, decided to get together to establish the Association of Chinese Americans (ACA). The first meeting was held at the International Institute in Detroit. Albert and I were among the 70 or more attendees who were the founders of ACA. (Detroit's ACA was the first chapter of the Organization of Chinese Americans (OCA) now with chapters in almost every state.)

ACA needed a newsletter so Albert encouraged me to volunteer for the job. I soon became the editor, and held that position for six years. In 1978, I resigned in order to work on other endeavors.

The ACA Newsletter took a big chunk of my time. Through that work I met Grace Chu and Spencer Lowe. Grace, a woman in her 70s, born in Mainland China, lived in Dearborn with her Chinese husband. She was a writer, and we liked each other immediately. She was childless and became my second mother. She was a great listener, and I didn't realize until many years later, that listening is an art unto itself.

Spencer Lowe, a graphic artist from Shanghai, was married to Alice, a nurse, and had four lovely children. With the help of Grace and Spencer and others including Mable Lim, Jessie LimPoy, David Wee, Lilian Tye Siak, and Ana YapChai, we put out a first-rate newsletter every quarter.

Computers were not in everyday use in the early 70s, so our newsletter was produced the old-fashioned way. Each article was typed manually, proofread, then keylined onto a board. Although our newsletter was just four pages (later expanded to eight pages) back to back, Grace, Spencer, a typist and several others, including myself, spent a long day putting all the articles into printable form. Every three months our home became the hub, with people in and out, with me serving coffee and tea, lunch, snacks, and sometimes even dinner.

The printed newsletter had to be picked up from the printer, then sorted out by zip code for bulk mailing. In the beginning, a group of volunteers did that. Later, the volunteers were the four in our family. Albert, Albert Jr., Tom and I took the bags to the post office. Although it was a time-consuming production, I liked using my writing and organizational skills.

At this time we felt we needed a bigger house. Our search narrowed down to the cities of Dearborn and Southfield. We finally chose Southfield, although it was a bit further north. We fell in love with a model home about a mile away from the freeway. While I had been driving since 1965, I had yet to learn to drive on the expressways.

Our corner house on Lathrup Boulevard was a big ranch with four bedrooms, a full-sized living room and dining room and a large family room. The finished full basement, tiled and walled with a half bath, was a bonus. The exterior was light grey brick with a 2 1/2 car garage and a fenced-in dog run. The decor, wall paper, drapes and light fixtures matched our taste and the house was ready for immediate occupancy. We loved it and bought it for $64,900.

Now we had to sell our other house. Instead of listing with a realtor, we put a FOR SALE sign on our lawn. Were we lucky. Within two weeks we had a buyer who paid our asking price, $24,900.

We were sorry to leave St. Mel's parish, the school and our neighbors and friends in Dearborn Heights, but we needed more room and better schools for Albert Jr. and Tom. I looked into Cranbrook, Country Day and Roeper Schools, as well as St. Michael's in Southfield.

Because Albert and I had full-time jobs, we couldn't drive our boys to those schools each day. We had no choice but to send them to the nearby public school, Schoenherr Elementary, where they were bussed to and from classes each day. We hired a high school student to be with them until I got home from work.

Once there we soon were entertaining and giving dinner parties, since we had a large basement that could easily accommodate 100 guests. That area came in handy when I became involved in the Committee for the Chinese Room (CCR) at WSU.

George E. Gullen, WSU president, wanted to create a series of ethnic heritage rooms like those at the University of Pittsburgh. He invited leaders of 15 ethnic groups from Metro Detroit for a meeting. I was selected to represent the Chinese Americans since I was active in ACA and Albert was a WSU professor.

After our first meeting, I was excited about the idea and determined to go ahead with the project. Although I had no training as a fund-raiser, I was willing to learn. Still as I look back to my early years in Manila, I recalled that as a 10-years-old, I was the top fund raiser for our Pasay Chinese School. It was a tradition, during All Souls' Day, for a group of students, accompanied by our principal and teachers, to bring lit candles to the mourning families assembled in the tombs and mausoleums. As the leader and spokesperson for our school for two years, I was totally unafraid and spoke to the heads of the families and asked for their financial support. In gratitude, the families would sign pledges to support our school. We succeeded in raising thousands of pesos for the school.

On the other hand, the fund-raising for the Chinese Room was quite different. The project was challenging and I was determined to put all my energy and effort into it. I overheard two ACA leaders discussing whether I would be able to complete the Chinese Room project. If I didn't, then the monies would be returned to the ACA coffer. Their skepticism steeled my resolve. I vowed to myself to prove them wrong. They didn't know my determination and tenacity.

At the same time Roman Gribbs, Detroit's mayor, was wooing the ethnic leaders of his city. He gathered a group of us in his office to discuss hosting ethnic festivals on the Riverfront. This was the first year we set up make-shift booths to sell ethnic food and drinks to visitors to raise funds for projects.

A month before the Far Eastern Festival, our committee met to plan our strategy. The festival started on Friday and closed late Sunday. Shifts were assigned to cook, man the booths, transport the supplies and clean up. Rice cookers and big utensils were borrowed from friends and restaurants. Albert learned to cook perfect steamed rice while he was in charge of the 12 rice cookers.

Albert also drove the borrowed WSU van to transport hundreds of pounds of meat and egg roll wrappers to our cooking station and later drove the cooked food to our booth on the Riverfront. I was responsible for shopping for the meat and other ingredients. When I visited the Eastern Market, store owners thought I must own a Chinese restaurant. "Not so. We're cooking for the Riverfront Festival to raise funds for our cause," I told them.

We also obtained a beer license and sold it along with Chinese tea and soft drinks. It was hard work, but gratifying - all for a good cause.

As the general manager, I set the menu - egg rolls, stir-fried beef with green peppers, and sweet and sour pork. I recruited volunteers, set the food prices and made decisions. At the end of the festival, we netted over $10,000.

After the festival, I cooked and hosted many fund-raising dinners at home. I remember one dinner in honor of Mason Yu's parents. His father was a retired five-star general in Chiang Kai-Sek's government in Taiwan. Eight other couples were invited. I shopped at Eastern Market for the best and freshest ingredients and was inspired to cook a 15-course banquet. It took two weeks to prepare, but it was worth it. After dinner I shared my dream of the Chinese Classroom at WSU. Each couple pledged between $500 to $1,000. Their pledges plus the $10,000 we earned at the Far Eastern Festival became the seed money for building our Chinese Room.

I was elected president of CCR. Others elected were David Hwang, vice-president, Ann Lee, secretary, and Y. S. Wang, treasurer. Our architect was John Shen. We picked a classroom instead of a lounge in the Manoogian Building, also labeled the Ethnic Heritage Center.

We wanted to expose the students to Chinese culture.

Consequently, every detail was Chinese. The ceiling tiles, reminiscent of those in the Forbidden City in Beijing, were hand-painted by the Chinese Youth Group of ACA. (Albert Jr. and Tom were among them.) The furniture, chairs and tables, designed by John Shen, were replicas of Ming dynasty furniture. The entire room was paneled in simple maple.

To raise public awareness, I chaired a gathering ceremony at WSU. Our guests included WSU President George Gullen, university board members and leaders and members of the Chinese community. The ceremony was scheduled for a Sunday afternoon. But on Saturday, we had a violent snowstorm. We couldn't cancel our celebration, since all the invitations were out, the hall rented and the performers were ready. Miracle of miracles, (after I prayed very hard to the Holy Spirit) that Sunday turned out to be cold, but sunny and bright and we had a record turnout for the event.

Aside from a dance and other musical programs, I gave a speech at the ceremony in which I painted a visual picture of the room as the committee wanted it to be. This enabled the participants to see the room in their mind's eye. It worked and our fund-raising caught fire. Check after check poured in and within six years, our Chinese Room was completed and we even had a surplus of funds. (Our budget was $50,000 and our committee donated the surplus to another non-profit organization.) Though the Chinese in the Greater Detroit area numbered but a few thousand, ours was the third room to be completed at the Ethnic Heritage Building at WSU. Classes are still held at the Chinese Room today.

At the final dedication ceremony, Dr. Thomas Bonner, the new WSU President, and many community leaders were present. How I wished Dr. Gullen, our friend and mentor, was with us, but by that time, he had resigned from his position at WSU. Before he died a year later I had the chance to visit him in the hospital and thank him for his help and support.

It took me weeks to plan the official dedication program. The rousing "Hwang Ho Concerto" (Yellow River), was beautifully performed on the piano by Vivian Yu. Rita Chan, dance artist, performed a traditional Chinese Fan Dance. At the conclusion I gave a brief "Thank You" speech. Corsages and tributes were presented to Carlene Bonner and Theresa, wife of architect John Shen. My friend, Chen Oi Hsieh, noticing that I didn't have a corsage, picked some flowers from the floral arrangements on the stage and created a token bouquet for me. That was thoughtful of her.

It was a proud and happy day for the Chinese Americans, and for me. After the celebration, I experienced a low and came down with depression and a bad cold.

Fortunately, Dr. Pang Man, a psychiatrist, and the fund-raising VP, consoled me saying, "Liz, you're the mother of the project. As a mother, your children take you for granted - that's very normal. It wasn't anything personal."

Albert and our two sons were most supportive toward my work for the Chinese Classroom. In 1976, before the Chinese Room was completed, I was involved in the mission of Chinese American Educational and Cultural Center of Michigan (CAECC) to promote Chinese culture among Chinese and Americans in Michigan.

During our first year, we solicited financial help from the Chinese restauranteurs, many of whom were members of the On-Leong Association.* They were supportive and donated the seed money to keep CAECC afloat. Later, Chen Oi, the executive

192

director, sent grant proposals to the Detroit Council of the Arts, the Michigan Council for Arts and Cultural Affairs; and the National Endowment for the Arts in Washington, D.C. She was very successful and we were able to sponsor many seminars and art exhibits.

We also organized the Miss Chinatown contest, much to the delight of On Leong and the entire Chinese American community. I loaned my beautiful *qi paos* to the young contestants. The Miss Chinatown Contest resulted in uniting two young couples and provided a summer job for me. The father of one of the contestants recommended me for a translation job with an American engineering firm which had recently established an office in China.

Alex Mark, CAECC president, left Michigan before the end of 1978, and I stepped in to fill his shoes. While Chen Oi was busy writing grants, Rita Chen was in charge of our cultural programs and the training of many young dancers. As public relations chair, I hosted some parties and made frequent appearances on local TV and radio.

Our Sons

Albert Jr. and Tom

While I derived much satisfaction from my involvement with the Chinese community, I tried to be a good mom to my sons. One of the reasons for my involvement in community affairs was to set a good example for them - in essence to show them how we must extend ourselves into the community, the country, and eventually to the world. A famous Chinese saying goes like this, "We are all brothers within the four seas."

As I look back, I wonder if I had invested too much time and energy in my community involvement in CCC, ACA, CCR and CAECC. During one of my visits with Fr. Thomas Liang, my spiritual director, I confessed guilt for not giving Albert Jr. and Tom more attention.

"You did what you thought was best. All that is past. Just look ahead and do what you can for them," was his advice.

During those years, Albert Jr. and Tom each had a full plate. They attended Chinese school every other Saturday, in addition to other extra-curricular activities. The Friday before their Saturday Chinese classes, I helped them study their Chinese. This started in 1972 when we founded CCC. They learned over 1,000 Chinese characters and could speak and understand Mandarin (Putonghua). Because they wanted more play time, they begged me to release them from the school. I was sympathetic, but their dad was adamant. They must continue with their Chinese studies.

One Friday evening while I attended a meeting, Albert supervised their Chinese lessons. He had such a difficult time that he eventually gave the boys permission to quit the classes. To this day, however, especially with China's emerging status as a world power and Mandarin as the dialect even taught in some Michigan schools, we wished we had insisted on keeping them in the Chinese school.

I also wanted to expose Albert Jr. and Tom to music. We bought a used upright piano for Albert and he started weekly lessons with Vivian Yu. Tom opted for drums so we bought a set of Slingerland drums for him and paid $2,000 - money I had saved for a long-awaited trip to Hong Kong. Each Tuesday afternoon, I drove Tom to his lessons with Mr. Gene Stewart at Mercy High School.

I also hired Greg Reid, a talented Henry Ford Community College art student, to teach them painting. But when they were more interested in washing their brushes than actually drawing or painting, I gave up. They started out playing T-ball at their school, St. Mel's, then graduated into Little League. Their Boy Scout activities were also at St. Mel's. Since Albert was so involved in his teaching, research and writing grants, I took them to all their activities, and was the secretary for the Scout Troup.

During the summer of 1978, Albert lectured and visited various labs in Europe, Asia and Australia. At this time it was prohibitive for the four of us to go, for we couldn't afford four sets of airline tickets. Albert's mother went with him instead.

At home, the boys and I had a busy summer.

I mustered enough courage to redecorate our home. I painted and wallpapered the boys' bedrooms, the kitchen and bathroom. It was quite an adventure. My first foray into paints and wallpaper was completely trial and error. On the first day of painting, we moved a big ladder into Tom's room and put a gallon of paint on the ladder shelf. As I climbed up the ladder, holding a paint brush in one hand and the ladder in the other, I slipped. The open can of paint fell and spewed its content all over me and the floor. Fortunately we had covered the carpet with oil cloth. Albert Jr. and Tom laughed and that defused my frustration, so I joined in.

Redecorating is a creative project. The boys picked their own patterns and colors and helped me in lots of ways. Albert Jr. and Tom still recall with fondness their special room and our time together that summer.

I also set a study regimen for them each day in reading, writing and arithmetic. They were assigned to write short essays each day, and I would outline the topic. Albert Jr. was an independent thinker, and tried very hard to use different words and ideas. Tom, my smart and easy-going son, would copy my words and use them exactly as I outlined them.

For fun, I took them and their friends from the neighborhood on Bob-Lo cruises and to baseball games, movies, the Detroit Zoo and the Detroit Institute of Art.

When Albert returned, the four of us spent a luxurious weekend at the Grand Hotel on Mackinac Island. We had gone to the Grand Hotel for lunches and dinners in the past but we were thrilled to be able to spend a weekend there and really live in style!

The Grand Hotel is renowned throughout the country. It has one of the world's longest front porches and the meals are world-famous. Proper attire is required of everyone in the dining rooms. The hotel was the setting of the movie *Somewhere in Time*. starring Christopher Reeve and Jane Seymour. Esther Williams, 1950s movie star, also shot some of her films there.

Our family at the Grand Hotel

New Ventures

Tom, Liz, Albert and Mom Helen celebrating the debut of
"Eating the Chinese Way in Detroit"

The years, 1979-1983, were full of challenges and excitement. My involvement in one activity dovetailed to another, and I soon found myself drawn into, and enjoying, new ventures and experiences.

In the spring of 1979, CAECC sponsored a symposium, *Food in Chinese Culture.* The speakers were Professor Ying-shih Yu from Yale University and Professor E. N. Anderson, Jr. from U. C., Riverside. As CAECC president, I organized and chaired the symposium. The topic was my heritage and that has always been my hobby and my love. Little did I know that it would launch me into a second career.

Albert and I were socially involved with his departmental colleagues. We formed an informal diners' club with six couples and met monthly at ethnic restaurants - French, Italian, Mexican, German, Hungarian, and others. Interestingly enough, we'd have Chinese every three months. One couple, Mike and Joan Rabins, suggested that I compile a translation of the menu terms in Chinese restaurants. For example, chicken is *kai, kei, chi;* while shrimp is *har, harr, ha.* Inspired by the recent food symposium and goaded by the encouragement of our diners' club members, I decided to write a critique of the Chinese restaurants in the Greater Detroit area.

Something else motivated me. The Mott Foundation offered $1,000 for a preliminary proposal for a community project. Since the Chinese restaurants and the On Leong Association were always supportive of CAECC and supplied us with complimentary food when we had our activities, I got to know the restaurant owners and workers. I learned that many of them didn't have health insurance which meant that their hard-earned savings could be depleted if they or their family members had medical emergencies. To help them, I wrote a proposal to find group health insurance for them. My competitors were qualified experts in the Chinese community, but my proposal won the grant. Unfortunately, my good intentions were just on paper. I encountered too many hurdles and had to give up the project.

I hadn't realized there were over 250 large and small Chinese restaurants serving everything from authentic Cantonese cuisine to chop suey in the Greater Detroit area. So my list of restaurant menu terms turned into a restaurant guide. I chose 66 of them which served reasonably authentic Chinese cuisine. They formed the backbone of my cookbook, *Eating the Chinese Way in Detroit.*

My choice was based on sampling their food. I paid for my lunch or dinner, since I didn't want to be biased. Wendy Thoryn, Louise Schlaff, Sandra Silfen and Spencer Lowe helped with that project.

Wendy was a reading and writing teacher engaged to help prepare Albert Jr. for his coming SAT. She came to the house to coach him and it didn't take us long to become friends. When I told her about my book idea, she was enthusiastic and jumped on my band wagon.

Louise Schlaff, my friend and colleague, was a journalism instructor at HFCC. When she heard of my plan to write a restaurant guide/cookbook, she immediately scheduled me for a talk to her class. I hadn't started to write, but I spoke to them about my dream, and how important it was for me.

Sandra Silfven was food editor for the Detroit News. Due to my involvement for CCC, CAECC and ACA, I became the spokesperson for the Chinese American community in Detroit and was called on whenever anything Chinese came up. That was how we met. When I showed her my first draft, she thought there was a possibility of three books, and suggested I focus on one at a time. I took her advice and wrote a restaurant guide and included essays on Chinese food and 30 recipes.

Spencer Lowe, the graphic artist whom I got to know in our work for the ACA Newsletter, came to help me. He had an eye for details and taught me to see beauty through his eyes.

Here I was working as a full-time librarian at HFCC and writing my first book. This was the year Albert Jr. graduated from Southfield-Lathrup High School. He was an all-A student, helped edit the school newspaper, and was on the debate team. I always made sure to set aside time to help with his work in the paper, and got to know his teacher/advisor.

Meantime Albert and I were searching for the right college for him. With his abilities, we were hoping he'd choose a career in the biological sciences and perhaps go on for graduate studies. We liked Kalamazoo College, a small liberal arts college about a three-hour drive from our home, renowned for its scholarship and faculty. But Albert Jr., a die-hard football fan, had his heart set on the University of Michigan. He applied at U-M, was accepted and convinced us to go along with his wishes.

In the fall, Albert Jr. went to Ann Arbor's Bursely Hall. We would usually drive to Ann Arbor on Saturdays and take him out for a good dinner. In the beginning, our visits were weekly, then later they became bi-weekly. Albert adjusted well to classes and life on a big campus.

Tom was a junior at Southfield-Lathrup High School. I knew his intelligence was above average, but he was clever enough to hide that from his teachers and remained on the B-tract. After I spoke to the vice principal, Tom was transferred to the A-tract curriculum. His grades soared - he just needed a challenge.

In 1980, Albert and I made a trip to Mainland China. I had not been back since I left China in 1948 and Hong Kong in 1955. Since President Nixon's visit in 1972, China had slowly opened her doors and I couldn't wait to see how she looked.

Our trip came through Albert's affiliation with Wayne State University. Dr. Thomas Bonner, university president, had accepted an invitation to visit from China's Minister of Science and Technology. Albert, representing the Department of Bioengineering, and I, were included in a party of 12 administrators and professors who accompanied Dr. Bonner. The others were Millie Jeffrey, WSU Board member; Marie Draper-Dykes; associate dean; Guy Stern, provost and his wife, Judy; William Brazil, administrator; and faculty members, Winnie Fraser, psychology, Stan Kirschner, chemistry, C.P. Lee, biochemistry, and P.K. Kuo, physics.

Beijing, Xi'an, Shanghai and Guangzhou were on the itinerary. When Albert first told me about the trip, I was ready to pack whether or not I could get official leave from my job at HFCC. But luck was on my side. When Dean Andrew Mazzara* of HFCC heard about the trip he gave me an official three-week leave and paid my travel expenses because he recognized China's increasing importance as a super power and the value of establishing good public relations with it. Since I was the only full-time Chinese faculty at the college at that time, he believed that I would be a good ambassador for the college.

Although I started out as simply Albert's wife, I soon found myself with more responsibilities - official hostess for WSU and personal interpreter for Dr. Bonner. My fluency in four Chinese dialects - Mandarin, Cantonese, Shanghainese and Fukienese - proved to be invaluable.

In Beijing, we visited the Great Hall of the People, the official state hall where heads of state and other dignitaries often met. We had lunch at the U.S. Embassy with Ambassador Leonard Woodcock and his wife, Sharon. We toured the Forbidden City, the Great Wall of China and the Ming Tombs. China had just opened her doors, and we were so privileged to be among the early groups of tourists there.

Our host picked us up in a minivan, a state vehicle, even though cars were very rare in China then. When we landed at

Beijing Airport, our plane was the only one in sight. We walked down the movable stairway, since there was no landing ramp. There were no megastructures, just one small building lit by a bare bulb hanging from a chord. The drive to the Friendship Hotel was free of traffic and we made it within minutes.

Everywhere we went, there were masses of people, on foot or on bicycles. Because they had not seen many foreigners, they looked surprised to see us. During our 12-hour flight to Tokyo where we transited overnight, I went around our group and gave each of them a Chinese name,* much like the fairy godmother in *Sleeping Beauty*. But instead of using transliterated characters, I asked for the particular virtues or qualities they admired, and gave them their Chinese names accordingly.

During our audience with the Minister of Science and Technology at the Great Hall of the People, Dr. Bonner received a gift of a Chinese seal engraved with his name in transliterated characters. I was ecstatic for I had a surprise for my friends when we returned to our hotel. I delivered a seal to each of my fellow travelers. Earlier I had asked our driver to take me to a chop shop where I purchased seals with their names engraved. Now, at last, every one realized the value and importance of a Chinese name and seal, and they had learned some Chinese culture too.

In Xi'an, we spent a day at the Cave of the Terra Cotta soldiers - and also enjoyed a *chiotze** banquet - *chiotze* are dumplings, with different kinds of stuffing made of pork, beef, seafood, vegetables and even peanut and sweet filling.

In Shanghai, we visited the Jiaotong University and campus, and had a delicious vegetarian banquet at the Jade Buddha Temple. We toured the Bund,* and ours was the only car driving on the Bund, the busiest street in the city. Our driver made U-turns whenever necessary and didn't have to worry about traffic jams.

In Guangzhou (Canton) we were housed in a beautiful hotel, The White Swan, located in Shamian, the island where I lived as a child. Albert and I, accompanied by our party, tried to locate my home on Po Ai Road. But the street names were changed, and the island was jammed with many makeshift buildings. Although I was able to find the Catholic Church where I attended mass and sang in the choir in 1947, we couldn't go in. It was padlocked. What a difference 33 years made. I wanted to spend more time in Shamian, but it didn't feel right dragging the others in our party. I vowed to return and search for it again.

Instead of returning to the U.S. with the others, Albert and I took a trip to Hong Kong. We hadn't been there since the 1950s. We wanted to visit our mentors - Fr. Fergus Cronin and Fr. Horace de Angelis. Fr. Cronin was still at Ricci Hall on the HKU campus, while Fr. de Angelis had already retired from Rosary Church, and lived by himself in a small flat on Jordan Road.

We returned to Detroit after three weeks, happy and energized, with many memories. But, I had another big project that needed attention - a new book was waiting to be completed.

For *Eating the Chinese Way in Detroit,* I used a standardized form and format listing the hours, location of the restaurants, and part of their menus. It was not simple, but an efficient and fair procedure. Spencer Lowe helped. I also added essays on Chinese food as well as 30 of my own favorite recipes.

With the book almost complete, the next hurdle was to find a publisher. I attended several writing conferences, hoping to find an agent who would sell it. I had read and studied books on the intricacies of publishing. One agent I met at the Detroit Women

Writers Conference was arrogant and insulting. He scoffed at my book and made fun of me. I finally realized that a neophyte has a hard time finding an agent and my only solution was to self-publish.

After consultation with Albert, I formed my own publishing company, the Chinese Cultural Publications, with a Southfield Post Office box address. I found a printer in Jackson, MI and ordered 5,000 copies. Printing less would not be that much cheaper. That was how *Eating the Chinese Way in Detroit* was born.

I vividly remember that Friday afternoon in September when Albert and the boys and I drove a rented U-Haul to Jackson to pick up box after box of my new book. I was so proud - an author at last.

The following Monday I brought a copy to show Dr. Harold King, vice president of Henry Ford Community College. He was my friend and I wanted to show him my new creation. When he asked about my plans for promotion, I didn't have an answer. He explained that promotion is the key to selling books and 5,000 copies would be hard to sell. He took me to the president's office. Within five minutes, he and President Stuart Bundy agreed that I should take a semester-long sabbatical. Since working there, I'd yet to take a sabbatical. Generally a sabbatical request had to be submitted a year in advance. An exception was made in my case. I filled out the forms which were quickly approved and signed by the boss.

The next step was to tell my library supervisor, Skip Rosenthal, the news. He was nonplused, "You're taking a semester off? Who am I going to hire in your place?" Since he couldn't override President Bundy's decision, I took the time off with pay.

Promotion was new to me. Fortunately, my involvement in the Chinese community provided me with frequent exposure in the media. I sent copies of my book with a cover letter to the newspapers, radio and TV stations. Responses were overwhelming. I was a frequent guest on Channel 7's (ABC) *Kelly and Company* and *Friday Feast,* and on Channels 2 (CBS), 4 (NBC), 52 and 60 and the local PBS stations. Sandra Silfven of the Detroit News interviewed me several times and wrote articles on me and Chinese cuisine. I also made friends with J. P. McCarthy, a popular radio talk show host on WJR, and was often a guest on his program.

It was serendipity that I connected with David McCarthy, book buyer for Hudson's. In those days, Hudson's had many branches throughout the metro area. Someone suggested I contact David, who could help me in promotion. After several unsuccessful attempts, his assistant told me the best time to reach him was between 5:30 - 6:00 p.m.

When I succeeded in reaching David, we talked for over 15 minutes. I told him about my book and how I came to write it. He listened and said he'd like to see it as soon as it came off the press.

As soon as *Eating the Chinese Way* rolled off the press the following week, I raced downtown to show it to David. He examined it from cover to cover and smiled as he flipped the pages. Then he telephoned his assistant, Nimrod Rosenthal, promotion manager. Curiously enough, I had already been in touch with Mr. Rosenthal. When Mr. Rosenthal first heard the title, he said, "It isn't a cookbook, it's just a restaurant guide."

"But, there are 30 recipes too."

"Those don't count," he said and hung up.

When Nimrod came to David's office, he voiced that same complaint. But by this time David was my champion. "She has 30 very good recipes in her book."

"But she didn't specify using a wok. How could I have her cook Chinese without the wok, since our aim is to sell woks?" Nimrod asked.

David turned to me, "Liz, you can easily cook your recipes in a wok, right?"

I nodded.

"See, she has no trouble using the wok. Now for the Chinese New Year demo in January, I want you to put her in the central station. The two other Chinese cookbook writers can be in subordinate stations to her left and right."

1981 was my year for promotions. I did the promo for Hudson's and was hired to do demos in every Hudson store - that is, Northland, Westland, Eastland and in the other metro area malls.

One Saturday afternoon, I was demonstrating at Hudson's Northland before 500 people - all standing, and crowding around me while I prepared and cooked three dishes. I spoke about my recent trip to China, my impressions of the people, and their way of life. My audience listened to every word, since China was mysterious and had barely lifted her bamboo curtain.

By 5 p.m. the people were still following my tales of China, her people, and her food. I was pleased by their attention, and could have gone much longer. It was not until Albert, who was in the audience, repeatedly pointed to his watch that I finally stopped. It had been well over three hours since I started. When Nimrod heard of what happened, he paid me double.

After that I was on fire and seized every opportunity to speak and demonstrate my cooking - at St. Beatrice (our parish church), cooking stores (mainly William Sonoma), in bookstores and libraries, at the Detroit Institute of Art, the Michigan Orthopedic Society, and Boy Scouts gatherings.

I also started to make and collect slides for my talks. My library of slides on the different aspects of Chinese cuisine and culture now numbers over 1,000.

After I sold over 3,500 copies, I approached the restaurants that were included in my book. This was where I encountered the greatest resistance. Many of the owners, even some whom I considered friends, were reluctant to buy 10 copies, even at a discount. It was ironic that they would spend hundreds of dollars advertising in the Yellow Pages and local newspapers, but wouldn't spend $60 for 10 copies of my book which they could sell to their customers for a profit. Here I was promoting their restaurants in all the media. The saying, "The prophet is not welcome at home," rang true.

But I did make many friends as I learned the secrets of promotion. For instance, David Louie of Channel 7, ABC, advised, "Just relax and be natural. Enjoy your work and have fun. That's the secret of a successful TV appearance." So on TV I made sure to always look my best and paid close attention to what I wore and how I looked.

This was also the year of Tom's graduation from Southfield Lathrup High. He had showed good judgment and common sense during his adolescent years and was becoming a well- adjusted young man. His grades were good, especially after he transferred from Tract B to Tract A curriculum.

After attending a few classes at Henry Ford Community

College and Wayne State University, Tom was still undecided as to what he wanted to do with his life - he was no different from many young people in this age - trying to find themselves

It was at this time the idea of sending him overseas came up. My brother, Francis, owned a chain of businesses in Guam - a gas station, a gift shop, a travel agency, and a tour company. We thought that by working in the real world, it would help Tom find himself. Within two months, Tom left for Guam. At the airport as I kissed him goodbye, my heart was filled with a prayer and a hope that he would learn something and return home a more mature young man.

After the success of *Eating the Chinese Way in Detroit,* I was ready to do more research on Chinese food and culture. That summer I went with Albert's mother, Mom Helen, to Shanghai where she had several brothers and a sister whom she hadn't seen for over 35 years. This was homecoming for her and for me too, since Shanghai was my birth place and I wanted to explore its food, its culture and its people.

During that month, she and I shared a room at the four-star Jin Jiang Hotel, within walking distance from the homes of her siblings. Thirty years later, Jin Jiang still stands and that district is one of the posh business areas in Shanghai. At the Jin Jiang, we had a room with two single beds, a full bath and a nice sized living room. This suite was very affordable.

Each day, Auntie Annie and Auntie Wen Sen (Mom Helen's sister and sister-in-law) would plan our itinerary - visits to relatives, shopping, eating and sightseeing. We were completely at their disposal and had a most enjoyable time.

This was also a time for bonding with Mom Helen. We were not only good roommates, but compatible in our likes, attitudes, and thinking. She regarded me as the daughter she never had, while I loved her as my other mother. I could easily share my feelings with her. It was a beautiful relationship and our time together in Shanghai was memorable.

Shanghai, in 1981, was not the mega metropolis it is today. (Since 1992, Albert and I have visited there often and found it to be different each time - more cosmopolitan with taller buildings and more traffic.) It had barely recovered from the Cultural Revolution. In 1981 her people were still simple and frugal, many dressed alike in blues and grays. Selections and qualities of goods in stores were limited and inferior compared to what is exported from China today. Restaurants were just beginning to pick up business and hadn't adjusted to occasional visitors, whether they were Caucasians or Overseas Chinese. Everything was inexpensive, compared to the U.S. dollar, and the exchange rate was over 8.2 to one.

Almost every morning, Auntie Wen Sen would come by our hotel to pick me up to go to the market. This was where fresh produce, meat, poultry, tofu, and every imaginable food could be found - piping hot *congee** accompanied by freshly fried *you-tiao*, steamed buns with meat and vegetable fillings, and a variety of other cakes and buns. I was anxious to try everything.

Before my departure from Detroit, I had arranged with J.P. McCarthy to telephone him when he was on the radio and describe the markets in Shanghai, the hustle and bustle, the cooked foods, freshly picked vegetables, and the atmosphere. Auntie Wen Sen was fearful. She reminded me over and over again to be very careful not to disparage the Chinese government and people on the air. She told me, "Don't talk about politics or economics. Don't tell the U.S. people that we are poor, that the market is dirty" (which by comparison to U.S. supermarkets they were.) "Don't, don't, don't." To pacify her, I visited the U.S. Consular Office to find out how safe it was to describe what I saw.

Their advice was to be careful what I said because the Chinese government monitored all outgoing calls and broadcasts. If I displeased them, they'd eventually track down my relatives and give them a hard time.

I understood the politics, but was still determined to phone J. P. After several attempts, I reached his manager, Hal Youngblood, who told me that my air time was preempted. J.P. was preoccupied with the announcement of the closing of all Hudson stores. Auntie Wen Sen sighed with relief.

A month flew by and soon it was time to leave Shanghai. Although we were both leaving on the same day, Mom Helen's San Francisco flight left at noon while mine was scheduled at 6 p.m. for Hong Kong. After a hearty breakfast, Auntie Wen Sen and her husband rode in a taxi with us to the airport. She was concerned, since I had six hours at the airport before departure. I assured her that I would be alright, since I speak Shanghainese and had a book to read.

We arrived at Hung Jiao Airport three hours early. Mom Helen had to go through customs and immigration immediately. I accompanied her through customs and was disturbed by the unpleasant attitude of the custom officers asking what she had in her suitcase and if she had any antique artwork.

Mom shook her head and answered in the negative. I helped her move her suitcase to the counter. They waited impatiently as she unlocked it. After a thorough search, they waived her through and pointed to the Immigration Section where she was to go. I barely had time to hug her.

Meantime I was nervous. I was carrying a beautiful 100-year-old celadon vase in my bag, given to me by Auntie Annie. It originally belonged to Albert's late grandfather who gave it to Auntie Annie to repay a debt. Because Albert was his oldest and favorite grandson, she gave it to me to take home to Michigan. What to do? How could I smuggle it through customs?

I thought of calling Auntie Wen Sen, but didn't, knowing that all phone lines were tapped. And to make things worse, I soon found the entire airport closed - the coffee shop as well as the counters. My flight was the only other one that day and was more than six hours away. I was the lone stranger and I was carrying a forbidden vase. If I suddenly disappeared Albert would have no way to find me. My only recourse was to return to Auntie Wen Sen's home and leave the vase in her safekeeping until our next visit.

I hailed a taxi and nervously showed him the address. When I arrived, Auntie Wen Sen and her husband had just returned, after taking different buses. I had to ask for some yuan to pay for my taxi, since we had given all of our Chinese money to them that morning. After I was given lunch, I blurted out what happened to Mom Helen and my fears. Later I was accompanied back to the airport without the vase. I had saved a family heirloom from being confiscated. (We managed to bring it home two years later and this vase is prominently displayed on the shelf in our living room.)

In June of 1983, Albert and I returned to China for the third time. Jiaotong University, one of the more prestigious universities in China, invited him and his colleague from General Motors, David Viano, to be guest lecturers. I went as Albert's companion.

It was the custom to put up big banners to welcome official guests so a big poster, WE WARMLY WELCOME PROFESSORS

KING AND VIANO, was hung at the University's main building. The first business of the day was to meet with the president and chief officers of the university in the guest lounge. Cups of Longjing tea, the best green tea from Hangzhou, hand- picked before the spring rain, were served while a video in English, touting the university's reputation, was shown to the guests. As we watched it, I noticed the English pronunciation and the production were inferior. Later I told the school authorities that I could, with my English background and my experience in the media, help them improve their video. My proposal was warmly welcomed, so during those three weeks when Albert and David were busy giving their talks, I rewrote the script and dubbed in my voice.

The Jiaotong University administration was so grateful that they paid for my flight to Beijing, the same as Albert and David. We were their guests for a week and had a private car and chauffeur who took us sightseeing and shopping. We were wined and dined and saw lots of interesting sights and landmarks in Beijing, including many temples and mosques. I was especially impressed with the statue of Kwan Yin, the Goddess of Mercy, in one temple. She was crushing a dragon at her heels, very similar to our Blessed Mother, the Immaculate Conception, who is often depicted as crushing a serpent at her feet. Indeed, our Holy Mother Mary is our Goddess of Mercy and Love.

Another interesting episode in Jiaotong in Shanghai happened because it is their custom to use a white bedsheet as a screen to show slides. When Albert offered to buy them a retractable screen, they declined and said that a sheet would do very well. It worked most of the time, except when it was windy, the slides were distorted. Life back then was simple and the people less materialistic.

Two Fathers

On our return from China, I stopped to visit my folks in San Francisco. Dad was suffering from esophageal cancer. He had lost a lot of weight and looked haggard. When Dr. John Yu, the oncologist, came to visit him at home, he advised me to tell Dad that he had only three months to live and should get his affairs in order.

I was sad to hear this and told Mom and my three brothers. But none of them wanted to tell Dad. Mom even tried to dissuade me from telling Dad the truth. I thought it was only fair that Dad knew what was happening.

I prayed for strength and courage.

"You mean John told you of my limited time?" he said.

"Yes, Dad, I'm afraid so. I'm so sorry. Can I do anything for you?"

"Yes. Please go to my office at New York Life and clean out my desk."

I spent a week going through every single piece of paper in his office. I organized and consolidated his 17 bank accounts and updated his will.

"Should I leave some money for the seven of you?" Dad asked.

"No, just give it all to Mom. All of us are quite comfortable. Mom will be alone and will need all the help she can get."

I drafted a simple will for him, leaving Mom all his money and real estate, and Dad signed it. After two weeks, I returned home, a sadder but wiser daughter. In late August, Mom was diagnosed with colon cancer and needed an operation. She was admitted to the same hospital as Dad, but in a different room. Classes had started at HFCC and I couldn't take extra time off to go to San Francisco.

On October 3, my brother James called to tell me that Dad had passed away peacefully in the hospital that afternoon, after ascertaining that Mom's condition was stable after the operation. I hurriedly took a leave from my job and flew with Albert to San Francisco.

While Mom was recuperating in the hospital, we held Dad's funeral - a simple but beautiful event. None of my brothers wanted to give the eulogy, so I delivered it. How I wish I had a copy of my speech. I remembered speaking about Dad's courage, tenacity and perseverance. How he helped to rebuild China after WWII, how he struggled to get his family to the U.S., and how he, as a young boy, knew hardship when his father died and his mother worked as a washerwoman to support him.

Dad studied hard. He worked hard and, as secretary to Tsinghua University's president, Dr. Mei Yi Chi, he won a scholarship to study at George Washington University in Washington, D.C. That was where he and Mom met. He always encouraged his children to study hard and make something of ourselves. He set a high standard of excellence for himself, and expected us to do likewise.

"We'll miss you, Dad," I said with a gentle sob. "Now rest in peace with your Heavenly Father."

Dad's most prized possession was his antique gold Rolex watch. I didn't realize that he had willed it to me until months later. I felt it belonged to one of my brothers, according to Chinese tradition. But Mom insisted that I take it since it was Dad's gift to me. His thoughtfulness and love were all that I needed. Anyway, I kept the watch in the safe and gave it to Mark Chiu, my brother James' oldest son, at his wedding 10 years later. The moment Mark put on the watch, it worked.

Dad's funeral was well attended. My mentor and friend, the former Father Thomas Liang, came. I hadn't seen him since he left the priesthood after his disillusionment with the Catholic hierarchy and its penchant for power and control. Before he left the priesthood, we spoke on the phone. "Please think kindly of me and my action," he pleaded.

I said, "I have no right to judge you...you'll always be remembered as Father Liang, my mentor and friend, and I'll always respect and cherish you."

At the funeral, Tom Liang and I made a date for dinner that following Wednesday. He wanted me to meet his wife, Eileen, a former nun, and was specific about having an early dinner at a certain restaurant. "We'll come by to pick you up. Please be ready by 5 p.m."

I agreed but wondered why we had to have such an early dinner. We dined at the Harbor View Restaurant in Emeryville. After our dinner Tom and I made plans to meet before my return to Detroit. His wife Eileen planned to attend her parents' 50th anniversary in Wisconsin, on that date.

But, it was not to be. Tom Liang died that following Sunday. He didn't want a funeral and his ashes, as he wished, were scattered in San Francisco Bay.

I returned home to Detroit several days later, completely

depressed. Within the week, I lost two fathers and that completely unraveled me. I was listless and Albert was worried and begged me to enroll in a Dale Carnegie Course. I enjoyed that course and learned much about positive thinking, as well as thinking and speaking on my feet, but my gloom and depression lingered. Then, Albert insisted I accompany him for a weekend trip to Boston. While he was visiting a lab, I saw and networked with my good friend, Nona Dreyer. That was uplifting and my depression lightened. In retrospect, I'm glad I took the time to mourn and heal, especially after losing two fathers at the same time.

Fr. Thomas Liang
Albert, Liz and Fr. Thomas Liang

The former Fr. Thomas Liang was my spiritual director during our first five years in the Bay Area. His wisdom, deep faith and philosophy influenced me in many ways.

I was thinking about him when a voice startled me. "Can I get you anything, Miss?" asked the stewardess on Northwest flight #342, from San Francisco to Detroit. It was mid-October, 1983. The sky was bright orange.

"Some Kleenex, please."

Hard as I tried I couldn't stop the tears. Here I was, seated by the window of a DC-10, in full view of a magnificent setting sun, feeling desperately alone.

I was returning home, after a 10-day stay in San Francisco, but it wasn't a vacation. I went to attend the funeral of my stepfather, Frank, the only father I had ever known. I always called him Dad. His death didn't come as a surprise. He was in his 80s when the cancer from his esophagus crawled slowly into his lungs, stomach and kidneys. In June, upon the advice of his oncologist, Dr. John Yu, I told him the truth about his condition.

The day after the funeral, I had arranged to meet Tom and Eileen Liang for dinner. I needed to reach out, touch, and interface with these dear friends, lost for 10 years. Tom, formerly Father Thomas Liang, was once a Catholic priest. I knew him as such in my graduate school days in Berkeley.

In the early 70s, after a rough ministry in a conservative parish in Castro Valley, he abandoned his calling and married Eileen, a former nun, who was coordinator of educational programs for the state of California. Tom remained a counselor to the few who still turned to him for guidance. I was one of them. To me, he would always be Father Liang, for whom I had the highest regard and respect.

He insisted that I be their guest for dinner. Our 5:30 p.m. reservations were at the Harbor View Chinese Restaurant in Emeryville by the sea. They picked me up at my mother's house at five. At the Harbor View, we had a table overlooking the ocean.

We had the last 10 years to recapture. I updated them on my family, my son, Albert Jr. majoring in cellular molecular biology at the University of Michigan, his brother Tom studying liberal arts at Henry Ford Community College, and my husband Albert, a full professor, busy as ever with his research at the Bioengineering Center at Wayne State University.

"And you?" he asked.

"I'm still searching for myself while being wife, mother, professional woman and writer."

"Elizabeth, look at the sun, the glorious sun. It's beginning to set now," Tom said. It was a beautiful sight, but so familiar that I had taken it for granted all my life. Again and again during our conversation he stopped to call my attention to the sunset. After about the seventh time, I grew impatient, "Why all this fuss, Father? It's a sunset and I've seen it hundreds of times."

"Ah, but today it's very special. Look, look." He was as exuberant as a five-year-old. "Isn't it glorious and magnificent?"

I was more interested in the food. We had Steamed Black Bass with Black Beans, Stir-fried Chinese Greens with Oyster Sauce, Chicken Broth with Winter Melon and Minced Ham, and Steamed Rice. A perfect combination of taste and texture, most fitting for our reunion.

In the short span of four hours, each of us covered a decade of happenings in our lives, mine in Michigan and theirs in Hawaii.

Two days later I called the Liang household, for Tom and I had agreed to meet again before my return to Michigan. I was shocked when Eileen picked up the phone. She was supposed to be in Madison, WI for her parents' 50th anniversary celebration.

"Eileen, you're still here? Not in Wisconsin?"

"Yes. Something happened and I had to stay here," she said.

"What? Where's Father Liang?"

"He passed away yesterday morning from an aneurysm."

I was stunned. "When's the funeral? I've got to see him one more time."

"Elizabeth, it was his wish to be cremated immediately, with no ceremony and no fuss."

"No, oh no. Where're his ashes? I must have some of his ashes, I must."

When my mother heard me crying she came and sat by me on the bed. "Poor child, you have lost two fathers in one week." (I distinctly remember these kind words, which were rare coming from Mom.)

Two fathers were gone. First my stepfather and now my spiritual father. Father Liang was special in so many ways. He was the one who got me a full scholarship to the College of Notre Dame in Belmont, California. Although I couldn't use that scholarship since I couldn't get a U.S. visa, that was how we met. When I finally came to the United States in 1955, he was the one person who made me feel welcome.

During my two years of graduate work at the University of California in Berkeley, he treated me to lunch week after week

221

and allowed me to air my frustrations while trying to adjust to life in the U.S. He waited outside the University of California Hospital when I checked myself in for what I thought was a nervous breakdown. He listened to my troubles over broken relationships and he hand-picked Albert, my husband, and encouraged our friendship. And of course, he officiated at our engagement and our wedding a year later.

So it was natural for us to name our second son after him. Years later, he was the one who instilled in me the belief that we are each unique in our own way and taught me that our Heavenly Father's love is totally unconditional. Fr. Liang was always there, ready to listen, to argue, to console, to encourage, and to dispel my doubts, about myself and my Albert.

As I watched the sunset from the window of the plane, our dinner at the Harbor View Restaurant made sense. I understood why he insisted that I keep looking at it. He left me a legacy – a legacy of love and beauty. I quietly mourned my teacher, friend, mentor and spiritual counselor. To me he will always be my Father Liang.

Finding Jonathon

Icontinued to speak and give food demonstrations, but I was itching to do another cookbook - a real cookbook, not a restaurant guide with recipes. My friend David McCarthy advised me to find an agent who could locate a reputable publisher. I took his advice and attended writers' conferences and networked with many people.

One day, Albert handed me a Northwest Airline Magazine from his recent trip. He showed me an article about a literary agent, Jonathon Lazear, who sold the novel of a budding Chinese writer for half a million dollars. As soon as I read the story I knew I had found my agent.

It didn't take me long to locate him - he had recently moved from New York City to Minneapolis. When I reached him by phone he was friendly. I told him about my book, my promoting experience, and my collection of 100 recipes. I was willing to go to Minnesota to meet with him and made a date for December 22 when Albert was available to go with me.

A week before our departure, I spoke to Jonathon's assistant, Joanne. I told her I wanted to cook a lunch for him and planned to bring all the equipment in a suitcase - pots and pans, knives, cutting board, and some spices. She gave me directions to their office and to the nearest supermarket. We had no trouble finding both.

When he learned of my plan, Jonathon said, "You can always cook for me another day. Let's just talk about your cookbook. How fast can your recipes be made? Can they be done in 15 minutes?" He had envisioned a series of ethnic cookbooks with recipes that could be prepared and cooked in 15 minutes. I thought for a moment and told him that I could easily adapt mine to 15 minutes.

"Great. Now work on these and get me first rate photos of the cooked dishes," he said.

We left his office after an hour, the utensils and spices unused. I left the fresh produce with Joanne. While Albert gave a talk at the University of Minnesota, I worked at the University library on my recipes. Within two hours I had the meat of a new cookbook. Now I had to tell my readers how to make the recipes in 15 minutes.

As with all creative projects, one thing dovetailed to another. Our world is always ready to fulfill dreams of people who think positively. I experienced this at that moment and was ecstatic. In two weeks, I came up with the game plan for *The 15-Minute Chinese Gourmet*. In no time I had an editor, Pat Cornett, and a first class photographer, Janine Menlove. Janine's photos were absolutely beautiful. Luckily I could use many of the handcrafted artifacts I've been collecting for my book. I was particularly fond of the little bamboo steamers I bought during my 1982 visit to Shanghai.

I sent the book with recipes, photos and index to Jonathon. He liked it and was ready to sell it to the highest bidder.

Our son Tom returned to Michigan from Guam. While my brother Francis owned the businesses, his partner, a shrewd operator, ran the day-to-day operation. He didn't like Tom, because he felt Tom was spying on him. Whenever Francis was away on business trips, Tom sent us SOSs asking for money since he didn't get paid. We finally persuaded him to come home.

One day, while cleaning his room, I found a bag containing over $2,000 in cash. Tom told us that the money was his retroactive pay from Uncle Francis. We felt it was unwise for him to have so much cash and suggested he buy a car. Tom had always been fond of cars and he certainly needed one to get around. He has a taste for fast and expensive cars, and found a black Firebird in great condition for $3,000. He used his $2,000 and we made up the difference. He was happy and so were we.

One morning, six months later, Tom stormed into our bedroom and said, "Someone ripped off the top of my car!" Albert and I ran out to look. His car was parked in our circular drive, right beneath our bedroom window. We asked ourselves how it was possible that we didn't hear any noise during the night and early morning. Our neighborhood was certainly changing. Sometimes four or five families lived in one house with cars coming in and out day and night.

With Albert Jr. at Ann Arbor and the three of us away during the day, we no longer felt safe there. We started looking for a house in another neighborhood. Shirley, my sister-in-law, a real estate agent, kept reminding us that the three crucial factors in buying a house were - location, location, location.

We found Millie Rzeppa who was charming and a good real estate agent. We told her what we wanted in a house, and she found a dozen for us to consider in the Birmingham/Bloomfield area. With each showing, we singled out the features we liked and disliked. In no time she knew what would win our hearts.

"Buying a home is like falling in love," she said. "Sometimes there's no logic, no rhyme or reason why one particular house appeals to you - you just love it or you don't."

How true. Within two weeks, we found our dream house in Bloomfield Hills. The house, in wood and glass, sat in a picturesque setting of trees and woods, with four large picture windows in the front. An unusual feature was its towering ceiling beams. The seller, a builder of log cabins in Upper Michigan, had this house especially designed for him and his wife. It was love at first sight for us. We made an offer without hesitation and it was accepted. Curiously enough, this house was featured on the cover of a real estate magazine for the greater Detroit area.

We had some misgivings about whether we could afford this house, which was six times more expensive than our other one. It was with stout hearts and a prayer that we signed the purchase agreement. We celebrated our signing with a dinner at Alban's restaurant that evening. In early December, we moved into our new home. Since our old house in Southfield was unsold, we left some of our furniture there to facilitate its sale which happened six months later.

Our dream home, smack in the center of the woods, is really a deluxe log cabin. Reality hit when I found a cockroach crawling on the living room floor. All I could think was, *Why has this critter invaded our home - of all places, this beautiful home. We had no such problem in Southfield or Dearborn Heights, or even in Detroit.* After some research, I found it was a wood roach, a denizen of the forest. I felt better knowing it didn't come from within, but from without.

In February, 1986, I took a week's leave of absence from HFCC to visit my mother in Sacramento, CA. She had been living there for two years but found the heat suffocating. I went to help her pack and move, as I did every time she relocated.

Celebrations

The following year, 1987, was filled with joy. Albert Jr. married Siew-Ling Lau in June and *The 15-Minute Chinese Gourmet,* published by Macmillan, came out in August.

Siew-ling is from Singapore. She had finished her second year at Bryn Mawr College and was visiting her cousin at the University of Michigan when she and Albert met at a party on campus when he was the disc jockey. They kept in touch after she returned to Singapore. She transferred to U-M that fall and rented a small apartment on campus. She had to accelerate her studies since Singapore was going through an economic downturn and her parents were anxious for her to graduate and return home.

Siew completed her degree in communications and public relations in three and a half years. Albert Jr.'s latent interest in music and dancing surfaced at this time and he became distracted and took a semester off from classes. He had been a bookworm in high school and during his freshman and sophomore years at U-M.

Grandma Rowena and Grandma Helen both met Siew and liked her so they kept hinting to Albert Jr. to be more serious in his courtship, since Siew would be returning to Singapore after graduation. With their encouragement and our approval, Albert Jr. proposed and she accepted.

They had a civil wedding at the Fourteenth District Court in Ypsilanti on March 26, 1987. Uncle Francis and Aunt Lucy, and Albert and I attended the ceremony and celebrated afterwards. Three months later, on June 26, they had an official church wedding at St. Beatrice Church in Southfield with Fr. Jim Sam as the officiating priest.

Siew's parents, Shirley and James Lau, and her little brother, Zhi Yuan, came for the church wedding. Siew's wedding dress was all-white. Her bridesmaids and flower girl wore white organza, with beautiful floral arrangements made by my friend, Masako Condo, an excellent florist. Siew's bouquet included strands of artificial pearls. The centerpieces for the round tables, were big, purple, onion flower balls - exotic and magnificent.

The bridal party sat at a big round table, covered with a hand-crocheted tablecloth that I bought during a recent trip to Formia, Italy. I am saving this tablecloth for the wedding of their son, Ian.

The wedding banquet was held at WSU's McGregor Center, designed by Minoru Yamasaki. His masterpiece certainly added an oriental dimension to the ambiance. The manager at the Marriott at WSU served a Chinese dinner to our guests, using many of my recipes. The DJ played many of Albert Jr. and Siew's favorite songs. Rebecca, Albert Jr.'s little cousin, did a solo dance. It was a beautiful wedding.

Jonathon Lazear called in early spring to tell me that Simon and Schuster had offered a $25,000 advance for my cookbook. At first I was reluctant to accept the offer and told him that I thought he could get me a million dollars. He said, "Liz, we're talking about a cookbook, not a novel."

I consulted my journalism colleague, Louise Schlaff. "Oh, Liz, $25,000 is a wonderful advance. Many only get no more than $2,000. Take it."

Just as I was about to call Jonathon, he called me. "Liz, I've auctioned your book and have four offers. Macmillan topped the others by offering $50,000. This is the best I can do - so take it," he said.

In the weeks following I finalized the 85 recipes. In two days, I literally tested and timed all of the recipes to make sure all details were correct. While Macmillan used Janine's eight beautiful photos, they provided additional black and white drawings.

I went to New York to meet with my editors, Arlene Friedman and Melinda Corey. They agreed that Janine's photo with the pearl balls in steamers would be perfect for the jacket and promised me an initial print of 10,000 copies. Alas, within a month, both Arlene and Melinda left Macmillan and my book became an orphan.

Macmillan's publicity department scheduled radio and TV appearances for me in California, Chicago, Cleveland and Pittsburgh. In San Francisco, I managed to get on ABC, with help from my friend David Louie, formerly from Detroit. I was also lucky to be interviewed by Paula Hamilton, the food editor of the Oakland Tribune in California. She gave me a full page coverage.

When I stopped at a Dallas bookstore while accompanying Albert to a professional meeting, I was delighted to see my book featured in the store's monthly newsletter. I identified myself to the bookstore manager who was thrilled and asked me to autograph all the copies they had in stock. In San Francisco, Los Angeles and San Diego, I did promotional demos at the William Sonoma and Neiman Marcus stores.

In mid-August I left for Hong Kong to do research for my third cookbook and take some cooking classes. I visited with John and May Pho, old friends from HKU. While there I was exhausted from work on promotions, and slept for two days straight. Later I reconnected with Fr. de Angelis and Fr. Cronin, priests who mentored me in my high school and college days in Hong Kong.

It was a Saturday morning when I visited Fr. Cronin. He told me he had to visit five patients in different hospitals and if I wasn't pressed for time, I could tag along. We took buses and taxis to the hospitals. After he made the rounds, we had time for tea. No sooner did we sit down than he popped this question,

"And now, my dear, how are you?"

I started to sob.

He patiently waited, handed me his handkerchief, then asked, "Want to tell me why you're so sad? Are you having trouble with Albert or your sons?"

I shook my head. No, I told him all of them were good to me, but my sadness came from searching for a way to grow spiritually. Attending daily mass, frequent recitation of the rosary, reading the Bible wasn't enough. I felt a hunger for depth and meaning in my soul. "I'm hungry for intimacy with Him," I said.

He was quiet for a moment, then recommended *Lectio Divina*, that is, reading a passage from either the Bible or spiritual book, and reflecting on it. He gave me a copy of *Shalom*, a small monthly magazine with daily excerpts from the Bible. "Read that day's piece, then meditate and pray." I gladly obeyed and used *Shalom* for two years. It helped me in my prayer life, but my emptiness lingered. Now, I realize this was my first foray into meditation.

It was during this HK trip that Fr. Cronin introduced me to Leon Cumber, Han Suyin's former husband. Suyin was one of my favorite novelists. I adored her book, *Love Is a Many-Splendored Thing*. When it was made into a movie, starring Jennifer Jones and William Holden, many of the scenes were shot in Hong Kong, one in particular, at HKU. I wanted to meet Leon and hear more about Suyin - how she lived and wrote. He described their life, emphasizing the loneliness and independence of a writer. That visit with Leon was over 20 years ago. At last, I was ready to embark on writing my memoirs.

I was considering an early retirement from HFCC. Although I had enjoyed my work at the college and had many friends on the faculty there, I wanted time to do research and write. At first Albert was vehemently opposed to that idea, saying I would be bored to death with time on my hands. Later I realized he was concerned I would lose my independence and income should something happen to him.

Mom Helen understood my reasons and became my advocate. She was able to convince her son to see it from my perspective. I had worked for 20 years, raised two sons, kept our home and helped Albert in his career. Now I wanted to pursue my dream of writing.

Albert I. King, Inc., our small consulting firm, was established in 1974. Albert had worked in the summer as an expert witness for lawyers in automobile related accidents to earn extra income since he was on a nine-month payroll at WSU. Although he had obtained many research grants, he preferred to distribute his share to his staff in order to keep them in the department.

Our First Grandchild

Baby Ian at three-months

On May 14, 1988, Albert and I beheld our bundle of joy - our first grandchild, Ian Christopher. We didn't realize the extent of our pride until we saw and held him in person.

That morning when Albert Jr. called to tell us that Siew was in labor, we rushed to St. Joseph Hospital in Ypsilanti, about an hour away. When we got there, Ian had already arrived. Fortunately Siew didn't have a long labor. As soon as Ian was bathed and presentable, the nurse handed him to me. I was a happy grandma! He was a healthy seven pounds, seven ounces, and my heart swelled with love and gratitude.

I went to Ann Arbor to help Siew during her first week of recuperation. She tried to breastfeed him, but had to supplement with baby formula.

In June I delivered the HFCC Faculty Award Lecture, an honor given annually to a faculty member. It is a coveted prize with a stipend of $500. The topic of my talk was "Food in Chinese Culture," and I had rehearsed it many times.

I wore my best outfit, a blue Valentino linen suit. There was a full house and more applause than I expected. In conclusion, I said, "Thank you, all, for coming. Words cannot express my gratitude for your friendship and support during the 20 years I've been at the college. This is my swan song because I'm taking an early retirement."

Gasps of surprise came from the audience for this had been my secret. I handed my letter of resignation to my library boss after the lecture, and he accepted it reluctantly.

Now retired, I had time to concentrate on family matters. We celebrated Albert's 54th birthday and Ian's one-month birthday in mid-June. It's a Chinese custom to have a one-month party to celebrate the arrival of a baby, since the nine-month gestation in his mother's womb counts as a full year.

The simple hand-written invitations were inserted in a red, *laisee* envelope imprinted with our surname in Chinese. Over 50 friends and relatives came to celebrate this double occasion with us. A 16-inch round, mocha creme and chocolate cake decorated with the letter *shou** (long life) in red was the piece-de-resistance, together with chocolate-dipped pretzels attached with "It's a boy," a gift from Bob and Faye Levine. I spent two weeks cooking a banquet of 15 entrees. Baked Salmon with Scallions and Ginger was one of them. Fish is prized as the symbol of plenty and abundance. (Recipe on p. 311)

On June 26, we also celebrated Albert's and Siew's first anniversary, together with their little one. It was at this time that my dear friend, Karen Chong, graduated from medical school at WSU. Her parents and sister came to her graduation and we hosted a dinner for them at our home. I had adopted Karen as the daughter I never had, and was sorry to see her leave Michigan. Karen returned to her home in Newport Beach, CA and now has a thriving practice as a plastic surgeon.

This was the year Tom was admitted to the Cleveland College of Podiatry and we were happy he had chosen a profession. His decision came as I was retiring from my fulltime job. He had turned 25 and it was time for him to be on his own. He applied for a government loan to help him through school.

In mid-August, we drove him in a U-Haul to Cleveland where he would share an apartment with an old grade school classmate, Gary Klein, who was studying podiatry at the same place.

In late August, Albert and I, accompanied by Siew and baby Ian, flew to San Francisco for the Chiu family reunion. We were proud of our first grandchild and wanted to introduce him to his two great grandmas.

Great Grandma Helen was overjoyed when she held him. He looked so cute in a bright red coat. She cuddled him and offered a prayer of thanksgiving. After all, Ian is the first son of Albert Jr. who is the first son of Albert, who is the first born of Yu-lo King, the first born of his father, for four generations.

Meeting Great Grandma Rowena was another matter. When Mom first saw Ian, she said, "Why, he's ugly!" That remark shocked me. I had purposely planned this visit so she could meet my first grandchild. I didn't understand why she would say such a mean thing.

I wasn't the only one who felt that way. My sisters, Mimi and Shirley, and my sister-in-law, Anna, told me that they too were upset with her. They made up by competing to carry, bathe and care for him. Mom continued to ignore him for three days. She intentionally focused her attention on Allison, the adopted daughter of my brother George and his wife, Janice. It was true that Allison was a little beauty with big, black eyes and a captivating smile, but she lived in the Bay Area and Mom saw her often. On the day of our departure, Mom said, "Let me hold Ian for a while." But, for me, the damage was done.

Albert, Siew and Ian went home after the reunion while I lingered behind since I had to attend the Institute of Wine and Food Conference in Napa Valley a week later. I asked Mom if I could stay with her in the interim, but she said that she didn't have room for me, since Shirley and Francis were staying with her.

When George and Janice heard her rebuff, Janice immediately invited me to their home. After Shirley and Francis left, Mom called and asked Mimi and me to stay in her apartment. I should have refused, but I didn't have the heart to. The three of us started a friendly chat one night that soon turned ugly and Mom walked away swearing, "You two were never my daughters - don't call me Mom anymore."

She was so angry because I asked her why she ignored Ian when we were at the Lawrence Welk Vacation Condo last week. She said that it was all in my imagination.

Tiananmen Square

On June 4, 1989, a cataclysmic event, which affected the whole world, took place at Tiananmen Square in Beijing. Thousands of college students rallied to protest the ousting and subsequent death of Hu Yaobang, a dissident high up in China Politburo. With worldwide news coverage, the rally grew bigger and more inflammatory. Crowds of students protested against the present Communist government and demanded democracy for China.

TV viewers from around the world watched as the action unfolded. Finally the Chinese government forced a crackdown. Army units from distant parts of China, with no loyalty to Beijing and her citizens, were sent in with tanks and machine guns. Thousands of student protestors were gunned down. Panic broke out. One courageous student who stood before rows of tanks to stop their entry to Tiananmen Square became a symbol of their courage and determination.

It was unbelievable. As Albert and I watched on TV, we were deeply moved. On Friday of that week I ran into Bernie McDermott, a part-time HFCC librarian, at a retirement party. He asked me what the Chinese Americans and I were doing about this big event at Tiananmen. I said nothing that I knew of.

"Nothing?"

His question rang in my ears and stung my heart as I was driving home after the luncheon. The more I thought about it, the more I knew I had to do something.

When I saw on TV that some Korean women in Greater

Detroit had formed a support group for the Chinese students in the area, I told myself that as Chinese, it was our duty to help our own. I called Tony Lee, president of the Association of Chinese Americans (ACA) in Detroit, and learned that the Chinese in Ann Arbor were conducting a meeting that night. I hitched a ride with two of ACA board members, David Chia and John Lee.

At U-M, we joined some 200 professors, students, and concerned citizens to discuss how to react to the Tiananmen Massacre.

Someone proposed a symposium on human rights. Another suggested we write a joint letter of protest to the Chinese government.

"All of these are good. But what should we do now?" I asked. Nobody had an answer. Finally we agreed that those who felt the need to do something immediately should meet and decide what action to take.

About 25 of us met and agreed to hold a public rally to protest the Tiananmen massacre. I volunteered to take notes and soon I was elected coordinator with David Chia as the emcee. We scheduled a rally in Detroit for the following Sunday, June 11, in Detroit.

The moment I returned home I was on the phone. I called all my friends and colleagues and was able to get a rabbi, a minister, and a priest to officiate at the rally. Detroit Councilman Clyde Cleveland got permission for us to use Kennedy Square in downtown Detroit at our designated date and time. Ginka Ortega, world-renowned flutist, and Val Palmieri, music teacher extraordinaire at Lahser High School in Bloomfield Hills, volunteered their talent and support. Word spread, and with Mason and Grace Yu and many others, we held our rally.

Over 800 people came and so did the media - WWJ, WJR radio, Detroit News and Detroit Free Press, and TV channels 2, 4 and 7. The rally was successful in awakening awareness throughout Michigan. Although I had spent a week organizing the rally, it was but one of many in major U.S. cities and around the world. After that, together with the Yus, we established Human Rights for China in Michigan (HRC). I was elected president and Mason, treasurer.

My involvement with HRC didn't end there. For a year, I criss-crossed the country, participated in student rallies, gave speeches, raised funds, organized and hosted dinners and get-togethers to promote our cause. In Ann Arbor I was the main speaker at its candlelight vigil. In San Francisco and Chicago, I met with student leaders. In New York City, I met with 30 student and professional leaders, all discussing how we could help the Chinese students. We pooled our resources with groups in other cities to buy a full page ad in USA Today for $50,000. It was a great joint effort and I felt good in my role as an activist.

When my literary agent, Jonathon Lazear, heard of my involvement with Human Rights for China, he asked if I would write a book on Tiananmen within three months. I declined saying that my involvement with the cause was too raw and I needed more time to process it. In retrospect, I wish I had said yes.

Home in the Woods

All my energy went into my food career. We decided to remodel our three-car garage into my second kitchen. I had planned to expand my culinary ventures into classes and TV programs. We wanted to use the existing cantilever beams as the setting for a studio kitchen, while building another three-car garage alongside the house. John Shen, architect and friend, designed the extension, and our contractor was Dan Ray. But John and Dan didn't agree on many issues. John resigned and Dan was solely responsible for the project. Because of my involvement with HRC, I didn't give enough attention to this remodeling project which later proved to be very expensive.

John's original design was to have the new garage built perpendicular to the house, facing the driveway and the street. But the City of Bloomfield Hills stipulated that garages in the city had to be out of sight from the street. It was huge and costly to comply with the city regulations. Over 600 tons of dirt and 12 trees were removed. It took almost a whole year to complete the project.

Initially I had asked Mom for a loan. She was about to sell her Lafayette home and promised to lend us $50,000 after its sale. When she sold her home in six months, she reneged on her promise. I was hurt and angry, but too proud to beg. We arranged a bank loan to meet expenses.

The second kitchen became our family room. Its restaurant-style stove and overhead fan made my cooking much more efficient. In this kitchen we've hosted many fund-raising parties for the human rights cause.

We were empty-nesters, since our boys have moved out and are on their own. Albert and I decided to spend 1989 Christmas and New Year's in San Francisco. We were actually away for three weeks, and managed to get the bargain of the year - the $75 a night included two full breakfasts for a suite at the San Francisco Marriott on Third and Market streets. This was possible for it was right after the big San Francisco earthquake where several highway bridges in the Bay Area collapsed. Tourism and business in San Francisco were dismal.

Our home in the woods

Grace and Mickey

In April of 1990, my good friend, Grace Chu, left for Los Angeles to be with her niece. We had been friends since we both worked on the ACA newsletter in 1972. She practically adopted me as her daughter and I considered her my Michigan mother. She was a great listener and it wasn't until I practiced meditation years later that I learned that listening is an art and the one who listens well loves well.

Albert and I once had a serious argument. He fell asleep before we resolved the issue. I was so angry I got up, dressed hurriedly, and drove off. Where could I go at midnight? Nowhere but to Grace's home. I didn't even have time to call, I just showed up at her door at that ungodly hour. Grace, in her loving and maternal way, was happy to see me and willing to listen and talk. My visit lasted over two hours, accompanied by a wad of Kleenex and many cups of tea.

She asked if I wanted to spend the night at her home, but by that time I was much calmer and at peace. I thanked her and told her that I should go home, for I knew that Albert and the boys would be worried about me.

Sure enough when I returned, the three of them had spent hours driving around different shopping malls looking for me.

How dumb. Why would I go to a mall at this time of the night?

When Albert asked where I'd been, I refused to tell him, since I needed to guard my secret in case a similar situation arose.

It had become a custom for Grace and I to celebrate our birthdays with *dim sum* in Windsor. One year when I drove to

Dearborn to pick her up for our *dim sum* celebration, Grace asked about my mom. No sooner did she mention her name than I had to pull over to the shoulder of the expressway to calm down.

Early that morning, Mom had called to wish me a happy birthday. In the course of our conversation, she dug up old wounds, accusing me of not being the same daughter and sister I once was, saying that I had grown selfish and self-centered and all I cared about was my own family.

How untrue. All these years, even after my marriage, I'd always been a good daughter. We sent money to her and Dad during our first Christmas when Albert and I didn't even have enough to buy each other a present. Through the years, she always called collect. Phone calls in those days were expensive and every month our phone bill took a big chunk out of our budget. At every Christmas and birthday, I emptied our piggy bank and sent her as much as we could afford. And my siblings? I always put them ahead of myself, and my husband and sons. Hadn't I taken care of my younger sisters when they needed help? How could Mom be so cruel and heartless?

Well, Grace listened and held me until I stopped sobbing. She told me that my mother was not as mature as her age and that I had to try to be forgiving and let it go.

Grace was an avid reader and she loved books. She was also a writer from the old school who was meticulous about every word, comma and period. She had written several pieces on the Chinese New Year for the Detroit News.

During the years I worked at HFCC in Dearborn, I would often visit her during my lunch hour or after work and would bring her some home cooking or fresh produce. She, in turn, would serve me cups of tea, or sometimes, a bowl of soup with wontons, which she wrapped herself. While she never mentioned her age, I would guess that she was in her late 70s. After her husband, Charles, died, she lived alone in the same home in Dearborn. I was concerned about her welfare and kept suggesting that I accompany her to look for a retirement apartment or home. She would pretend to agree with my proposal, but kept postponing the visit.

Later I noticed Grace had become impatient and irritable. When asked if she was alright, she would snap at me, "Why shouldn't I be okay? I feel fine." But I could see that she was in denial. I knew she had a lump in one of her breasts, but she refused to show it to me. Nor was she willing to consult a doctor. Her good friend, Dorothy, was equally exasperated and worried. After several telephone conversations with Dorothy, we decided to call her sole surviving relative, a niece, in Los Angeles. When Chi Ching heard of her aunt's physical condition, she flew to Detroit. Within a week, she was able to whisk Grace to her home in California.

On May 17, Chi Ching called and told me that Grace had a happy month with her and her family and passed away peacefully the night before. I didn't attend Grace's funeral but made Chi Ching promise to bury her in the black brocade jacket I gave her before she left. *Rest in peace, dear Grace. I love you very much and I shall miss you.*

In June, we held another big rally for human rights for China at Kennedy Square in downtown Detroit. This was to mark the second anniversary of the Tiananmen Square Massacre. Because HRC (Human Rights for China in Michigan) was already well established, we had no trouble getting public and media support. Over 700 people gathered for the event and the Detroit City Council affirmed our cause by presenting us with a special plaque.

In November, Ian and I joined Albert and traveled to the STAPP Conference in Orlando, Florida. (This conference was named after Colonel John Paul Stapp, M.D.,* a scientist who became known as "the fastest man on earth.") Ian was barely two and half years old and we couldn't wait to take him, our first grandchild, to Disney World and Epcot Center.

On the first day, Albert accompanied us to Epcot Center where we enjoyed all the exhibits. One was about the human body, and strangely enough, Ian noticed the eye and kept repeating "the eye, the eye."

On the second day, while Albert was attending a meeting, Ian and I visited Disney World by ourselves. I had his stroller and diaper bag, and was ready for an adventure with my little one.But Ian refused to ride in the stroller and insisted on being carried. So there I was, carrying Ian with one arm and lugging the stroller and diaper bag on the other. Somehow, it didn't occur to me to find a place to deposit his stroller. We visited Mickey Mouse and Donald Duck and when we returned to our hotel room that afternoon, I was thoroughly exhausted.

On the third day, when Ian and I returned to Disney World. I left the stroller in the hotel and packed the minimum in his diaper bag, but we only stayed half a day. At dinner that evening, Bess Patrick (wife of Albert's professor, Larry Patrick) said, "Remember, Liz, God gave babies to young mothers, not to aging grandmas." How true.

On the fourth day when Ian asked, "Mickey today?" My answer was a firm NO.

1991 - A Year of Joy and Sadness

In May 1991, Tom graduated from Cleveland Podiatry School, and we celebrated this with much fanfare. The entire King clan came to Cleveland for the party. In addition to Albert, Albert Jr., Siew, Ian and me, relatives included: Grandma Helen, James and Shirley, Lucy, Francis, Anthony and Rebecca. On the Chiu side were Grandma Rowena, George, Shirley and Bill, Sherri, Matt and Christopher for a total of 19. All lodged at the Cleveland Marriott as our guests. Auntie Shirley and Uncle Bill hosted a Chinese banquet for us the next day. Now, at last, Tom was Thomas Ignatius King, DPM, Doctor of Podiatric Medicine.

In July, Albert and I had an interesting adventure. After seeing a Gene Hackman movie, *Narrow Margin,* where the entire action takes place on a train, we thought it would be fun to take a slow train from Windsor to Vancouver on the VIA, Canada's official railway. We booked a first class cabin with a full bath. But we were distressed to find only a half bath in our first class berth. When we complained to the purser, he told us that the train didn't have an en suite bathroom.

Our first day on board was great - the a la carte menu in the dining room was superb, and the scenery breathtaking. The second day, however, was bad. The train broke down before we reached Winnipeg and we were bussed to that city. They told us the delay might be for a couple of hours, so we should check at the office for updates. After several hours, the delay was pushed further and further back. At lunchtime, first class passengers were given coupons redeemable in nearby restaurants, while second class passengers were ignored. This was grossly unfair so I organized a committee to petition for equal treatment. After much negotiation, VIA distributed meal tickets to the other class passengers as well.

As the delay dragged on, Albert and I went to the nearest hotel and rented a room for half a day so we could shower and rest. After dinner, while Albert was busy with his work, I went to the VIA office to check for departure time. On my way back to the hotel, I had the uncanny feeling I was being followed.

Since our hotel was two blocks away, I felt it was foolish to continue walking by myself. I ran to the gas station at the corner and told the attendant behind the glass window that I was being followed.

"Just stay where you are now so I can see you," he said.

Soon a neatly dressed young man came by. He pretended to be interested in buying something from the station. After a few minutes, he chose a pack of gum, paid for it, and left.

Immediately after that, the gas station attendant said, "Run quickly to your hotel. I'll keep a close watch on you."

I did and was out of breath when I arrived at our room. Phew! That was a close call.

Next time Albert went to check for departure time. The VIA office still had no answer. I telephoned the local TV and radio station to report the derailment and delay.

"Lady, this isn't news to us - the VIA is often derailed and late."

Finally around midnight, we returned to our compartment on the train. We would continue our journey, but the power in the dining car couldn't be restored. For the remainder of our trip to Vancouver, only sandwiches, hot dogs, and hot and cold drinks were available. Fortunately these were on the house so that pacified most of the passengers.

We arrived in Vancouver, a full day late. Luckily we were on holiday and didn't have to keep a schedule. We were so glad to see Albert's relatives - Auntie Bao Hwa and her brother, Uncle S. Y. King, both in their early 70s. The last time we had seen both of them was in Hong Kong in 1980. They treated us to several excellent Chinese meals, since Auntie Bao Hua was a "Chinese Princess," who always carried a small notebook with the names and phone numbers of her favorite restaurants. We also did quite a bit of sight-seeing. Vancouver is a beautiful city, much like San Francisco.

Back home our Human Rights for China (HRC) association was still very active. When I got wind of the pending visit of Professor Fang Lizhi to WSU, I seized the opportunity to invite him to speak to the Chinese Americans in the Greater Detroit area. Professor Fang was the astrophysicist who sought refuge and asylum at the U.S. Embassy in Beijing. The professor, an advocate for democracy, was hailed as a hero by the students. He accepted my invitation and the visit was set for mid-November. In the meantime, as HRC president, I started planning for the event. During the first week of October, we hosted a banquet for 70 at our home for people from whom I hoped to get help. After dinner, committees were formed to take care of details for this historic event.

In early November Albert and I were in Paris to attend one of his conferences. While Albert was at the meeting, I visited the Louvre and other museums, shopped and walked around the city. We stayed at our favorite hotel, Grand Haussman, which is near

L'Opera, and the room and breakfast were good.

One morning I attended a fashion show at Galerie Lafayette. A breakfast, with croissant, fruit and either coffee or tea, with champagne, preceded the program. I shared a table with a lady from South Carolina. We introduced ourselves, shared our backgrounds as well as our opinions about the models and their outfits. One model wore an attractive canary yellow suit that caught my fancy. Later, we both fell in love with a blue woolen coat and decided to check it out. Fortunately the store had two in stock, sized M and S. My friend bought the M and I the S. I still own that coat and enjoy wearing it from time to time.

When Tom met us at the airport on November 11, he asked, "Do you want the good news first or the bad news?"

"What's the bad news?" I asked.

"Matt (my sister Shirley's son) had a motorcycle accident in San Diego yesterday. He's in intensive care and his parents are flying back to the U.S. from Seoul, arriving tomorrow."

What a shock. Matt was a freshman at University of California, San Diego (UCSD), hoping for a career in medicine. It was only in late August that Shirley accompanied him from Seoul to get him settled on campus. While I didn't get to see them, we had spoken on the phone several times. And now this? Poor Matt, poor Shirley and Bill, their lives would never be the same.

I phoned my mother and siblings for more details. After some discussion with Albert, I flew to San Diego and visited with Shirley and Bill for a few days and visited Matt in intensive care.

Here's what happened. Matt was asked to leave the UCSD dormitory when he acted unruly toward some of his dorm mates. He moved out to live with his cousin, John Chiu, near campus.

248

John owned a motorcycle and had taken Matt for a ride one time. One day when Matt went to look for John, John was out, but the keys to the motorcycle were on the table. Matt took the keys and decided to take a spin. Within minutes he came to a curve on the expressway. The motorcycle hit the shoulder. He was thrown off, landed on his head, and injured his brain stem. He wasn't wearing a helmet nor did he actually know how to drive that vehicle.

Now he was teetering between life and death. Poor Matt, at 19 his life was in jeopardy. His parents had such high hopes for him - he was to be an opthalmologist.

I listened and talked to Shirley and Bill, together and separately. Bill was depressed, but realistic, realizing that if Matt recovered from his coma, he could be almost like a vegetable. Shirley, the mom, kept hoping and kept telling Matt, "Wake up, Matt. No matter what, Matt, I'll always be here to take care of you."

It was indeed hard for Shirley, a mother, to let go. How could one mother counsel another mother to let her child die? I didn't have the answer. Now, 21 years later, Matt, half-paralyzed, is still in a wheelchair and has to be fed and bathed at home.

In between visits to San Diego, I managed to chair Professor Fang's talk at home. We had close to 2,000 attendees at the Mercy High School auditorium. He gave a rousing address, exhorting Chinese Americans to continue their support for struggling students. Afterwards, people came up to the stage for photo ops with Professor and Mrs. Fang. Table after table was filled with Chinese hors d'oeuvres and sweets, courtesy of the Chinese restaurants in town.

Donna and a New Cookbook

In the spring of 1992, my friend Diana Chang recommended that I attend a weeklong workshop to help me know myself. I took her advice and enrolled in a one-week course, *Intensive Journal*. Dr. Ira Progoff, a student of Carl Jung, pioneered this method of building self-awareness after 25 years of using psychotherapy with his patients. Instead of recording their history, he let his patients write their own story (his-story or her-story). His idea was that when patients take time to write their story, they will grow in self-knowledge and self-reliance. Dr. Progoff devised a system by which his patients journal with their right brain and write with the flow. His system is divided into four sections: 1. Life/Time 2. Dialogue 3. Depth 4. Meaning.

The course was held at a retreat house in Menlo Park, CA. I didn't mind flying to the West Coast for a week, since I was intent on self-discovery. I wanted to find out who I was and how I could fulfill my mission on earth. On the first day every student was given an empty binder with marked subdivisions and a stack of loose leaf paper. Each session started with a talk given by a trained instructor, followed by 45 minutes of non-stop writing. We were taught to write with our right brain, without judgment or editing. In this way, we eventually plumbed deep into our center, to the living source, which is the Holy Spirit. At the end of the week, my binder was filled with my journaling. I not only learned an effective way to solve my problems and dilemmas, but also gained self-knowledge. I bought many books and tapes on this method of self-discovery. I also invited a trained Progoff instructor for a workshop, first at my home and a year later, at Manresa Retreat

House nearby.

It was at this workshop that I met Donna Dean, a former nun, now a public health specialist. We became friends the first day we met. As we talked, she about her work in low-fat cooking and eating and I about my Chinese cookbooks, we suddenly had an "aha" moment. Why not collaborate on a low-fat Chinese cookbook? Although the book market was glutted with Chinese cookbooks, we hadn't seen one on low-fat Chinese cooking. Donna could help me with the low-fat concept and be editor and graphic designer, while I would be responsible for creating and testing the recipes. I returned to Detroit excited and energized. Not only had I found a way to understand and know myself, but I had met a collaborator for a third cookbook.

We agreed that I would send Donna 10 recipes at a time. She would edit and comment on the style and format and return them to me. I was happy for I had an exciting project to focus on.

In early October, I made a business trip to Portland, OR to meet with Donna. A tastefully decorated guest room awaited me when I arrived. We spent a week planning and finalizing the format of our book. During my visit, I shopped and cooked most of our meals at her home. I met Bob Wilson, a nutritionist, and engaged him to analyze the caloric content of each recipe. After some discussion, we three agreed to simplify the process. Only calories from fat and the percentage of fat would be included in each recipe. The three of us worked well as a team and made great progress.

In February 1993, I went to San Francisco to take care of Mom. She had a cataract operation on her left eye. Since Mimi was in Manila, Shirley in El Paso, and Maria in Chicago, none of them was available nor willing to take care of her. During that week, I shopped, cooked, and accompanied her to the ophthalmogist for her post operative checkup.

In April I was back with Donna and Bob in Portland. This time, Donna and I gave a big party to promote our forthcoming book, tentatively entitled, *The Low-Fat Chinese Gourmet.* We shopped for food and party supplies and I bankrolled the purchases and cooked the food. Donna cleaned, decorated, and spruced up her house. The guests were her relatives, friends and neighbors.

After the party, Donna went berserk. In the kitchen there were piles of dirty dishes and platters of food everywhere. She couldn't stand the mess, and disappeared for a few hours. When she returned, she apologized profusely, but I had already washed all the dishes and cleaned up the kitchen myself. I was not only tired, but angry.

When Bob drove me to the airport, I found a book on the passenger's seat - *A Course in Miracles* (ACIM). I had heard of this title and thought it was an actual course. But when I held the book in my hand, I was mesmerized and determined to read it. I couldn't wait to buy a copy for myself. At the neighborhood bookstore I bought 100 copies - for myself, my siblings and close friends.

A Course in Miracles, printed on paper similar to that in a Bible, was dictated to Helen Schucman by a voice in her head. Helen, a non-Christian, is a psychology professor at Columbia University School of Medicine. Together with Bill Thetford, a colleague, they hid the manuscript for many years, not wanting to expose themselves to the ridicule of their peers. But circumstances dictated otherwise. After its publication some years later, the book attracted many readers and followers. Classes and study groups in ACIM popped up all over the country. At first I thought of joining a group in my neighborhood, but eventually decided to study it by myself. I spent a whole year going over it, line by line, page by page. Finally I found it too heady, since it is based more on psychology than theology. Jesus Christ is mentioned only twice, while the Holy Spirit shows up more frequently. Its main thesis is:

"Nothing real can be threatened. Nothing unreal exists. Herein lies the peace of God. There is no order of difficulty in Miracles. One is not 'smaller' or 'bigger' than another. They are all the same. All expressions of love are maximal." (ACIM, page x)

So in addition to Progoff's *Intensive Journal,* I now have ACIM as a guide in my search for intimacy with my God.

In mid-August, 14 of our family, including Albert and I took the Alaskan cruise on the Holland American line boarding at Vancouver. This was my brainchild - I wanted to see the beauty of our 49th state, together with my mother and Albert's mother. Originally I was preparing a trip just for the four of us, then Auntie Bao Hua and Albert's two brothers, James and Francis, wanted to come along with their families and parents. How I wished Albert, Siew, Ian and Tom could have joined us. They were busy with their jobs and I didn't offer to take four-year old Ian with us, since I wanted to give more time to our mothers.

We cruised for a week. Albert and I had our own room with a balcony. Mom Rowena and Mom Helen shared a room with Auntie Bao Hua. When I ordered their tickets, I specified a room with three beds, but didn't know that the third bed was a rollaway. When the three ladies saw the rollaway, they lost their graciousness and made a beeline for the beds. Mom Rowena and Auntie Bao Hua were faster and each took the more comfortable single bed. Mom Helen was stuck with the rollaway. What could I do or say? Either way I'd be blamed. Whose side should I take?

My mother's or Albert's mother?

Sure enough, throughout the cruise, Mom Rowena and Mom Helen were at odds. I was hoping to have a happy, family reunion, thinking that both of them, in their 80s, would be gracious, mature and compromising. But I was wrong. I was so stressed out during the cruise that I had to walk away from both of them many times. Fortunately, Shirley and Lucy, my sisters-in-law, were present. They helped to defuse many situations. The end of the cruise couldn't come soon enough for Albert and me.

When we returned home, Albert asked whose bright idea it was that we take both our mothers on the same cruise. I confessed that it was mine, but I had been too idealistic. I was so angry after the cruise that I finally found some consolation when I could scream out a nasty word in the privacy of our home. To de-stress, Albert and I decided to take a vacation by ourselves. This time we opted for Europe.

We had a few free days before Albert's professional meeting at Aachen, Germany. So we went to visit our friends, Aatje and Dick Van Kempen, in their lovely home in Eindhoven, a suburb of Amsterdam. We were their houseguests and Aatje spoiled us with her love and hospitality. We talked about spending a weekend to see Brussels and Antwerp.

"Belgium is a very small country and you don't need a weekend to see it all - one day would do it. Dick and I will drive you there in our car," she said.

We toured Belgium and enjoyed their company. After that, we still had a long weekend free. Where to this time? Prague? When we stopped by a railway station, the attendant who spoke very little English, kept saying, *Nein.* No, we couldn't use our Eurail pass to go to Prague. What to do and where should we go? Albert suddenly suggested Berlin. As a World War II buff, he had always been intrigued with that city, the stronghold of Hitler's infamy. I agreed with his suggestion, but where should we stay? I suggested the Grand Hotel. At first Albert was hesitant, thinking that it would cost a mint for a weekend there. Why not find out what it would cost? It turned out that they had an inexpensive weekend rate and we gladly accepted that.

What made me suggest the Grand Hotel was a happy coincidence. Just before we left home for the airport, I had time on my hands. Since we were packed and ready to go, I turned on the TV and watched *The Grand Hotel,* starring Greta Garbo. That was how I knew about it.

Our time at the Grand Hotel in East Berlin was memorable. Although it was bombed during the war and rebuilt later, much of its former grandeur remained.

When the bellman took us to our room, he said excitedly, "Your tenor is coming."

"My tenor? Who? Pavarotti? Domingo?" I asked.

"No, your emperor," he said.

"My emperor? Oh, we're Chinese, not Japanese, we don't have an emperor."

Our room wasn't a suite nor was it exceptionally grand, but it had class. The queen-sized bed had a lace duvet and comforter, the windows were decorated with lace curtains, and reprints of old masters' paintings hung on the walls. The old-fashioned bathtub had four feet in the European tradition.

After we unpacked, we decided to look around. In the lobby, we were surprised to see everyone in rapt attention. It turned out the Emperor and Empress of Japan, together with their retinue, had just arrived.

"Let's stand at the back," I said to Albert, since we could easily be mistaken for Japanese. His Majesty, Tenno Heika, was the first in line, followed by the Empress. To my surprise, he suddenly turned back to look at me and smiled. At that instant, I curtsied while Albert snapped his photo. Months later, when we showed this photo to our Japanese friends, they were in awe and wanted a copy. We didn't know that it was prohibited for a commoner to take a picture of The Emperor, let alone a non-Japanese commoner – Albert.

We were in for another surprise that evening. When Albert and I went to the formal dining room on the top floor for dinner, we found it was fully occupied by the Emperor and his party. The waiters at the entrance thought we belonged to his party and waved us in. Now, if we had been able to converse in Japanese, we might have crashed the party. But since our Japanese was limited to hello, good morning, thank you and goodbye, we dared not join the revelry.

In October, I attended a mid-week retreat at the Manresa Jesuit Retreat House, about a five-minute drive from our home. As one of the captains of the retreat, I had the opportunity to speak to Fr. John Snyder, the priest leading the retreat. Fr. John, a Jesuit from St. Louis, was very friendly and personable. When I went to say goodbye, he asked if my husband and I would be interested in joining a group of American Catholics on a Gregorian trip to the Vatican next April. Since Fr. John was staying at Manresa through the weekend, I invited him to our house for dinner. I wanted him to meet Albert and perhaps persuade Albert to go to Rome.

It turned out that Albert agreed to join the Vatican trip since he wanted to straighten out a controversy. He was doing cadaveric research using bodies donated to the University. Nagging questions about the ethics of doing simulated crash tests in the lab using human bodies came up. The U.S. Government didn't have a religious position on this issue and there were conservative Catholics who thought that the testing was unethical. The recent brouhaha that prompted *L'Osservatore Romano* to condemn the use of cadavers worried him. Albert wanted to go to the Gregorian University in Rome to ask the theologians about this.

For the dinner for Fr. John, I cooked Braised Lamb Shanks, one of my specialties. He loved it and was going to take more, but I asked him to save some room for the other entrees I was cooking. When I returned from the kitchen with the other dishes, Fr. John had a guilty look on his face. Albert had served him another lamb shank during my absence. Aha, his hand was caught in the cookie jar!

Liz, the chef and cook book author

6

Silence and Stillness

In early January 1994, I had a yen to take *Transcendental Meditation* (TM), popularized by the Beatles in the 60s. I found three TM centers in the Yellow Pages - in Detroit, Ann Arbor and Madison Heights. Since the last one was only about a 20 minute drive from my home, I phoned, but got no response. I finally drove there, only to find it closed. A note posted on the door listed a Detroit address.

I called the Ann Arbor office, asking them to notify me if and when a class in my Birmingham/Bloomfield area was offered. Within a week a call came saying that a teacher would conduct a small class in Birmingham, and if I signed up, I would be her fourth student. I paid $1,000 for the course and justified it to Albert, saying that I really wanted to learn meditation, and that would be his and my birthday present to me. He encouraged me to go right ahead and do my thing if it would help me find peace.

The others were a college girl from U-M, and an Indian couple in their mid-50s. In a private session with each of us our teacher gave us our mantra which we were to use to start our meditation - one mantra per person, not to be shared with anyone. Our class met daily for two hours during the first week, then weekly during the first month. At last I was meditating and in the stillness and silence I found peace and harmony.

One day, the Indian woman came and asked for my mantra. I told her that it was private since our teacher emphasized that it was not to be shared. But she kept insisting and told me that she and her husband found out that their mantras were the same. Then she repeated their sound and asked if mine was the same. Sure enough, it was.

I was angry. Why did our teacher lie to us? I wouldn't have minded if she told us that while we all had the same sound, it would later become our personal sound since we each added our own individuality to it. But to say that we each had our own private sound or mantra wasn't true. Right away I switched my mantra to Abba, which means father in Aramaic, our Heavenly Father. I continued using the TM technique, but my mantra was Abba.

In April I had the chance to use meditation when Albert and I joined 25 American Catholics from different U.S. cities and met in Rome for our Gregorian Trip.

Even though our seats on the plane were comfortable during our seven hour trip from Detroit to Rome, I couldn't sleep. By the time we arrived at the Holiday Inn in Rome, I was totally exhausted. We landed a day early, so we could rest before we joined the official party the next day. Fortunately a room was available for us right away. Albert suggested I meditate before we took our nap. Sure enough, after 30 minutes of silence, I was refreshed and relaxed and slept soundly.

After we woke up from our nap, Albert and I went outside to see where the Crowne Plaza, our hotel for the week, was located. We were joined by a Jesuit priest who lived in Rome. This priest began to point out the buildings around the hotel and paid special emphasis on a long building nearby. He said it was where the Inquisition was held and where Galileo was condemned to house arrest. Albert wondered quietly how the Jesuit knew what he was going to ask the theologians.

A few days later we were driven to the papal residence at

Castel Gandolfo, 15 miles southeast of Rome. There, we were shown the telescopes and lab equipment used by Galileo while he was incarcerated. Interestingly, there was a free booklet for all visitors entitled, *Galileo Forgiven after 400 years.*

Our Gregorian trip was fabulous. Each day was filled with activities - visits to the Gregorian University, the Vatican, the Pope's summer home, Galileo's lab, various papal institutions of higher learning and churches. Each day before breakfast, I meditated 30 minutes and was ready then to be an energetic tourist.

By five o'clock in the afternoon, I ran out of steam. I would again meditate and be ready for our evening activities. It turned out that the other travelers in our group were regular supporters of the Gregorian University in Rome - people who donated a million dollars without batting an eye. Later I asked Fr. John Snyder, SJ, our host, why he invited us to join this august body of high rollers. His reply was, "We need little fishes too."

On the day before we left Rome, Albert sought out a moral theologian to ask about the ethics of using human cadavers for research. He told him he would have to think about it and would get back to him. A month later, Albert received a four-page theological report on that issue. When the paper arrived, it was filled with theological terms which were incomprehensible to Albert.

My friend Diana Chang asked why was I praying with a mantra the Hindu way. I explained that I was just using their technique, but my mantra *Abba* (Father) was Christian. Within a week, she sent me a copy of John Main, OSB's *Christian Meditation: The Gethsemani Talks.* It is a 54-page booklet. After reading and digesting it from cover to cover, I was elated. I didn't know the early fathers of our Church also prayed and meditated in a similar way.

Fr. John Main, a Benedictine priest from London, recovered the contemplative tradition that was lost through the centuries. Armed with this information I went to see Fr. Bernie Owens, SJ, a friend at the Manresa Retreat House nearby.

"Why didn't anyone tell me that meditation was practiced by our desert fathers and mothers in the fourth century?" I asked.

His answer was that this tradition was lost in our church and even in his many years of Jesuit seminary training, he only had one lecture on contemplative prayer.

Fr. John advocated using *Maranatha (Come, Lord* in Aramaic, the language used by Jesus) as the mantra. I obtained permission from our pastor at St. Regis, Fr. Dan Murphy, to start a Christian meditation group at the parish.

Fr. Jack Schuett, a Jesuit from Manresa, and Deacon Brian Carroll from St. Regis, came to help me start our first meditation group. About 20 of my friends, Catholic, Protestant, and non-Christian, were invited to the first session. I told them that this was a gift, and that it wouldn't cost them $1,000 apiece. The only prerequisite was that they join us once a week as a group, and practice it twice daily by themselves. After the first month, our group dropped to 15, later to 10, and finally we had only six to eight regulars.

Hope and Disappointment

In May of 1995, Albert, Tom and I were in Nashville, TN, to attend Albert Jr.'s graduation from nursing school. Although he has a B.Sc. from U-M with a major in cellular molecular biology, he didn't pursue graduate studies. After his graduation, he worked as a manager for Taco Bell. The title was impressive, but it was low-pay work with long hours and lots of responsibility.

When Albert, Siew and Ian moved to Nashville in 1992, he worked for Opryland, a huge hotel near the Grand Ole Opry, home of country singers. Fortunately, he decided later that working as a waiter and room service server wouldn't benefit his family in the long haul. Siew was assistant to the provost of a medical college. That was the reason they moved to Nashville. Siew's boss at WSU, Dr. Walter Strong, was offered a position at the medical school there and he wanted Siew to transfer to Nashville too. Siew and Albert discussed his offer with us and we thought it was a wonderful opportunity for her to follow her mentor. Little did we realize that it would mean their settling in a new place without any family support and that we would miss them and Ian very much.

When Albert Jr. decided to switch careers and get a certificate in nursing, he called us with the news. We listened then suggested medical school. We told him we would help him financially. He said medical school was too demanding and would take too long, and he'd rather be a nurse in order to have more time for Siew and Ian. He graduated from the University of Tennessee in two years. Now he could get a better job with more pay.

In June, Albert and I took the upstream Yangtze Cruise. We

had hoped to catch the cruise on the Regal Cruise Line, but since we were a party of two, we could only travel on the smaller Victoria Cruise Line. While the scenery along the Yangtze was majestic and beautiful, the food on board was terrible.

Whoever thought of losing weight on a cruise? Well, we did. At the first evening, when we boarded the boat and insisted on being fed per our itinerary, we were served a special egg drop soup. (My nephew Aaron would often relate this "joke" to his friends. It went something like this, "Let me tell you how to make egg drop soup. It's so easy. All you need is a pot filled with some broth, then you take an egg and drop that in it.") That night ours was a fried egg dropped into clear broth. At first I thought I had stumbled on a new recipe until I found out later, after many meals on board, that the Chinese cook didn't know how to cook.

In the morning when we were served *jook* or congee, we had fresh kohlrabi, not the preserved variety. Whoever heard of serving fresh raw kohlrabi with *jook*? That pickled vegetable was so common and inexpensive, but if the cook didn't know that, his knowledge of Chinese cuisine was nil. Time and again, the entrees served were below one star and each time the maitre d' came by to ask for my opinion, my answer was, "Please don't ask me. You'd be totally depressed with my answer."

Our cruise lasted for five days and we needed some activities and recreation. While the ship's crew performed a variety show each evening, we had to keep occupied during the day. We finally found a mahjong set and wanted to use the table in the recreation room. Imagine our surprise when we were told that we had to pay a fee for using that room and table. I protested and finally convinced the purser that it was our privilege, as passengers, to use the facilities on board.

The farewell banquet was one to remember. I mused, *Finally, we'd be treated to a good meal.* Sure enough, the waiters started the dinner with a beautifully arranged hors d'oeuvres platter. We were all anxious and hungry and couldn't wait to dip our chopsticks into it. Imagine our disappointment when we were told that it was just for "our eyes only," not to be eaten. So much for the Victoria Cruise on the Yangtze.

In December, I returned to Portland, OR, to work with Donna on our cookbook. I finally realized that she works in spurts. Whenever I sent her a batch of 10 or more recipes, it was months before she edited and returned them to me. Now, finding an agent who was willing to sell our cookbook wasn't as easy this time. I approached Jonathon (my literary agent) first, but he turned me down, since his specialty was novels and movies. While I did connect with other agents, none of them were enthusiastic - the market was glutted with cookbooks, Chinese and otherwise.

Singapore

Albert was invited to spend the summer of 1997 doing research at the University of Singapore (U-S) Medical School. En route to Singapore, we stopped in Hong Kong for a week. We always enjoy returning to the place of our youth and seeing old and dear friends - Julian and Doris Chang, Che King and Gloria Chow and others. We filled ourselves with mouth-watering fare from different Chinese restaurants, gaining an extra inch or more at our waistlines. Hong Kong restaurants still serve the best Chinese cuisine of all the places I have been.

From there we flew directly to Singapore. This time our visit to that island state was three months. Siew's parents, Shirley and James Lau, asked us not to eat lunch on our flight, for they planned to take us to try out a new restaurant. But Thai Airline's lunch was hard to resist - lobster and crab on noodles. The Laus picked us up at the airport, with our many suitcases which contained gifts and the usual necessities.

After a second lunch, the Laus took us to the apartment provided by the University of Singapore. It was a large, third floor flat, with three bedrooms, two full baths, a full kitchen, a large living, and dining room. The bedrooms were air-conditioned, but not the kitchen, living and dining rooms. A washer was provided, but no dryer.

"This is where you hang your wash. The heat will dry it up quickly." Shirley pointed to the small verandah by the kitchen where several poles were hinged. We had to buy our own hangers. After Shirley and James walked through our apartment, they left saying, "Call us if you need anything."

I soon discovered there was no toilet paper. I tried to call for help only to find the phone wasn't connected. We couldn't send an SOS to the Laus, and our host, Dr. Kamal Bose at the U-S, was nowhere in sight. Albert and I walked around the compound area and found a small convenience store where we purchased toilet paper, soap, and other necessities. We also found the apartment office where we picked up sets of towels and sheets on consignment.

That was how we were inducted into our stay in Singapore. Now, whenever we have newcomers to Detroit and WSU, I go out of my way to help them adjust. I drive our visitors to the grocery, drugstore and department stores so they could pick up whatever they needed during his stay. One never truly understands a situation unless he has experienced it firsthand. Truly, we cannot walk someone's walk until we wear his moccasins.

Singapore is right by the Equator and has only one season - hot, steamy summer. From 8 a.m. to 7 p.m., it is hot and humid. A 15-minute walk is enough to make one sweat from head to toe. Albert reported for work each day and left the apartment before 8 a.m. to catch the shuttle to the medical school. He didn't return until 6 p.m.

The university campus wasn't that close, neither was the library. While I visited the library often, I didn't stay there all day. Once a week I'd walk to the markets. Singapore has two kinds - the wet market and the dry market. The dry markets are like our grocery stores, filled with fresh produce, dried, canned, frozen food and other household needs. The wet markets, however, are very different. They have fresh vegetables and fruits of every variety, seafood of all kinds including shrimp to shellfish, and freshly butchered meat and chicken. The fresh fish balls were absolutely divine - very crunchy and sweet.

There were stalls selling clothes, housewares and things, such as Chinese *laisee* envelopes and gift items. Small "hawker" food stands were everywhere. My favorites were the ones selling fresh tofu pudding. A bowl of tofu pudding, topped with liquid cassia sugar, sold for 25 cents, Singapore currency. I occasionally stopped at the nearby mall for lunch and I enjoyed soup rice noodles topped with greens and fish balls.

On most Saturdays, the Laus picked us up for 5 p.m. mass at their parish, the Holy Family Church. Then we all had dinner at a fancy restaurant chosen by Shirley and took turns picking up the check. Singapore has a mix of Chinese, Malaysian and Indian people, so we enjoyed many choices of ethnic foods, all of which were great.

Weekdays I'd take the subway downtown to shop. Although the fashions in Singapore aren't as stylish as those in Hong Kong, I enjoyed milling around with the crowds and window shopping. Interestingly enough, each subway station had groups of shops and eateries, sometimes, even a movie house.

Another highlight of our Singapore visit was the time we spent with the Wongs. Hee Kit is an orthopedic surgeon at the medical school at U-S, while Mei-li, a general practitioner, has her own office. They are the parents of three lovely daughters, Ying Xi, Ying Mei and Ying Li. We shared several meals with them and Mei-Li was kind enough to take time off from work to accompany me shopping.

In early July I visited Taiwan at the invitation of my friend Diana Chang. That week sped by - we were like young girls having our first pajama party. We talked, ate, shopped, attended concerts, and visited museums.

I returned to Singapore with an extra piece of luggage which exceeded the allotted weight allowance and paid a substantial surcharge. When I went to check-in at Eva Air, I was told that because I failed to confirm my flight, my seat was taken. My options were to either upgrade to first class for an extra US $1,000 or wait for a vacancy on that flight, second in line. If all else failed, I had no choice but to take the next day flight.

I was desperate. I wanted to fly back to Singapore that day since Albert was leaving for a week's visit to Detroit the next day and I wanted to see him before his departure. Why didn't I remember to confirm my flight? I didn't want to pay for the upgrade, so I kept praying and hoping and waiting. Soon I overheard someone remark, "Gosh, one of the women in our group lost her passport and couldn't join us."

My hopes soared. Could that be my good luck? But there was someone wait-listed ahead of me. Then I heard my name called and learned that the other passenger couldn't wait and purchased a first class ticket. So I was next in line. I said a silent "thank you" to the Father.

I flew back to Singapore on schedule and was able to spend some time with Albert before his trip to Detroit. Being alone in that big apartment was very different, although the Laus promised to pick me up for our usual Saturday get-together. Several hours after Albert left, I was surprised to hear the doorbell ring. I rushed to the door, not knowing whom to expect. Lo and behold, it was a courier delivering a large bouquet of yellow orchids - a gift from my beloved Albert! He knew I would be lonely and would miss him. That beautiful bouquet was my companion until Albert's return a week later. But each time I looked at it, my eyes were moist for I felt like Little Orphan Annie, all alone in Singapore.

Since the Laus are Siew's parents, we suggested the four of us invite Albert, Jr, Siew and Ian to Singapore for a week. The seven of us could tour Malaysia, spend quality time together, and share expenses. Alas, we couldn't find a big enough van to accommodate all seven of us. We had to drive two cars. Siew rode with her parents, and Albert Jr. and Ian with us.

We stopped at Johor Bahru, then Genting Highlands, Kuala Lumpur and finally Penang. In each place we booked three rooms: one for the Laus, one for Albert and I, and the third one for Albert, Jr, Siew and Ian. Ian, however, chose to share our room most of the time. Throughout the trip I couldn't help but feel the coolness between Albert Jr. and Siew.

"They've been married for 10 years, is this the end?" I asked Albert. I persuaded him to have a serious talk with his son. He tried, but Albert Jr. was tight-lipped. *This isn't like him because he's usually very open and effusive,* I thought.

Once back home Albert and I, Francis and Lucy, together with several other couples, founded the Chinese Catholic Society of MI (CCSM). This had been a gleam in our eyes for some years. When my friend, Diana, helped me draw up a list of questions for potential members, we felt it was time to take action. Ten Chinese couples were invited to our home. After dinner, we officially drew up the by-laws and launched CCSM. I also contacted the Detroit diocesan chancellor, Sr. Barbara Celesky, and worked with her and her office for the next few years.

Vicissitudes of Life

As parents, Albert and I endured the ups and downs, the joys and sorrows of our sons. On March 7, 1998, our son, Tom tied the knot with Marlowe Muske in a Royal Oak chapel, while Albert and Siew were divorced a month later.

Tom introduced Marlowe to us after they had been dating for six months, so by then they were almost engaged. Marlowe had a cute little son, Austen.

The wedding was held on March 7 in a non-denominational chapel. Two-year-old Austen, attired in a tux, was the ring bearer. He had a good time running up and down the altar steps during the wedding ceremony.

The dinner reception was held at the Red Fox on Woodward and Long Lake in Bloomfield Hills. About 100 guests from both sides of the family attended. My Mom and several of my siblings came, as well as Albert's two brothers and their families. Mom Helen, Albert's Mom, begged to be excused since she couldn't fly the long distance to Detroit from San Francisco. Many of the Muske relatives were present, together with some of our close friends.

My relatives came a day earlier. On March 6, we hosted two tables at New Wah Court Restaurant in Windsor, Ontario to celebrate Rowena's 86th birthday and the coming nuptial. On Sunday I cooked a big dinner for everyone, and hosted the Chinese tea ceremony at home. Marlowe donned an aqua Chinese brocade pantsuit, a gift from Auntie Theresa Shen, and received many *laisees* and jewelry. It was joyous occasion.

We were much saddened by Albert Jr.'s breakup with Siew, knowing how painful it must be for our beloved Ian, who was only 10 at that time. But what could we do? Ian's parents were adults and their decision was final. When Siew first broke the news to us after the New Year, I suggested marriage counseling. I registered them with the Marriage Encounter group in Nashville only to be told later that it was canceled due to insufficient participation. Such was fate.

Both of them were working hard at their jobs, and Albert Jr. was working two jobs at the same time - full-time nursing and part-time in Opryland. They were like ships passing in the night. Without any family support and few friends, things must have been very difficult for them.

It was in March that my third cookbook, *A Wok A Week: 52 Lite and Easy Meals,* was published by China Books and Periodicals in San Francisco. As I reviewed the gestation period of my new baby, I realized how stressful it was. First of all, none of the three agents I engaged could sell my book. Then, Donna and I repackaged the recipes twice, and even then, we couldn't sell it.

While I managed to get an interview with a top publisher in New York, I brought along a suitcase full of pots and pans and was ready to cook several recipes for the editor to sample. But she didn't buy our proposal. In a whimsical moment, Donna and I decided to do an 8 x 8-inch mock-up version of my cookbook. When I showed it to her, she thought that was what the final book would look like and turned me down immediately. My explanation couldn't change her mind. I also talked to a local publisher, but found the terms unacceptable. Finally, my good friend, Theresa Shen, suggested that I contact China Books and Periodicals in San

Francisco. That did it and we agreed on a cooperative venture.

I was responsible for getting the book edited, finalized and printed. They would market it for me under their imprint. Although the process was expensive and time consuming, I welcomed the challenge. For six months, I was in constant touch with Singapore about the color separation for the cover photo; with Kuala Lumpur for printing; New York with the printer's agent; Portland with Donna and Bob; and San Francisco with China Books.

The last hurdle with Donna was heart-wrenching. I had been paying her regularly each year for the last three years we worked on the book. This time, she demanded another $2,000 before she would surrender the completed manuscript to me. She claimed she had invested more time than she thought. Sure, but I spent months waiting for her to edit the recipes, not to mention the time needed for me to test and finalize them.

Albert was furious and felt that Donna was taking advantage of my kindness and generosity. She was signed on as co-author and I promised her 40 percent of the book sales. Still, the recipes were all mine, I had paid to have the recipes analyzed, the photos taken, and for printing and shipping. Albert felt that this was the last straw and I should just let the book go.

But I couldn't. I had carried it for six years and wanted to see it born. Finally Albert relented and sent Donna the sum she requested. When copies of *A Wok A Week* arrived, they didn't bring the joy and exhilaration that my two previous cookbooks did. No matter, it was in print and I was thankful.

Now a quick story about my friend, Lin Xi'an, who did the Chinese ink and brush drawings for the cookbook. We met quite by accident. I had just parked my car at Sam's Club, when a

Chinese woman came toward me speaking Mandarin.

"Are you Chinese? Would you mind taking me to the store so I can buy some ice cream for my son?" she asked.

"Not at all, come with me," I said.

I even offered her a ride home if she could wait for me to finish shopping. She lived close to Sam's. Before she got out of my car, she insisted on inviting me to her apartment for a cup of tea.

I was hesitant and told her that I could only spare half an hour. That 30 minutes extended to two hours. Lin Xi'an was not only an artist, but a sculptor. She had just immigrated to Detroit from Hunan, China with her husband and her nine-year-old son, Henry. Her husband, an engineer, worked for a Detroit firm and was quite tight with money. They had an argument that morning when Henry asked for some ice cream. His dad refused, saying that ice cream was a luxury. His mother felt that he was only a child and they could afford to buy him some ice cream now and then. So she walked to Sam's and that was how we met.

She brought out some of her paintings and sculptures and showed me brochures of her exhibits in Beijing and other cities in China.

"A 20 x 20 feet mural of mine hangs in the Beijing Airport," she said. I also saw photos of her work with the minority tribes in Southwest China.

Our friendship blossomed during the next few months. When she found out that I was working on a cookbook, she volunteered to draw Chinese ink and brush paintings for me.

"Just tell me what you want and I'll do it for you," she said.

When I needed her drawings, she came to my home and within two hours, produced 30 brush drawings. She refused to be paid but when I insisted, she compromised. I could buy two of the water color paintings of her dear friend in China.

Within a year, she and her family moved to the New England area. I saw her once, near Myrtle Beach, when she cooked a six-course dinner for Albert and me at their apartment. After that they moved and I lost track of her. It is my hope that someday, we may find each other again.

Lin Xi'an, your kindness and generosity will always stay in my heart. As I write these words, I say a silent prayer for you and yours, that Our Lord will keep you all in His loving care.

After the divorce, Albert Jr. moved into a rented room in Nashville, TN. I knew he was depressed and made time to visit him often. Finally he agreed to buy another house for himself - big enough for him to live comfortably. Albert Jr, a bachelor, became a home owner again together with his cat, Blue.

In August, we were excited, awaiting the arrival of our third grandchild, Tom and Marlowe's baby. On August 13, Makenzie Marilyn, AKA Kenny, was born in Beaumont Hospital. Marlowe wanted Albert and me, as well as her parents, to be at the actual birth. This was the first time we witnessed the miracle of birth and it was awesome. I couldn't imagine what it would be like until I saw a little head with dark hair pushing out into the world. When the baby emerged, the attending obstetrician caught the newborn and announced, "It's a girl!"

Albert and I hosted a small banquet for her when she was a month old, true to Chinese custom. Now, at last, we had a baby girl to love and it was quite serendipitous that she was born on

August 13, so close to Mom Helen's and Helen Rowena Maria's (the baby I lost in 1970) birthdays on August 15.

Little Makenize

The New Century

We had big plans for 1999. On August 15, Mom Helen (Albert's mother) would be 90 while on August 13, our granddaughter Kenny would be one. How wonderful it would be to celebrate the two birthdays together since the dates were so close. Albert and I made plans to take our whole family to San Francisco (where Mom Helen was living) for the double celebration.

But it was not to be. On July 23, Jack Preston, Mom Helen's long-time companion, called to tell us that she had passed away peacefully in her sleep. She was so quiet that when he went to wake her in the morning, she didn't move. After several vain attempts, he used a mirror to check her breathing and that was when he realized she was dead.

His news brought us much sadness - our beloved Mom Helen had returned home to her Heavenly Father and be with her beloved Yu-Lo (Albert's father). Come to think of it, didn't we detect a slight slurring of speech when we talked on the phone a couple of days ago? Did she suffer a mild stroke then? We didn't really know.

After consultation with Albert's brothers, James and Francis, we asked Jack to make arrangements to fly her body back to Detroit. Lynch Funeral Home picked up her casket at the airport and prepared her for the funeral Mass and burial the next day.

Mom Helen had a simple wake and funeral. While there were many flowers from us and other out-of-state relatives, we had few visitors. The three brothers were rather private and didn't want to publicize her passing to their colleagues and acquaintances. Only those who were very close to us were notified. James and Shirley, Albert Jr. and Ian flew over immediately.

The Requiem Mass at St. Regis was beautiful. Lucy was the organist and together with her daughter, Rebecca, provided the music and liturgy. Fr. Dan Murphy, pastor of St. Regis, officiated at the mass. The procession of cars to St. Hedwig Cemetery in Dearborn Heights was short and Mom Helen was laid to rest in the plot beside Yu-lo, her husband for over 35 years. Now, at last, they were reunited in their Father's mansion.

We all missed her - her gentle and wise guidance, and love. She had been like a mother to me, in more ways than one. I still vividly remember our month long visit to Shanghai in the early 1980s. Many thought we were mother and daughter and we were. *Rest in peace, Mom Helen, we will miss you but will always carry your love in our hearts.*

In October I had the opportunity to make a true pilgrimage to China, different from my other trips because our purpose was to visit churches, seminaries and convents. The three-week pilgrimage was organized and led by Fred and Marie Brandauers and included my friend Diana Chang, and five others and me. Each of us was to bring a small carry-on suitcase as our luggage. We stayed in two-star hotels, ate frugally and traveled on crowded buses and trains to the 11 villages and towns on our itinerary.

The Brandauers were old China hands. Fred, son of Methodist missionaries, was born and raised in Hubei, China, and spoke fluent Mandarin and Cantonese. He was a former Methodist minister, who later converted to Catholicism. His wife, Marie Materi, a former nun, shared her husband's missionary zeal and was equally passionate about helping the Church in China.

When Diana Chang first informed me of such a pilgrimage, it was natural that I would say yes. To be with her and to share a room with her for three weeks would be a joy since she was one of my best friends and I had respected and loved her as an older sister. To visit many major and minor seminaries, to meet priests, sisters and bishops in Beijing, Shanghai as well as other remote towns and villages was another attraction. I started preparations for this trip months ahead and even ordered a special safari jacket with 12 pockets for my necessities. When I arrived at the airport on departure date, I realized that I had left that jacket at home.

The 21 days of our pilgrimage passed quickly. Each day and each visit brought new adventure and insights. I saw the poverty, the hunger and thirst in the eyes and hearts of the faithful in China. Many of them were 13-generation Catholics, dating back to the time when Fr. Matteo Ricci, SJ,* went to China as a missionary in the 16th Century. This made me more determined than ever to do what I could to help them. I prayed for guidance and for light and asked the Holy Spirit to lead me in my mission.

That New Year's Eve - the end of the 20th century and the beginning of the 21st - was very special. We hosted a dinner party for the faculty and students of WSU Bioengineering Center at our home to celebrate this milestone. Since Tom and Marlowe were away in Kaua'i, Hawaii, we took care of little Kenny.

Kenny was barely a year old and as cute as a bunny. Dressed in a fancy bordeaux velvet dress with black patent leather shoes, she was the toast of our party. After dinner, Albert and I tried to keep her awake till midnight - the magic moment. Poor baby, she couldn't wait, she fell asleep on my lap. That night, we lit many candles, including a set of maroon ones, ranging in height from 18 to 6 inches, with a diameter of four inches. These were my

Y2K candles, bought from the House of Bombay at one fourth the original price. I purchased four sets. One for Albert Jr., one for Tom, one for Karen Saunders, my goddaughter in San Diego, and one for us. These candles are still usable after many years. No wonder Albert teased me saying, "They will last us until the Y3K year."

The New Year also brought us a big gift. Albert was elected to the National Academy of Engineering (NAE). Members are elected "based on their distinguished and continuing achievements in original research." This was a prestigious honor, since membership in the entire academy include about 2,000 U.S. and foreign engineers. Our entire family flew to Washington, D.C. to celebrate the induction ceremony. Later, President Irvin Reid of WSU hosted a special reception for Albert at his home. Many friends and colleagues came to celebrate this happy occasion. Now WSU has two National Academicians, one in Medicine and one in Engineering.

September 2001

Everything that occurred this year paled before September 11 - the day the terrorists crashed two planes into the Twin Towers in New York City and changed the world forever. My spiritual life also changed when I met Fr. Laurence Freeman OSB, Spiritual Director of the World Community for Christian Meditation (WCCM)* at Manresa Retreat House the day after we returned from San Francisco.

On September 7, Albert and I had left for San Francisco to join the protest rally against the 1951 signing of the treaty with Japan, instigated by General Douglas MacArthur. It was in this same city, 50 years ago, that the U.S. forgave Japan for its imperial aggression against the United States. It was also here that Japan, though the defeated aggressor, was given unparalleled rights and privileges which made it possible for her to become the great economic super power she is today.

As an active member of the Nanjing Massacre and the Michigan Historical Society for WWII, I wanted to march and protest the injustice and inhumanity of the Japanese Imperial Army. We were among the thousands gathered at the square by the San Francisco Opera House. Our visit was so secretive that neither my mom nor my brothers in the Bay Area knew we were in town.

"Stay away from the camera," Albert warned, "for we don't want your mom or brothers to know we're here." We went just for the weekend to do our thing and have a day or two of leisure by ourselves before flying back to Detroit.

It was here that we connected with Collin Quock, one of the

ushers at our wedding 41 years ago. He is a cardiac surgeon. A year before, he arranged a reunion with Bernice Woong, one of my bridesmaids, and Faye Chan, whose niece was my flower girl. Former Legionnaires (Legion of Mary members) from St. Mary's Chinese Mission also came.

On Monday, September 10, Albert and I had planned our departure. After a dinner of fish congee at a Burlingame restaurant, we returned our rented car. To do this we had to drive from Burlingame to South San Francisco, then wait for the shuttle to return us to the Airport Marriott by San Francisco Bay. We wanted to take our time and leisurely board our noon flight home the next morning.

We woke up about 8 a.m. and before breakfast, Albert called Northwest to check on our flight. I was surprised to hear his comments,

"What? Our flight is canceled? What? We are at war?"

Before I could question him, he turned on the TV. In front of us was a horrifying scene of smoke and fire. Two tall buildings were aflame and crumbling. I thought this was a scene from a movie, until I realized that the station was CNN. It was actually the Twin Towers of the World Trade Center in New York City, when American Airline Flight #11 hit the North Tower and United Airline Flight #175 hit the South Tower.

As soon as reality set in, we pulled up our window shade to look at the airport. What we saw was row after row of planes, all standing still. No wonder we didn't hear any flying overhead. All was silent at the San Francisco Airport.

We knew we'd probably be stranded in town for several days. I called the front desk to be sure that we could keep our room until we could get a flight home. Then Albert said,

"Run to the Hertz Desk in the lobby and get another rental car otherwise we'll be stranded completely."

I dashed down and found a compact car at $50 a day.

"Why, that's highway robbery," I said to the Hertz receptionist.

"Well, ma'am, this is the last car I have. If you don't take it, I'm sure someone will and I may get double the price."

I signed the lease and took the keys.

With time on our hands, I wanted to call my mom, but Albert cautioned, "If you do, she'd never believe or trust you again. It's better not to let her know. Besides, let's enjoy the time we have together."

We managed to see a few, long lost friends. Dora and Frank Kuo were one couple we haven't seen for ages. Dora, a landscape architect, had lived many years in Hawaii, while her husband, Frank, was a retired professor of computer engineering at Stanford University. Frank was actually the "father" of the internet, but it was his enterprising student who marketed it worldwide. We treated the Kuos to a meal at the restaurant we had enjoyed earlier, fish congee and trimmings.

Our visit with the Kuos was pleasant and we traveled down memory lane. I found out that Dora's sister, my Hong Kong classmate Vivian Lee, with whom I spent a beautiful day just before Tom's birth, commuted regularly between Seattle and Washington, D.C. in her legal practice.

We also visited Ada Tom, my classmate from the University of Hong Kong. We usually visit each other whenever I'm in the Bay Area, to renew friendship and catch up on the latest news in

Hong Kong and the Bay Area. Besides, Ada never fails to treat us to great meals at her family restaurant, *The Empress of China,* on Grant Avenue in San Francisco's Chinatown.

We drove by the houses I lived in during my five years in San Francisco, August 1955 - June 1960. The first was on 33rd Avenue and Balboa, then 121 Clement Street, and finally, 1400 Washington Street.

We remained in San Francisco for two days before we could get a return flight to Detroit.

7

Coming Home

I was anxious to get home since I had already registered for a four-day retreat at Manresa that week. This retreat was far from ordinary. It was led by Fr. Laurence Freeman OSB, spiritual director of the World Community for Christian Meditation (WCCM)*, whom I had yet to meet. Little did I know that after meeting him, my life and Albert's, would never be the same.

While I had been a meditator for seven years, and was leading a meditation group at St. Regis on Sunday afternoons, I wasn't involved with WCCM. I didn't learn about it until two years later, when I ordered books from Sr. Miriam McCarthy of Medio Media, the publishing arm of WCCM. Sr. Miriam sent me a copy of their quarterly newsletter. Fr. Laurence Freeman's name came up frequently, since he usually wrote a long article entitled *Dearest Friends,* where he shared his message and interactions in the community.

One day, Fr. Bernie Owens SJ of Manresa, said to me, "Well Liz, who's this Fr. Laurence? Don't you think it's time we invite him to lead a retreat here?" Fr. Bernie was already converted to meditation after reading my copy of Fr. John Main's *Word into Silence.*

"Good idea," I said.

So I contacted Steve Cartwright, WCCM's Midwest coordinator, who, in turn, invited Fr. Laurence to come to Manresa. He arrived on Thursday, September 13. The retreat started with two meditation periods - one at 7 a.m. and the second

45 minutes later. I wondered why two periods were so closely packed together. After the first meditation I was ready to leave when Fr. Laurence gave me a curious look. Since it has always been my habit to sit in the first row, I stayed and meditated again. The next day when Fr. Laurence posted a schedule for individual visits with him, I signed up. Our meeting lasted for more than an hour.

Although this was our first meeting, I couldn't stop myself from pouring out my whole life story to him. I told him about my family life and relations with Albert, my dominating and controlling mother, and my mission in life. After that, he had two questions, "Would you like to help us coordinate the Midwest? How about becoming a Benedictine oblate?" Although I didn't know anything about being a Benedictine oblate, I answered "yes" to both requests.

In return, I asked, "Have you been to China? Would you like to go and teach Christian meditation there?"

He said "yes" and we had a deal.

Since my 1999 pilgrimage, I had waited for the opportunity to alleviate the hunger and thirst for God I had seen in China. Ever since that first meeting with Fr. Laurence, I sensed that I had found my mission as well as my teacher. (Although I had several spiritual directors at different times in my life, I finally found a teacher who could guide me in my mission.) I was very willing to walk my path with him as my guide.

He certainly had leadership charisma. He inspired confidence and I trusted him implicitly. No question he was the teacher I had been waiting for all these years. Later during the retreat, I told him, "When the student is ready, the teacher appears. Yes, I'm ready and here you are."

He appreciated my role in organizing the retreat. While Steve Cartwright was the person who invited him to come, I worked with Fr. Bernie to make it happen. He wasted no time in asking the U.S. Coordinator, Mary Sue Anderson, to officially welcome me to WCCM/USA.

"You should hear what he had to say about you," she said.

Fr. Laurence also has the talent to recruit volunteers, people who like me will give him our all.

By the end of the year, we accepted the fact that Tom and Marlowe were definitely heading for the divorce court. Although my heart ached for my granddaughter, Kenny, meditation had helped me realize that there was nothing I could do. I could empathize, love, and listen, but their lives were theirs to live and choose.

At Last, Answers

Until January 22, 2002, I had had a big black hole in my soul. I couldn't understand why I, who have been blessed with a wonderful husband, two fine sons, three lovely grandchildren, a successful career as author and librarian, respected and admired as the "superwoman" in the Chinese American community and an activist for human rights, was sad and depressed. I often felt that life wasn't worth living. I had tried for a long time to find the answer.

In 1972, I saw my first therapist, JF. This continued with biweekly visits for 10 years. When JF left, I went to see NP. Again the weekly therapy sessions helped. Ten years later, before NP moved away, she said,

"Liz, do you know that when you're with your mother, you're nothing but an extension of her right hand?"

The truth of her statement hit me. After NP, I tried several other therapists, but didn't feel connected to any of them. I then sought spiritual counseling and realized that big black hole was due to the fact that I had never received unconditional love from my parents.

My surrogate fathers and mothers (priests, nuns and my amah) had shown me unconditional love. While they nurtured me through my adolescence and college years, I hadn't internalized the true value of their love. I was still yearning for love and approval from my mother. My stepfather, Frank, passed away in 1983. We children seldom saw or spent time with him, but when we did I could count myself fortunate to have more of his attention, since I studied hard to excel in order to earn his affection.

While living in Michigan, I saw Mom at least twice a year. Her visits always coincided with our vacations. She never came nor took time off from her job as a saleslady to help me when I had my babies. Still we included her in almost every vacation we took, whether it was a long weekend or an entire week with our family.

When my second cookbook, *The 15-Minute Chinese Gourmet,* was released by Macmillan and I was sent across the country to promote it, I took turns taking either mom or my mother-in-law with me. While the latter was so proud and couldn't boast enough about me to the media, mom was nonchalant and took my success for granted. I particularly remember that trip to Los Angeles when I did a cooking demonstration at a Williams Sonoma store in Beverly Hills. She tagged along, but didn't show any pride or joy. Instead she was busy checking on homes that she could buy.

Many times when we had angry discussions, she would remark, "You think you're so smart, eh? Don't forget it all came from me." Time and again she kept reminding me not to forget my roots.

I remember my 40th birthday. She called early that morning to wish me a happy birthday. Later our conversation touched on my siblings and their affairs. Suddenly, she burst out, "How you've changed. You no longer care for your family. Don't ever forget that were it not for me, you wouldn't be here today. I could have easily aborted you…"

Wow, that was a blow. After she hung up, I sobbed about the cruel remarks coming from my own mother. Oftentimes I would ask myself: *Why I, now a grown and mature woman, still wanted my mother's attention and affection, like a little girl? Why did I need her approval? Was I not good enough as I am?*

I started my odyssey of self-discovery in the early 70s. Whenever I had the chance to write I kept asking myself these questions: *Who am I? Why was I born? Why didn't Mom abort me as she was advised to? What is my purpose in life? My mission?* I was on a perpetual quest, hungry to find out who I really am and why I was put on this earth.

I read voraciously - psychology, philosophy, theology - books that were recommended and others that appealed to me, Catholic, Protestant, and Buddhist. I was dying to learn and discover.

I sought self-help programs. I flew to California to attend Ira Progoff's Intensive Journal, which taught me how to write with my right brain without judging or censoring. I dialogued with myself, my body, society, with relatives and friends, past and present. It was a great way to self-understanding.

And it was not pure accident that I came across a copy of *A Course in Miracles*. I immediately bought a copy and spent over a year studying it. Later, I bought 100 copies to pass out to relatives and friends. I even handed one to Pope John Paul when we were near him in Rome in 1994.

Then came *Attitudinal Healing,* championed by Jerry and Diana Jampolsky. I took the trouble to find their center in Sausalito, CA and attended one of their seminars in Kalamazoo, Michigan.

But these weren't enough. I was restless and impatient. Something inside me was yearning for fulfillment. I remembered how in the early 60s the Beatles promoted *Transcendental Meditation* ™. I enrolled in a TM class and started to use a mantra to quiet my "monkey" mind. I did find some measure of peace.

The turning point came when I found Christian Meditation. I felt like Christopher Columbus discovering a new continent. It is also known as contemplative prayer, where in total silence and stillness, without sound, images, thoughts or ideas, we can be with God and can experience His presence and love.

Thus began the amazing grace of my total healing. After reading all of Fr. John Main's books as well as those of his disciple, Fr. Laurence Freeman OSB, I knew that I had found myself. I knew why I am here on this earth, what my mission is, and how I can achieve it.

I can live my life to the fullest and realize my potential. In meditation, I keep in contact with the creative center of my being, and am in a constant and continuous state of expansion. In meditation, I am rooted in myself, hence rooted in God. At the same time, I am confident of my own being, my own capacity for goodness, for loving and being loved.

Slowly but surely, as I meditate day after day, in the morning and in the evening, I have not only found my peace, but also realize I am loved, loved for myself, loved because I am a child of God, loved unconditionally with all my faults and warts. Slowly the big black hole in my soul has begun to heal.

Now, I no longer needed Mom's acceptance, attention and love. In silence and stillness, I know I am lovable and that I am loved unconditionally. This is what led me to stand up to her that fateful day in January 2002. I wasn't only free, but independent. I cut her apron strings, my umbilical cord, and became a whole person.

Surprised by Grace,
Ten Years Later

Two weeks before my 76th birthday, I flew to San Francisco to visit my mom once again. Albert and I would be taking a four-week trip to Europe and Asia, but before that I wanted to spend some time with her should God call her home in our absence.

I prepared for this visit. I consulted several books, especially on how to listen and talk to the lonely, depressed, and the dying. I wanted to help her banish her fear, accept her suffering and offer it up as redemptive suffering for those she loved. Above all, I wanted her to see death as the next phase of life, an entry into our true homeland.

I prayed for grace and the Holy Spirit came to my assistance. A friend from our meditation group loaned me a book, *The Invisible World,* with chapters on suffering, death, dying and judgment. I felt this approach would be most appropriate and acceptable to her. *The Stephen Ministry Training Manual* was also very helpful in preparing me for our discussion.

That week was the best week I had with her in my 76 years. We were able to talk and she opened up quite a bit. In view of her short attention span, and poor hearing and eyesight, I only read her salient parts of the chapters on suffering, death and dying. We had lengthy discussion on the subject, in both English and Chinese. I believe I succeeded in calming her fear of death and encouraged her to put her entire trust in God. She had to forgive, especially forgive Dad (Frank) for whom she still held anger. I kept reminding her to love, trust and believe – the way to prepare herself for the important journey.

Since she was a gourmet chef and still has a healthy appetite, we frequented quite a few restaurants. I cooked some of her favorite foods, such as stir-fried thin rice noodles with chicken, pork and bean sprouts, ox-tail soup with onions, carrots and tomatoes, braised ox-tail with oyster sauce and onions, steamed fish with scallions and ginger, among others. It was especially gratifying to see her pick up an oxtail vertebrate and suck its tender, juicy meat.

We played her favorite game, mahjong. After several hands, I was so glad to see her regain much of her former acumen. Mahjong, the favorite pastime of Chinese around the world, consists of 144 tiles. While the rules may vary with the game, it is nonetheless, a good stimulant for the brain. What was so amazing was that when she was so absorbed in the game, she was no longer hungry, itchy or in pain. That really captured her attention and gave her much joy. While four players are needed for a regular game, three can also play. So during those two days, we recruited Ah Heung, her full time caretaker and maid, to play with us. Mom was elated when she was able to clean Ah Heung out of her chips.

One evening while Ah Heung was busy in the kitchen, I had to help Mom with her bath. How I ached when I saw her emaciated body, her frail limbs which were mostly skin and bones;her ingrown toenails all curled up because of her years of standing as a sales person. I could no longer be angry at her.

I had forgiven her for all the hurt and pain I received and endured these years. I had come to accept her as she is, with her faults and shortcomings. I had come to accept her as she is, not as

I'd like her to be. I know now that I cannot change others, only myself. When I change, others are changed because we're all part of one world and one consciousness.

In the past, I was resentful because I couldn't accept her abusive treatment of me. Yet I took time to visit and help her – more often than my sisters - even while I was working full-time. And I didn't feel good about our relationship since the true affection of mother/daughter was never part of that relationship. Oftentimes I felt revulsion at hugging her. While I knew that I had to do my duty as a good Chinese daughter, that is, take time off from my job and fly to the West coast to see and help her, I didn't feel comfortable being close to her. We hardly talked or shared our feelings. Although we would eat or cook together, or even go shopping or visiting.

When I went to say goodbye to her that morning, she sobbed and said, "I don't think I'll see you again in this life." While I realized that she has been saying this each time one of us left her, I said, "Mom, let's leave our lives in God's hands. Who knows? I may return to visit you again. If you're already in heaven, then wait for me."

By being silent and still, I have learned to be, to be a true a human being, not a human doing. By being rooted in my center and in myself, I am confident of my capacity for goodness, for loving and being loved.

These lines from St. John's First Epistle: 4: 7-9 are most appropriate:

Dear friends, let us love one another, because love is from God. Everyone who loves is a child of God and knows God, but the unloving knows nothing of God. For God is love, and his love was disclosed to us in this, that he sent his only Son into the world to bring life.

Meditation provides an entry into that fullness of life, rooted in ourselves, rooted in love, rooted in God. Writing my memoirs has helped me see, understand, and accept. There are many things I don't like, but need to accept. And in the process, I grow and learn. Hardships make us stronger and more independent. All these years of catering to Mom have made me stronger and more compassionate.

Grace, which is a gift from God, is amazing. If we're humble and simple enough, we can be transformed. I don't know whether Mom is thoroughly transformed or whether she can remember our recent talks and discussions. It doesn't matter. All I know is that I tried. I tried to help her, as a good Chinese daughter, or for that matter, as a human being. At 99, she may be called home anytime, but at least she is ready.

While writing these lines, I am wearing one of her short-sleeved silk blouses. Even though she can't tell me she loves me, I know in my heart, it doesn't matter. It's okay. I am loved anyway and I am at peace.

Mom's Passing

Mom died on April 14, 2014. She lived for 102 years, one month and eight days. We weren't optimistic about her living much longer since she had constant pain and eczema. A recent X-ray on her right heel showed a hairline fracture while a CT-scan found a big lump near her bladder. Since she was over 100 years old, the doctors advised against invasive surgery. Pain pills and itch-relieving ointment were her only recourse.

I visited her in early February. At that time she was fading in and out of consciousness. Her appetite was poor and even when we managed to wheel her to her favorite Chinese restaurant, she didn't want to eat.

The Marriott Courtyard where I stayed was just kitty corner from her apartment. I was assigned Room 414 on the fourth floor. I should have, but didn't, ask for another room. Although I'm not superstitious, many Chinese don't like the number 4, for it sounds like "death" in Cantonese. Four fourteen literally translates "sure to die."

That week in Oakland was quite routine. I would walk over from my hotel to her apartment to check on her several times during the day even though she was usually napping. She got up more than 10 times during the night and slept poorly. Although she wore a diaper, she refused to soil it. Ah Suen and her husband, her caregivers, took turns helping her to the commode.

During that week, my sister Mimi, my youngest brother George and I took care of details to prepare for her final departure.

We picked out the coffin, the mortuary which was to cremate her, the church and priest for the memorial Mass, the flowers, and the prayers. I realized that it would be hard for George, the youngest and the closest to Mom, to take care of all this when it finally had to be done. We also shopped for a headstone and prepared the Chinese engraving.

The three of us were able to finalize all the preparations during that week. It was time for me to return to Detroit for I had a household to run, a working husband to take care of, in addition to other commitments.

March 6 was her birthday, but since I had just returned from visiting her, I didn't fly to San Francisco this time. This was the only birthday I missed in over 20 years. But I sent a check to my brother Francis, asking him to invite Mom, George and family to dinner to celebrate the occasion.

March came and then April. Mom was definitely fading, since she didn't eat or drink much. The caregivers tried their best to spoon feed her, but each attempt was a battle.

On Monday, April 14, George was constantly on the phone with my siblings and me. Between 10 and 11 p.m., she died. Albert and I were meditating at home at that time, and I had the distinct feeling that Mom's soul was leaving her body. I prayed for her and implored the Good Lord to have mercy on her soul.

How did I feel? I felt partially relieved. Relieved that she was no longer suffering and that she had now passed on to a better life. I knew that the Good Lord in His mercy would forgive her faults, just as I had to do. For how could I recite *The Lord's Prayer* if I didn't forgive her in my heart? I do believe that everything I have experienced, especially in coping with her abuse, has been necessary to make me stronger, to enable me to become what I am today. She did what she could for me or the best she knew how, even though it wasn't what I would have liked. It's OK.

Mom's body was cremated the next day and her ashes stored in a beautiful Imari vase with a lid. This special piece of China was given by Mom to my sister Shirley years ago, so Shirley now wanted Mom's ashes in it.

James, Francis and Anna (my two younger brothers and sister-in-law) were away on a month-long cruise to Tahiti. We postponed the memorial service and burial until their return in early May.

The memorial service, held at St. Leo's Church on Friday May 9, was a grand one. George and Lin, had arranged for her urn to be carried on an ark. The ark was bedecked with flowers and carried by her three sons, James, Francis and George. The fourth bearer was grandson John Chiu. Her other grandchildren all had a part in the ceremony.

Fr. Ignas Kilolelo, the Kenyan priest who baptized her months earlier, officiated at the memorial Mass. The music played during the Mass included her favorite hymn - *"Amazing Grace."* James, the oldest son, gave the eulogy, while I wrote her biography for the Mass program.

Here's the eulogy I was supposed to give at her burial, but didn't, since it was rainy and we didn't have time.

Thank you all for coming to celebrate our mother's life and thank you, George and Lin, for coordinating this event. We're here today to honor Mom's long and full life – imagine 102 years - a century plus two!

She was a woman of both worlds - the old and the new. Born and raised in Canton (Guangzhou) China, she received a traditional education and was well versed in Confucian classics as well as in Chinese literature and history.

o Her Chinese penmanship was bold and strong.

o She adjusted well to a new life in the U.S.

o She spoke English and even wrote in English.

o She had a zest for life and loved to sing and dance.

o She was a champion mahjong player and was so skilled that we children would wait for her return from the game to count her winnings which paid for our dim sum the next day.

o She also loved to cook and entertain and continued to do so well into her late 90s.

o She was a great chef and used her cooking to win hearts. After serving as her sous chef for four years, I later authored three books on Chinese cuisine.

o She had a phenomenal memory and could remember the phone numbers of her children at the snap of a finger.

o She was an ardent student of the Bible and could easily recite passages from memory.

o She was astute. To this day, I partially owe my 54 years of happy marriage to her. It was she and Fr. Thomas Liang who encouraged my friendship with Albert.

I still remember one of my last visits with her. When I was leaving, she sobbed, "I don't think I'll see you again in this life." I replied, "Mom, let's have faith and leave everything in God's hands. Next time when I fly from Michigan to visit you, I look forward to seeing you, but, if you're already in heaven, then wait for me."

After the burial, all the guests and relatives were invited to a banquet at the Three Brothers from China Restaurant in Pleasant Hill, about a five-minute drive from the cemetery. A full 12-course dinner was served to the seven tables of guests present. In addition, a roast pig, Mom's favorite BBQ meat, was brought over from Oakland. Additional testimonials and memories were shared during the dinner. All left knowing that Mom certainly led a rich full life.

Love Is All

T his memoir covers my life journey until 2002, the day I cut my apron strings and became independent of my mother, except for Chapter 7.

As I examine my life - it's like viewing a tapestry from the underside. Knots and tangles, threads of gold, silver, greens, blues, reds, yellows and black intertwine. Although I can't see the "pattern" the Master Weaver has planned, I can detect strands where His hand has directed and guided me. I can see how He has led me through my happy and bright days as well as the dark and sad ones. His grace strengthened and nurtured me. With the unconditional love of my mentors and the gifts I've been blessed with, I got to where I am now.

In my search for *Who am I? Where am I going? What is my mission on earth?* I finally realized that we are all created for love, by Love. "Our heart is restless until it rest in You," St. Augustine wrote. Only He can satisfy me, fill my big black hole. It was after I'd been disciplined to follow Christian Meditation and incorporate the twice-daily periods into my everyday life that I experienced peace and harmony in my soul.

Yes, love is the answer. All my life I've been searching for love, unconditional love, from my parents. There was this insatiable hunger in me to win Mom's approval, no matter how successful my career and community service were to become.

The upside of trying so hard to win her love and approval had made me try harder, to do my best, to excel. This discipline instilled in me perseverance, tenacity and the importance of hard work which led to my maturity, and for that I'm grateful.

Mom is no longer a presence in my life, but her influence and legacy live on. No matter how different we were, part of her still lives in me. I'm the good Chinese daughter, conditioned by my Chinese culture and tradition and my Christian upbringing. Now I've finally matured and am my own person.

I've forgiven Mom for all the mental and verbal abuse she heaped on me all these years. I've come to realize that she did what she knew best. She never received unconditional love from her mother, although her father did care for her in some ways. In the same way her mother never received unconditional love from her parents either. The vicious cycle which passed from one generation to the next must be broken. I've broken the cycle and became whole.

I'm grateful she sent me to study at St. Mary's in Hong Kong. It was during those five years that I experienced the loving attention of the mothers, as well as that of our pastor. They not only converted me to Catholicism, but taught me how to give and serve and later how to forgive. Forgiveness frees and allows me to grow, to be who I am and who I was created to be.

My habit of attending annual retreats (to recharge, regroup and refuel) started during my time at St. Mary's. It helped me grow in my faith. When my soul yearned for intimacy with Him, the stepping stones were there: *Intensive Journal, A Course in Miracles, Attitudinal Healing and Transcendental Meditation -* finally. *Christian Meditation.*

By practicing *Christian Meditation* twice a day for the last 22 years, I've found the peace of soul I longed for. In silence and stillness, I know who I am, I know that I am loved.

In retrospect, I realized that I'm very much like my mother, especially about food. We shared a love of Chinese food and cooking. Chinese cuisine is all embracing and it's the index to our culture. Mom and I totally embraced this culture. We loved to cook and eat, loved to share and entertain. We used food to please and nurture people and to win hearts.

Since Ah Woo's influence and cooking has been part of my heritage, it's no small coincidence that I authored three cookbooks and have orchestrated many dinners and big banquets. For 20 years, I've cooked for my husband Albert's Bioengineering Department at Wayne State University. Our annual Christmas/Chinese New Year party was first served to 30, then 50 and finally 200 which included the Engineering College. It was the College's event of the year. On two separate occasions I've also cooked a 15-course dinner for 100 as a fund raising project for the Church in China.

My family life has come full circle. Albert, my husband and soul mate, has been supportive of me and my activities throughout our 55 years of marriage. He has helped me find myself and given me space and time to do it.

After more than 50 years in teaching and research, Albert is now working half-time at the University and planning retirement in 2018. In addition to teaching, he's presently writing a textbook for Springer: *The Biomechanics of Impact Injury: Biomechanical Response, Mechanism of Injury, Human Tolerance and Simulation.*

We have downsized to a condo. It was hard to leave our beloved home in the woods, but a simpler lifestyle leaves more time to write and to promote *Christian Meditation* locally. Albert

303

helps with two of our three meditation groups.

While I've resigned as China Coordinator and a member of WCCM's Guiding Board, I'm still in regular touch with several priests, sisters and seminarians in China. The WCCM in Hong Kong celebrates its 10th anniversary in April 2016 and I plan to be there for the occasion. In 2002, Hong Kong had one meditation group. Now, with the support of Cardinal Tong and led by Lina Lee, the coordinator, there are 14 groups and the number is still growing.

Our sons lead independent and happy lives. Albert Jr., a nurse, and his wife Sheila, are raising three lovely children in Nashville, TN. Our oldest grandchild is an entrepreneur in information technology in Berkeley, CA.

Dr. Tom, Michigan podiatrist, and his companion, Sherri, are both successful in their careers and also helping to raise Tom's two teenagers.

Meeting and working with my teacher, Fr. Laurence Freeman OSB, director of WCCM (World Community for Christian Meditation) has further motivated to me continue. I'm now on course to fulfill my mission.

And that dear reader, is the subject of another book.

Recipes

China and her food are inseparable - each defines the other. Her food illustrates the way of life of the Chinese, and eating, to the Chinese, is an activity of the highest order. When we Chinese greet each other, we almost immediately ask, "Have you eaten yet?" Chinese cuisine is truly a celebration of the senses. It is on par with the other art forms that are an integral part of Chinese culture.

It is with joy that I've included 13 (a baker's dozen) recipes in my memoir. Except for the Shanghai Red-Cooked Pork and Baked Salmon with Scallions and Ginger which are in print for the first time, the rest are excerpted from my two cookbooks, *The 15-Minute Chinese Gourmet (15 Min CG) and A Wok A Week: 52 Lite & Easy Meals (AWAK.)*

MENU OF RECIPES

Appetizers: Chicken on Skewers (pp. 306-307)

Lettuce Rolls (pp.307-308)

Soups: Hot and Sour Soup (pp.308-310)

Tomato and Egg Soup (pp.310)

Entrees: Baked Salmon with Scallions and Ginger (pp. 311)

Pepper Steak (pp.312-313)

Scallops and Shrimp with Spicy Sauce (pp.313-314)

Shanghai Red-cooked Pork (pp.314-315)

Vegetables: Asparagus Spears (pp.316)

Sweet Sugar Snap Peas (pp.316-317)

Staples: Cold-Tossed Noodles with Bean Sprouts (pp.317-318)

Fried Rice with Ham and Eggs (pp.318-319)

Steamed White Rice (pp.319-320)

CHICKEN ON SKEWERS (AWAW, p.194)

Ingredients: 1 medium chicken breast, skinned, boned and
partially frozen
24 to 28 8-inch bamboo skewers

Marinade: 1 teaspoon cornstarch, 1/2 teaspoon sugar
1/2 teaspoon baking soda, 1/8 teaspoon white pepper
1 tablespoon hoisin sauce, 1 tablespoon ketchup
1 tablespoon oyster-flavored sauce, 1 tablespoon whiskey
1 teaspoon grated gingerroot, 1 teaspoon
minced garlic

1. In a large bowl, mix the marinade ingredients until smooth.
Set aside

2. Trim the fat and cut the breast into very thin slices, about 3
inches long and 1 inch wide. You should get about 25 slices.
Add the sliced chicken to the marinade. Mix well and let
stand for 30 minutes or longer.

3. Prepare the outdoor grill or preheat the oven on broil for
5 minutes. If cooking indoors, line a cookie sheet (one that
has edges) with aluminum foil.

4. After the chicken has marinated for at least 30 minutes,
weave a skewer like a needle through the center of each
slice of chicken. If slices are short combine two or more on
one skewer. Place the skewers side by side on the cookie

306

sheet for inside broiling or on a platter to take outside to the grill. Mix the remaining marinade with 1/4 cup of cold water and pour over the skewers.

5. Cook about 4 inches from the heat for 8 minutes on the first side and 7 minutes on the second side. Serve hot.

Serves 8.

LETTUCE ROLLS (*15-Min CG*, p. 44)

Marinade: 1/2 teaspoon cornstarch, 1/2 teaspoon sugar
               1/8 teaspoon baking soda, 1/8 teaspoon black pepper
               1 teaspoon soy sauce, 1 teaspoon oyster sauce
               1 teaspoon cold water, 1/2 teaspoon sesame seed oil
               1 teaspoon dry sherry, gin or vodka, optional

Ingredients: 1/4 cup hoisin sauce, 1/4 cup oyster sauce
               1/4 cup lean ground chuck or lean ground pork
               4 large whole leaves from head or leaf lettuce
               ice cubes and water
               4 fresh Shiitake mushrooms or 4 small presoaked
               Chinese dried black mushrooms
               8 water chestnuts
               1 tablespoons corn, vegetable or safflower oil
               1/4 cup frozen green peas, well-thawed
               1/4 teaspoon salt
               1/8 teaspoon black pepper

1. Mix marinade ingredients together in small bowl and set aside. Place hoisin sauce and oyster sauce in separate small bowls and set aside.

2. Add ground meat to marinade in bowl and blend well. Set aside.

3. Soak lettuce leaves in large bowl filled with ice cubes and water. Set aside.

4. Wash fresh Shiitake mushrooms. Cut off and discard stems. Place mushrooms and water chestnuts in food processor. Fine-mince and set aside.

5. Heat skillet or wok on high for 30 seconds. Add oil to coat skillet for 30 seconds longer. Add mushrooms, water chestnuts, and peas. Stir-toss and blend well for 1 minute. Add salt and black pepper and mix again. Add marinated beef and stir-toss for 2 minutes, until meat loses its pink color. Remove to serving platter.

6. Drain lettuce leaves and place on separate platter.
Diners wrap their own lettuce roll. Place a leaf on a plate, spread a little hoisin or oyster sauce, then spoon 1/4 of beef mixture onto the leaf. Roll, wrap and enjoy!

Serves 2 to 4 (4 lettuce rolls)

Note: This recipe can easily be doubled or quadrupled. The filling can be cooked ahead of time and reheated just before serving. Lettuce leaves can be crisped a day ahead and refrigerated in a covered container.

HOT AND SOUR SOUP *(15-Min CG, p.51)*

Ingredients: 1/4 cup presoaked crunchy mushrooms (won yee or cloud ears) or 1 tablespoon
dried crunchy mushrooms
1 cup boiling water
1/4 cup lean ground pork, beef or turkey
4 cups homemade chicken stock or canned broth
1/2 cup firm tofu, drained and diced

2 tablespoons diced scallions
1 egg, well beaten

Seasoning: 1 tablespoon cornstarch, 1 teaspoon minced fresh garlic
1/2 teaspoon sugar, 1/2 teaspoon black pepper
1/4 teaspoon salt, 2 tablespoons Worcestershire sauce
2 tablespoons cold water, 2 tablespoons wine vinegar
1 tablespoon soy sauce, 1 teaspoon sesame seed oil

Marinade: 1/2 teaspoon cornstarch, 1/4 teaspoon sugar
1 tablespoon cold water, 1 teaspoon soy sauce
1/2 teaspoon sesame seed oil, 1 teaspoon dry sherry,
gin or vodka, optional

1. Mix seasoning ingredients together in cup or small bowl. Mix marinade ingredients together in cup or small bowl. Soak dry crunchy mushrooms in 1 cup boiling water for 5 minutes.

2. Add ground meat to marinade in bowl and mix well. Set aside.

3. Pour chicken stock into saucepot, add marinated meat, and bring to boil.

4. As the soup stock is boiling, squeeze dry the crunchy mushrooms. By this time they should be soft and have expanded to 5 times their original size. Remove hard particles and shred finely with Chinese cleaver or sharp knife. Set aside.

5. When stock boils, add tofu and mushrooms. Cook on high heat until soup comes to a second boil.

6. Add seasoning and stir well. Add scallions and turn off heat.

7. Pour egg slowly into hot stock in thin stream. Stir again and mix well. Cover until ready to serve in individual bowls.

Serves 4 to 6.

Note: This soup is easy to make ahead of time and reheat at

dinnertime. For a hotter, spicier flavor, keep a bottle of hot chili sauce and a black pepper shaker on hand for diners to add to the soup.

Variation: For a vegetarian soup, use freshly made vegetable soup stock or canned vegetarian stock and omit the meat and marinade.

TOMATO AND EGG SOUP (15-Min CG, p. 48)

Ingredients: 4 cups chicken broth, freshly made or canned
1 large firm tomato
1 egg, well beaten
2 tablespoons diced fresh scallions
1 teaspoon sesame seed oil
salt and pepper to taste

1. Bring soup stock to boil in cover saucepot.

2. While stock is boiling, wash tomato and cut off front end. Cut tomato in half, then slice thinly into 1/8-inch wedges. Add tomato wedges to boiling soup stock, cover, and continue cooking on moderate high heat for 4 minutes.

3. Turn off heat. Slowly pour in beaten egg and stir gently, until egg is cooked, about 30 seconds. Add diced scallions and sesame seed oil. Add salt and pepper to taste.
Ladle to soup bowls and serve.

Serves 4.

Variation: For a vegetarian soup, use freshly made or canned vegetable soup stock.

BAKED SALMON WITH SCALLIONS AND GINGER

Ingredients: 1 salmon fillet, about 1-1/2 lbs
2 scallions, thin sliced
1 50-cent knobs of fresh gingerroot, peeled, thin sliced and cut into strips
1 1/2 teaspoons sugar
2 tablespoons olive or canola oil
1 1/2 tablespoons Maggi seasoning or soy sauce
Pam spray

1. Rinse salmon fillet under cold water and pat dry with paper towel. Set aside.

2. Preheat the oven at broil for 5 minutes.

3. Use a sheet of heavy aluminum foil, large enough to fold and cover the fillet. Spray Pam or brush oil on the foil before placing the salmon. Cover the fillet completely and place in a baking pan large enough to hold it.

4. Broil for at least 8 to 10 minutes, depending on the temperature of the oven and the thickness of the salmon fillet.

5. Test for doneness with a fork. If the fillet flakes easily, then it is done.

6. Transfer the fillet in foil to a large platter. Carefully unwrap the foil, but do not remove it from the fillet. Spread the sugar evenly on the salmon, then the sliced scallion and ginger over the fillet.

7. Heat the oil in a small saucepan until it is smoking. Ladle the hot oil over the fillet. Spread the Maggi or soy sauce over the fillet and serve.

Serves 4 as a main entree, 6 to 8 with other entrees.

PEPPER STEAK (15-Min CG, p.60)

Ingredients:2 (8 ounces each) strip or sirloin steaks, well-
trimmed of fat and bones

1 large green pepper

1 large onion

4 tablespoons olive, corn, or vegetable oil, divided

1/4 teaspoon salt

Marinade: 1 teaspoon sugar, 1/4 teaspoon black pepper
1/4 teaspoon baking soda, 2 tablespoons soy sauce
1 teaspoon sesame seed oil, 1 tablespoon dry sherry,
gin or vodka, optional

Binder: 2 teaspoon cornstarch, 1/4 cup chicken soup stock
2 tablespoons oyster sauce or Worcestershire sauce

1. Mix binder ingredients together in cup or small bowl. Mix marinade ingredients together in large bowl.

2. Cut steaks into 1-inch wide strips, then into 1-inch cubes. Add steak cubes to marinade in large bowl and blend well. Set aside.

3. Wash and cut pepper in half, lengthwise. Scoop out seeds and cut off caps. Cut into 1-inch pieces. Set aside. Cut off both ends of onion and peel. Cut onion in half, then each half into quarters. Set aside.

4. Heat skillet or wok on high for 30 seconds. Add 2 tablespoon oil and swirl to coat skillet for 30 seconds longer. Add onions and pepper. Stir-toss for 1 minute. Add salt and blend well. Remove to serving platter.

5. Swirl 2 tablespoons oil in hot skillet for 30 seconds. Add beef cubes and marinade. Stir-toss for 3 to 4 minutes or until meat loses its pink color. Add onions and peppers to beef and

mix well.

6. Add well-mixed binder to skillet and blend well. Stir-toss for 1 minute longer. Transfer to serving platter.

Serve over hot rice or noodles, together with a vegetable or salad.

Serves 4.

SCALLOPS AND SHRIMP WITH HOISIN SAUCE (AWAW, p.160)

Ingredients: 1/2 pound sea scallops

1/2 pound large shrimp in the shell, about 12 or 13

Poaching Liquid: 2 quarts warm water, 4 tablespoons diced scallions

1 tablespoon grated gingerroot, 1 teaspoon minced garlic

Sauce: 1 teaspoon sugar, 1 teaspoon cornstarch

1/4 teaspoon black pepper, 1/2 cup chicken broth

2 tablespoons hoisin sauce, 2 tablespoons ketchup

1 tablespoon oyster-flavored sauce, 1 tablespoon dry white wine

Seasoning: 1 tablespoon oil (to coat wok), 2 tablespoons diced scallions

a 1-inch knob fresh gingerroot, 1 tablespoon whiskey

1. Bring the 2 quarts of warm water to a quick boil in a 4-quart covered saucepan. Add the scallions, gingerroot and garlic for poaching. Bring to a second boil in about 1 minute. Turn off the heat.

2. Rinse the scallops and pat them dry with paper towels. Halve each scallop into two rounds of equal thickness and set aside.

3. Peel the shrimp but leave the tail on. Make a 1/4-inch deep

313

cut along the back of each shrimp to butterfly it. Devein and rinse them. Pat them dry with paper towels and set them aside.

4. In a medium-sized bowl, mix the sauce and set aside.

5. Turn on the heat under the poaching liquid and bring it to a quick boil. Turn off the heat again and remove the pan from the stove. Add the scallops and shrimp. Cover and let stand for 2 minutes. With a slotted spoon, remove the scallops and shrimp, drain and place them on a serving platter. Set aside.

6. Heat a wok on high for 30 seconds. Add the oil and swirl to coat the wok for 30 seconds. Add the seasoning ingredients. Stir-toss for 15 seconds. Add the sauce and bring the mixture to a quick boil. Continue cooking for 1 more minute.

7. Drain the seafood again to remove any residual water from the serving platter. Ladle the sauce over the seafood and serve.

Serves 4.

SHANGHAI RED-COOKED PORK

Ingredients: a 3-lb. pork butt
12 dried medium Shiitake mushrooms
1 can (12-ounces) bamboo shoots, preferably in slices. If not, thin slice each shoot
2 green scallions, with ends removed, cut into 2-inch segments
4 slices gingerroot, smashed
3 tablespoons cooking oil
1 cup cold water

Seasonings: 1/2 cup dark soy sauce
1 1/2 tablespoons sugar

1-1/2 tablespoons wine or vodka
1/2 teaspoon black pepper

1. Cut the pork butt into 1-1/2 inch cubes, but do not trim the fat and set aside.

2. Soak the mushrooms, caps down, in a bowl of hot water for 15 minutes until they are soft.Squeeze the mushrooms dry, but reserve the mushroom water for use later. Cut each cap into 2 and set aside.

3. Heat a wok or skillet on high for 30 seconds. Add the oil and swirl to coat the wok for 30 seconds. Add the ginger and green onions, then the pork and toss to brown the pork for about 2 to 3 minutes.

4. Add the seasoning ingredients and stir-toss the pork again for a minute.

5. Add the mushrooms, the water, and mushroom water, and bring to a boil.

6. Transfer the contents to a large saucepot with lid. Turn heat to medium low and cook for about an hour.

7. Add the bamboo slices and mix in with the meat and mushrooms. Cover and let simmer on low for another hour or so, until the meat is tender.

8. If the water level is low, add another cup of hot water.

9. Skim off the fat from the top. Ladle to a dish and serve with steamed rice.

Serves 4 to 6 as a single entree. This can serve more than 6 when combined with other entrees.

ASPARAGUS SPEARS (AWAW, p. 47)

Ingredients: 1-1/2 pounds fresh asparagus spears
1/4 cup chicken broth
2 teaspoons minced garlic

Dressing: 1 teaspoon sugar, 1/4 teaspoon black pepper

2 tablespoons lite soy sauce, 1/2 teaspoon sesame seed oil

1. Snap off and discard the tough end of each asparagus spear. (If you bend the stalk using both hands, they will usually break at the woody part of the stem.) Wash and drain the spears. Place them in a microwave-safe dish. Add the chicken broth and garlic.

2. Cover the dish and microwave on high for 3 minutes. Pour off the liquid. Mix the dressing ingredients in a small cup and add to the cooked asparagus. Blend carefully but well.

3. This dish is delicious hot or cold. To chill for serving, refrigerate at least 1/2 hour.

Serves: 4

SWEET SUGAR SNAP PEAS (AWAW, p. 72)

Ingredients: 1 pound fresh sugar snap peas
2 50-cent-size fresh gingerroot
1/2 tablespoon oil
1/2 teaspoon salt
1/2 cup chicken broth

1. With kitchen shears, snip the ends off the peapods. Rinse, drain and set aside.

2. Smash the gingerroot to release its full flavor. Set aside.

3. Heat a wok on high for 30 seconds. Add the oil and swirl to coat the wok for 30 seconds. Add the smashed gingerroot and stir-toss for 30 seconds. Add the salt and peapods. Stir-toss for 1 minute. Add the chicken broth, cover, and cook for 2 1/2 minutes more.

4. Ladle to a bowl and serve.

Serves 4.

Note: Fresh sugar snap peas have a firm, tender skin. No stringing is necessary.

COLD-TOSSED NOODLES WITH BEAN SPROUTS
(15-MinCG, p. 106)

Ingredients: large kettle of boiling water
1/2 pound very thin noodles, fresh or dried
1/2 pound fresh bean sprouts preferred, or 1 can (14-ounces) bean sprouts

Seasoning: 1 tablespoon soy sauce, 1 tablespoon sesame seed oil
1 tablespoon Hunan chili paste or any brand of Chinese chili paste, optional
1 teaspoon wine vinegar, 4 tablespoons diced fresh scallions
1 teaspoon minced fresh garlic

Marinade: 1 tablespoon sesame seed oil, 1/2 teaspoon sugar
1/2 teaspoon salt, 1/4 teaspoon white pepper

1. Mix seasoning ingredients together in large bowl. Mix marinade ingredients together in medium bowl.

2. Cook noodles according to package direction until just

tender (al dente.) Rinse in cold water and drain well. Add noodles to seasoning in bowl and toss to coat well. Set aside.

3. While noodles are cooking, add 3 cups boiling water to 2-quart saucepot. Add fresh bean sprouts and parboil for no more than 15 seconds. Drain under cold water. Add bean sprouts to marinade ingredients in bowl. For canned bean sprouts, drain well, then add to marinade in bowl. Toss to coat well.

4. Add marinated bean sprouts to seasoned noodles. Mix together well. Spoon to serving platter.

Serves 4 to 6.

Variation: The noodles may also be served plain without bean sprouts or substitute 1 to 2 tablespoons oyster sauce for the Hunan chili paste. Another variation is to substitute a raw cucumber, sliced into thin slivers, for the bean sprouts. Then top it with any cooked meat or chicken, thinly sliced.

FRIED RICE WITH HAM AND EGGS (15-Min CG, p. 101)

Ingredients: 4 cups cooked long grain rice, cooked at least a day in advance

1 package (10-ounces) frozen peas and carrots, drained
4 tablespoons corn, vegetable, or safflower oil, divided
2 eggs, well beaten and seasoned with dash of salt and white pepper
4 tablespoons diced fresh scallions
1/2 teaspoon salt
1 cup diced ham

1. Separate kernels of cooked rice with your fingers and set aside.

2. Rinse peas and carrots under hot water for 1 minute. Drain well and set aside.

3. Heat skillet or wok on high for 30 seconds. Add 2 tablespoons oil and swirl to coat skillet for 1 minute longer. Add eggs and stir-fry until liquid is set but eggs are not dry or browned. Transfer cooked eggs to small bowl and break into small pieces with fork or chopsticks. Set aside.

4. Swirl remaining oil in hot skillet for 30 seconds. Add scallions, salt and rice. Stir-toss for 1 minute. Turn heat to medium low and stir-toss for 2 minutes longer until all grains of rice are coated.

5. Add peas, carrots, and ham. Stir-toss for 2 to 3 minutes longer. Add eggs and mix well.

Serve hot together with a soup, salad, or entree of your choice.

Serves 4 to 6.

Note: Fried rice can be reheated in the oven at 250 degrees for 15 minutes or in a microwave oven in a covered dish on high for 5 minutes.

Variation: Any cooked meat, shrimp or poultry, finely diced, can be substituted for ham.

STEAMED WHITE RICE (AWAW, p.13)

Ingredients: 1 cup long grain white rice, 1 3/4 cups cold water

1. Put the rice in a 1-quart saucepan and rinse it twice with cold water. Pour off the excess water by cupping your hands over the rice grains. Do not use a strainer or colander. Add the cold water and bring the rice to a boil, uncovered, over high heat.

2. When the water bubbles to the top of the saucepan, in

about 7 minutes, turn the heat to medium and continue cooking, uncovered. Stir with a fork or chopsticks occasionally to prevent sticking.

3. After about 5 minutes, when the water has almost evaporated, reduce the heat to simmer. Cover the saucepan with a tight-fitting lid and steam for about 20 minutes. Do not lift the lid during this time.

4. When steaming is complete, fluff the rice with a fork or chopsticks. Replace lid and let stand until you are ready to serve.

Yield: 3 1/2 cups of cooked rice.

Note: You can use the following formula to cook more rice:

2 cups of rice to 2 3/4 cups of water, yields 7 cups cooked rice; 3 cups of rice to 3 3/4 cups of water, yields about 10 cups of cooked rice. To succeed with these proportions, the rice must be rinsed twice (so that it can absorb more water) and drained by pouring the water off the rice instead of using a colander. Cup your hand over the rice as you pour off the water. Use larger saucepans for larger quantities and allow for longer cooking time.

An electric rice cooker makes perfect rice without supervision each time. It is a good investment if you serve rice regularly.

(For more recipes, check my cookbooks, *"The 15-Minute Chinese Gourmet"* and *"A Wok A Week: 52 Lite and Easy Meals."*)

Notes*

Chapter One
Mother

It is a tradition in a Chinese family for younger siblings to address their elder siblings by their birth order. In this case, Mom's brother ranks No.3 among the family children, therefore he's addressed as No.3 Brother.

Mahjong, a game of 144 tiles, has many variations with different rules and scoring systems. The points range from six to 56. The southern variation, played by my *Pau Pau* and *Kung Kung*, is quite simple, with a maximum of six points. It usually requires four players and if the players do not play regularly, they must first agree on the rules and scoring system.

Lo Po Beng (Wife's Cake is a traditional flaky pastry filled with either candied melon, sesame paste or coconut. It is popular in the southern part of China and Hong Kong and is usually included in the dowry the bridegroom gives to the bride's family.

Me

Lun Lun (Cantonese pronunciation) or Ling Ling (Mandarin), represents the *qilin*, a creature in Chinese folklore. It is depicted in Chinese art and sculpture with a dragon head and a body of a tiger with scales. Although it may look fearsome, it is a gentle and peaceful creature. It is often thought to be a symbol of good omen - prosperity, success and longevity.

U.S. $52,000 in 1935 is almost 18 times its value today, equivalent to close to a million U.S. dollars.

Amah is the term used for a nana or maid.

Manila

Uncle Ko, Uncle Wang and Uncle Sun - it's a Chinese custom, as a gesture of respect, to address our parents' friends as uncles and aunts.

After World War II

Even though my studies in Chinese were limited, I kept my spoken fluency in Mandarin, Shanghainese, Cantonese and Amoynese. This has proved invaluable since I go to China, Hong Kong and Taiwan for my missionary work to teach and nurture Christian Meditation.

Intramuros, also known as "Walled City", is the oldest historical district of Manila, the capital of the Philippines. It was totally demolished during the Japanese retreat in WWII. It has since been restored and declared a National Historical Monument.

Lechon is a popular dish in the Philippines and other Spanish-speaking regions. It is prepared for festivals, holidays, and special occasions. The pig (usually a suckling pig) with entrails removed, is first seasoned, skewered on a large stick, roasted in a pit filled with charcoal and roasted on all sides for hours until done. The crispy crackling skin is the distinctive feature of the dish.

Chapter Two

Canton

Shamian is a small, beautiful island of 330 acres, surrounded by a moat in the southwest corner of Canton. It was one of the ceded territories to the Foreign Alliance that defeated the Boxers in 1900. It is a self-contained haven with consular offices, a Catholic church, bank, hospital, post office, stores, and a school. (For more information on the Boxer Rebellion, see note in Chapter Four, 1967-1968 – Years of Simple Blessings.)

Litchi Wan (Li Zhi Wan, in Mandarin) also known as Lychee Wan Chung, is a scenic bay along the Pearl River which attracts many tourists and vacationers.

It is customary in Chinese household to hang scrolls of couplets portending good fortune, harmony and prosperity along doorways. This couplet is a typical example:

Harmony, Happiness and Blessings to the Entire Family
For All Seasons throughout the New Year
（ 和氣吉祥全家樂，四季平安過旺年 ）

Hong Kong

The Legion of Mary, founded in 1921 by Frank Duff in Ireland, was very welcome in Hong Kong. The Catholic diocese embraced it whole-heartedly for its disciplinary training of young and older Catholics in spiritual and corporal works of mercy. It is modeled on the Roman army, with the presidium as its smallest unit, while the Curia supervises many presidia.

The University of Hong Kong (HKU)

HKU was very exclusive, only the brightest and best of scholars could pass the matriculation to qualify for admission. The student population, in the early 50s, was under 1,000. Today, HKU has an enrollment of over 26,000 students.

Mimi and Philip were happily married for 50 years. Philip passed away in Manila in November, 2004, two weeks after celebrating their golden anniversary. They have seven children, 20 grandchildren, and 7 great grandchildren. Mimi now lives in California.

A Time of Change

U.S. is known as "the land of the Golden Mountain," because of the Gold Rush in California in the mid-1800s.

Catholic Society of HKU (KATSO) formed in January 1955 by the four of us who attended the Pax Romana Seminar in Madras, India, just celebrated its golden jubilee in 2006. Albert, Albert Jr. and I returned to Hong Kong for this auspicious celebration. This was indeed a joyous and sentimental journey for us as founders of KATSO and we reconnected with many old friends: Michael and Ruby Lau, Patrick and Connie Sum, among others.

Chapter Three
Hello America

Dim sum, the Cantonese term for delicious tidbits, is literary translated as dainty morsels that "touch-the-heart." For indeed they do. These small, delightful concoctions are usually made with meat, seafood and sweets, scarcely larger than bite-size. They come steamed, fried, baked or boiled.

Our First Christmas

Qi pao (Mandarin) or cheung sam (Cantonese), is the traditional Chinese dress with a Mandarin collar and side slits. They come in various lengths and in the old days, were custom-made to fit.

Chapter Four
Detroit, Here I Come

Fox and Fisher theaters. The Fox Theater, fully restored in 1988, and designated a National Historical Landmark in 1989, is now a performing arts center. The redesigned Fisher Theater of rose wood and brass now hosts shows bound for Broadway.

1967-1968 – Years of Simple Blessings

The Boxer Rebellion: The Boxers, so called because they practiced martial arts and calisthenics, were Chinese nationals and farmers who claimed to have supernatural invulnerability to gunshot blows and knifes. Together with the Imperial Army of the Qing Government, they attacked the foreigners in China. The uprising was in response to grievances ranging from opium traders, political invasion and economic manipulation to missionary evangelism. But when they lost their war (1899-1901) to the united coalition of eight nations - Russia, Japan, Germany, Austria-Hungary, France, United Kingdom, Italy and the U.S. - China had to pay an indemnity of 450 million taels of silver equal to 67 million pounds (more than the Chinese Government's annual tax revenue) over a course of 39 years. In addition, certain large cities (as in the case of Shanghai and Shamian in Canton) were ceded to the nations where the countries established their special territories, called concessions. The French concession in Shanghai, where I lived as a child, and Shamian in Canton were two of the settlements. (Source: Wikipedia)

The U.S. used a large portion of the reparation received for the education of Chinese students in the U.S. universities (and Britain later followed her example.) To prepare the students for this,

an institute was established to teach the English language to prospective students, and this led to the formation of Tsing Hua University, now one of the leading institutions in China.

Chapter Five
New Horizons

On Leong Association: is the Cantonese name for the restauranteurs and merchants' association. It is very supportive of CAECC's (the Chinese American Educational and Cultural

Center of Michigan) activities and programs and readily supplies us with food and financial support.

New Ventures

Andrew Mazzara later served as the third president of Henry Ford Community College (HFCC) from 1990-2005. In 2006, HFCC Board of Trustees officially named the college's administrative building in his honor.

Chinese Names are very important, for they represent the virtues or qualities parents hope to instill in their children, much like those names given to *Sleeping Beauty* by her loving fairy godmothers.

The Bund, along the Huang-Pu River, skirts the metropolis of Shanghai. It is now the busiest section in Shanghai.

Congee or rice porridge, is known as *jook* in Cantonese and *hsi fan* in Mandarin. It has a light consistency, usually made with 1/4 portion of rice to 3/4 portion of water or clear broth. It is the best antidote for a cold or hangover, and can easily be paired with any meat, chicken or seafood and even served with nuts and fruits as a sweet dish. In Hong Kong, Taiwan, China and elsewhere, there are *jook* houses/eateries that only serve different varieties of *jook*.

You-tiao is a popular accompaniment to *jook*. It is an elongated deep-fried donut.

Grace and Mickey:

Col. John Paul Stapp, a pioneer in automotive safety, was an air force officer whose mission was to prevent injuries to pilots who eject from disabled jet aircraft. He rode a rocket sled in Alamorgordo, NM in the1940s to expose himself to wind blasts at speeds exceeding the speed of sound. When the sled stopped at very high deceleration levels he sustained an eye and wrist injury and became interested in automotive crash research. He became an advocate for the use of seat belts in cars and was influential in the passing of the seat belt law for cars in 1966, mandating that all cars be equipped with lap belts. The Stapp Car Crash Conference is held every year, in his honor, to discuss new findings in automotive safety.

Chapter Six
The New Century

Matteo Ricci (1552-1610) was an Italian Jesuit priest, who lived in China for over 25 years. He not only mastered the Chinese language, adopted Chinese customs, but dressed and lived like a native. He composed the first European-style map of the world in Chinese, helped develop a system for transcribing Chinese words into the Latin alphabet and compiled the first Portuguese-Chinese dictionary. In 1601, he was invited by the Emperor Wanli to become an adviser to the Imperial Court, thus becoming the first Westerner to be invited into the Forbidden City. His love for China and the way he lived and taught won him many converts to Catholicism. His beautification as a saint is in progress at the Vatican. (Source: Wikipedia)

Chapter Seven
Coming Home

The World Community for Christian Meditation (WCCM), with Fr. Laurence Freeman, OSB as director, is headquartered in London, with more than 2,500 groups and 25 centers in over 140 countries. Please check their website: www.wccm.org for more information on Christian Meditation.

Glossary of Chinese Words*

Although there is only one written form of Chinese, there are many different dialectic pronunciations for the same word. To preserve the authenticity of the region, it is necessary to stick to the dialect used there. Cantonese is usually used in the southeastern part of China and Hong Kong, while Putonghua (Mandarin) is the universal dialect of China.

CANTONESE WORDS:

chai (齋) pronounced as spelled

    A vegetarian dish or meal

Chiu Sheung (超常), pronounced as: ciu shoeng.

    This is my mother's name, which means "most exceptional."

chow mien (炒麵), pronounced as spelled

    Stir-fried noodles

dim sum (點心), pronounced as dim sum.

    Delicious tidbits, literary translated as dainty morsels that "touch the heart."

    These small delightful hors d'oeuvres are made from meat, seafood and sweets, scarcely larger than bite-size. They can be steamed, fried, baked or boiled.

ho fun (河粉), pronounced as spelled

    flat rice noodles

kailan (芥蘭), pronounced as gaai laan.

Chinese greens, with texture similar to broccoli, and often
called Chinese broccoli

kung kung (公公), pronounced as gung gung

Maternal grandfather

jook (粥), pronounced as zuk

Rice porridge, usually eaten at breakfast or late night snacks.
Its popular name is congee.

laisee (利是), pronounced as lei si

Small red envelopes used for "lucky" money, usually given
by elders to children or younger generations during special
occasions, especially during the Chinese New Year, birthdays,
or special occasions.

lo po beng (老婆餅), pronounced as lou po beng.

Boxes of wife cakes are usually included in the dowry the
bridegroom gives to the bride's family and relatives. These
traditional flaky pastries are filled with candied melon,
sesame paste or coconut and are popular in the southeastern
part of China and Hong Kong

Lun lun (麟麟), pronounced as spelled

This is my Chinese nickname. It represents the qilin, a
creature revered in Chinese folklore. It is depicted in Chinese
art and sculpture with a dragon head and a body of a tiger
with scales. Although it may look fearsome, it is a gentle
and peaceful creature. It is often thought to be a symbol of
good omen - prosperity, success and longevity. The
Mandarin equivalent is Ling Ling.

pau pau (婆婆), pronounced as po po.

Maternal grandmother

san nin ffai lok! san tai gin hong! maan si jyu ji! (新年快樂！身體健康！萬事如意！)

Pronounced as spelled.

Happy New Year, wishing you good health, prosperity and blessings

tai tai (太太), pronounced as spelled

Mistress or lady of the house

PUTONGHUA (MANDARIN) WORDS:

baofu (包袱) pronounced as spelled.

A bundle of things tied together with a big scarf or kerchief

chang ming bai sui (長命百歲), pronounced as spelled

May your life be long, and may you live to a 100 years old.

chiaotze (餃子), pronounced as jiao zi

Dumplings with different fillings

Guangzhou (廣州), pronounced as spelled

Used to be the city of Canton in Southeastern China

Jinhua ham (金華火腿), pronounced as jin hua huo tui

The ham from the city of Jinhua is considered one of the best hams in China.

Ling Ling (麟麟), pronounced as spelled

My Chinese nickname in Putonghua (See Lun Lun in Cantonese section.)

Litchi Wan (荔枝灣), pronounced as li zhi wan

Name of a scenic bay along the Pearl River

Po Ai Lu (博愛路), pronounced as bo ai lu

　　Street of brotherly love, a street in Shamian Island

Qi Pao (旗袍) pronounced as chi pow

　　Long Chinese dress with Mandarin collar and side slits,
　　usually custom-made

Shamian (沙面), pronounced as spelled

　　Name of a small island in southwest corner of Canton

Shou (壽), pronounced as spelled

　　Longevity

Tai Tai (太太), pronounced as spelled

　　Mistress or lady of the house

　　(In this case, the Cantonese and Mandarin pronunciation are
　　very similar.)

Wen Huei (文慧), pronounced as wen hui

　　My official Chinese name, which denotes culture and wisdom

Xin Nian kuai le! Shen ti jian kang! Wan shi ru yi! (新年快樂！
身體健康！萬事如意！)

　　Pronounced as spelled.

　　Happy New Year, wishing you good Health, prosperity and
　　blessings.

You Tiao (油條), pronounced as spelled

　　A popular accompaniment to jook. It is an elongated deep-
　　fried donut.

Zhejiang (浙江), pronounced as spelled

　　An eastern coastal province in China

Acknowledgments

I have so many people to thank, especially all those whose names
appeared in my memoir, for having touched my life – they
were the angels who lifted me up when I forgot to fly.

My mother and father who in their own way molded me to what I
am today. As I look back I understand that they did the
best they knew how.

My many mothers and fathers, Ah Woo, Mother Piera, Fr. De
Angelis, Fr. Fergus Cronin, SJ, and Tom Liang as well as
my mother and father-in-law, Helen and Yu-Lo King, for
their unconditional love.

My beloved husband and soul mate, Albert, who is always behind
every venture I embark on.

Our two sons, Albert, Jr. (and wife, Sheila) and Tom, who are my
pride and joy.

Our grandchildren, Ian, Austen, Kenny, Maxwell, Albie, Allison,
and James for bringing joy and sunshine into my life.

My sisters, Mimi, Maria and Shirley, whose love and support I
lean on.

My brothers, James, Francis and George, who are there to listen
and to encourage.

My brothers-in-law, James and Francis and their wives, Shirley
and Lucy, for their love, friendship and support.

My many dear friends, Janet Enguehard, Katie Mielock, Vincentia
Hepp, Ginka Ortega, Theresa Shen, Elizabeth Hsu, for their

insightful comments.

My assistant, Dawn Li, who helps me in many ways.

My architect friend, Frank Ho Asjoe, for drawing the sketch of my home in Manila at a moment's notice.

My beloved shepherd and mentor in Hong Kong, John Cardinal Tong, and his assistant, Sr. Emilia, for their guidance, encouragement and support.

My wonderful teacher and guide, Fr. Laurence Freeman, OSB, and all my meditator friends in Hong Kong, China, the U.S. and elsewhere, especially Lina Lee, Celina Chan, Ann Wong Chan, Stella and Albert Li, Augustine Xiao and Tony Hu, for their support and prayers.

My dear friends, Dr. Julian Chang and his lovely wife, Doris, for their loving and attentive care of me every time I visit Hong Kong.

In particular, Iris Lee Underwood, James King and Fr. Greg Hyde, SJ, for reading my manuscript and offering invaluable suggestions.

And especially to Lilian Siak, for introducing me to Alex and Dorothy Chan, who helped me launch this book.

Last but not least, to my dear friend and editor, Corinne Abatt, who worked with me painlessly during the last three years.

Finally, my eternal gratitude to the Holy Spirit for inspiring and guiding me, especially in the writing of this memoir.

Elizabeth Chiu King, author of three popular books about Chinese food, finally shares her own life story. Her new autobiography, *"The Good Chinese Daughter: Growing up in China and in America,"* leaps across time and space like and automated jumping bean.

Born in Shanghai, she and her family lived in Manila during World War II. She was educated in Hong Kong, and came to the U.S. in 1955 with her family. She attended the University of Hong Kong, the University of San Francisco, the University of California, Berkeley and the University of Michigan, holding graduate degrees in English and Library Science. She has worked as a librarian and teacher at Henry Ford Community College in Dearborn for 20 years.

Since settling in the Greater Detroit area in the 1960s, she has been active in community and church affairs. She founded and chaired five organizations and also served on the Guiding Board of the World Community for Christian Meditation (WCCM) as its China coordinator for over 10 years.

She says, "There are so many needs in our world – each of us must find our way to help make it better, more human and more understanding. I've tried to do my part, and to encourage others to find a way to share their gifts and experience."

Photograph of Elizabeth (p. 258) by Michelle Andonian

Jacket Design by Icicle Group